BEASTS OF THE WORLD

VOL. 2

WATER MONSTERS

ANDY MCGRATH

HANGAR 1 PUBLISHING

World (Vol. 2): Water Monsters
McGrath
gar 1 Publishing

ug Hajicek

There is no doubt in my mind we are looking at an animal that hasn't been classified yet.

— ARLENE GAAL

A MESSAGE FROM THE AUTHOR

Scan for message.

CONTENTS

FIENDISH FISH

SUPER SHARKS

A READER'S GUIDE

This book has been sympathetically crafted to foster a case-specific and non-linear exploration, allowing readers to engage with its varied content in a manner that suits their preferences. The structure encourages curiosity, enabling readers to dive into the topics that intrigue them most without feeling constrained by a sequential narrative. This flexible approach acknowledges people's vast range of interests in studying cryptids.

Each subheading distils complex topics into manageable segments, presenting intriguing facts, folklore, and contemporary theories surrounding these remarkable creatures in a digestible format. This design is intentional and aimed at ensuring that individuals of all ages and varying levels of expertise can absorb the material effectively. Whether a reader is a casual observer or an avid researcher, the content is crafted to engage everyone's sense of wonder and inquiry.

The cases are presented objectively and analytically, an approach that is vital for clarity amid the diverse information the author has meticulously sifted through. This objectivity ensures readers have a balanced view, considering various perspectives on each cryptid. As a result, individuals are invited to take on the role of detective, piecing together clues and evidence to formulate their theories regarding the potential existence of yet-to-be-discovered fauna. This interactive element fosters critical thinking and creative reasoning, empowering readers to draw conclusions based on the evidence.

Importantly, it is essential to note that the cases vary in length and depth; some cryptids, such as the Loch Ness Monster, are accompanied by rich historical narratives that have been chronicled through the ages, while others, like the Dobhar Chu, are steeped more in folklore and myth. These variations highlight the multifaceted nature of the material and illustrate how cultural context plays a significant role in the stories we tell about these creatures. The author encourages readers to approach these differences with an open mind and an inquisitive spirit, inviting them to appreciate both the historical and speculative dimensions that contribute to the allure of cryptids.

I hope this book serves as a valuable reference for newcomers and seasoned enthusiasts alike. It strives to bridge the gap between entertainment and education, offering a thoughtful compilation of research and narrative that can cultivate a deeper understanding of the topic. I wish for it to be enjoyed in the spirit in which it was written—a celebration of the mystery that surrounds these peculiar creatures. So, make yourself comfortable, and get ready to explore the wonder of the unexplained.

WHAT ARE WATER MONSTERS?

Water monsters, particularly those associated with lakes, represent captivating figures in folklore and cryptozoology. These mythical entities are thought to inhabit both freshwater and saltwater environments, with notable examples such as the Loch Ness Monster. Often depicted as resembling prehistoric reptiles like plesiosaurs, these creatures are characterized by elongated necks and substantial bodies, alongside features like flippers and scales.

Categorizing these elusive beings is complex due to inconsistent eyewitness accounts influenced by optical conditions and cultural narratives. However, they can be broadly classified into several groups, including:

- Lake Monsters
- Sea Serpents
- Cryptozoological Krakens & Massive Medusas
- Terrifying Turtles
- Pernicious Pinnipeds,
- Secret Sirenians
- Mystifying Mustelids

- Strange Cetaceans
- Fiendish Fish
- Super Sharks

Proposed explanations for reported sightings range from the existence of surviving prehistoric species—such as basilosaurids and ancient marine reptiles—to oversized cephalopods, including giant squids, and misidentifications of common species like otters. Additionally, natural disturbances, such as boat wakes, may lead to erroneous interpretations of ordinary animals as extraordinary entities. The inquiry into these water monsters raises the question of whether traditional explanations suffice or if advancements in technology will reveal a hidden array of undiscovered aquatic species, perpetuating the allure and mystery surrounding these creatures.

LAKE MONSTERS

Def.

Lake monsters are often depicted in various forms, including large creatures with horse-like heads, eel-shaped beings, plump plesiosaur-like reptiles, and sleek, amphibian-like entities. Their historical and mythological origins span thousands of years, as evidenced by art, ancient texts, folklore, and legends on almost every continent except Antarctica.

NESSIE

What's in a Name? The term "Loch Ness Monster" comes from the Gaelic word "an Niseag," which is a feminine diminutive derived from the name of the loch. The legend originated from sightings reported in 1933. It is believed that the term was first used by Evan Barron, the editor of the *Inverness Courier*, in a story published on May 2, 1933.

The scientific name for the Loch Ness Monster is *Nessiteras rhombopteryx*. This name was proposed by Peter Scott and Robert Rines in 1975, based on underwater photographs taken in 1972 and 1975. The name translates to "the Ness wonder with the diamond-shaped fin." Other names for the creature include Bobby, Lady of the Lake, Loch Ness Monster, and Niseag.

Monstrous Measurements: The most common descriptions of the creature indicate that it resembles a large, rounded object, similar to an overturned boat. Witnesses often report seeing several humps in a line or a long neck accompanied by a hump. The creature typically measures between 10 and 45 feet in length. Its color is grey, dark grey, or black, although some sightings have noted a sandy or lighter shade. The skin appears mottled and rough, resembling that of an elephant. The underparts are sometimes described as white.

It has a small, flat head that seamlessly blends into the neck, featuring two horn-like protrusions on top and oval-shaped eyes. The neck is about 4 to 8 feet long, and it usually has one to three humps, though reports of up to eight have been made. Sightings on land suggest that the creature has four short, thick flippers. Its tail measures 5 to 6 feet in length and has a rounded end.

Terrifying Tracks: The tracks of this creature are rarely documented, and while several reported sightings have been reported, some were later proved fake, and others were too ambiguous to ascertain. Descriptions of the tracks vary; they are sometimes said to be three-toed and flipper-like, while at other times, they are described as large drag marks near the shore or extensive areas of flattened vegetation leading to the loch.

Beastly Behaviours: The creature has been described as gliding effortlessly through the water, sometimes moving in a graceful zigzag pattern. It frequently travels against wind currents or just below the surface, creating a distinctive V-shaped wake. Occasionally, it lashes out at the water with vigour. It possesses the ability to sink like a heavy stone. Its most active times are during dawn and dusk. Occasionally, it can be seen on land, where its movements appear awkward. It appears solitary in nature, as sightings of two or more individuals together are rare.

Deadly Diet: It has been observed eating trout and eels and chasing salmon, which will occasionally beach themselves to escape its predations.

Watery Abode: Nessie is believed to inhabit Loch Ness, a huge glacial lake in the Highlands of Scotland and Britain's largest body of fresh-water. It is thought that "Nessie" prefers to reside in the dark waters of the loch, rarely visiting the surface. The visibility is poor due to suspended peat particles from the surrounding hills, which give the water a rusty colour. Nessie is also reported in the adjoining Lochs of Oich, Lochy, and Garry, which it reaches by traversing the River Oich and Loch Dochfour via the River Ness, which leads to the North Sea via the Moray Firth. Some researchers have theorised that Nessie is an ocean visitor who randomly frequents Scottish lochs for some unknown purpose.

Scary Sightings

580 A.D: The Irish Missionary, St. Columba, is said to have been the first to see Nessie when he exorcised a Water Horse near the mouth of the River Ness. This account is often viewed with scepticism due to its mythological roots, but it is frequently cited as the earliest mention of a creature resembling what would later be called the Loch Ness Monster.

1871/72: D. Mackenzie of Balhain was standing on a rock off Abriachan when he observed an object resembling an overturned boat churning the water as it moved across the loch from Aldourie. This sighting is one of the earliest recorded modern encounters with the creature, sparking local interest and rumours.

1919: Margaret Cameron and three siblings witnessed a 20-foot monster move from the trees into the water at Inchnacardoch Bay. They described it as having two short, round feet and moving like a caterpillar. This sighting added to the local folklore surrounding the Loch Ness Monster and ignited further curiosity among residents and visitors alike.

1923: Alfred Cruickshank reported seeing a large, humped body that stood about 6ft high roughly fifty yards ahead while driving along the loch. When the creature barked sharply, it slipped into the water, a detail that left many curious about the mix of terrestrial and aquatic characteristics.

1933: John Mackay and his wife saw a large black body with two humps swimming with a forward-rolling motion at the northern tip of the loch, a description that matches the classic depiction of Nessie. This sighting led to increased reports and interest in the creature, coinciding with other sightings from the same year.

1933: George F.T. Spicer and his wife witnessed Nessie crossing the road before them. Their detailed description of a long neck and high back with a total length of about 25ft became one of the most cited among enthusiasts and sceptics.

1934: Brother Richard Horan of St. Benedict's Abbey watched the creature's head and neck for five minutes before it submerged. This sighting was critical in establishing ongoing interest throughout the 1930s.

1934: Housemaid Margaret Munro saw a colossal creature rolling on the shingle beach in Borlum Bay. Her account of the animal, which had a giraffe-like neck and an absurdly small head, has been noted for its vivid detail.

1934: Sir Edward Mountain headed the first organized surveillance of the loch, which resulted in eleven sightings and several photographs. Many photographs captured unclear shapes resembling boat wakes or other inconclusive images, yet this attempt marked a notable effort in studying mysterious phenomena.

1934: Veterinary student Arthur Grant saw Nessie while riding his motorcycle, and his description contributed to the growing list of extraordinary accounts that captivated the public's imagination.

1936: Fifty observers, including local man Duncan Macmillan, described a creature with a small head and black humps. This mass sighting significantly bolstered local legend, increasing awareness and media attention on Loch Ness.

1947: J.W. McKillop saw a large head and neck making a wake near Drumnadrochit. Multiple motorists' independent confirmation of this sighting lent credibility to the reports.

1952: Greta Finlay and her son Harry observed a humped animal at Aldourie Point with distinct projections on its head. This detailed account has become an essential part of the lore surrounding Nessie.

1957: Christine Fraser witnessed a 25ft animal with three humps near Strone. Her experience became one of the key sightings recorded in the 1950s.

1962: Writer F.W. Holiday saw a blackish-grey creature estimated to be 40-50ft long. His observations further fuelled speculation about an unknown species within Loch Ness.

1965: Ian Cameron and William Fraser observed what they described as an upturned boat at the South shore. When several witnesses verified their claims, it became one of the longest and most corroborated sightings.

1967: Biochemist Roy Mackal reported seeing an 8ft back and a pectoral flipper while servicing hydrophones. This encounter solidified his belief in the monster's existence and pushed the scientific community to investigate further.

1970: In the boat Roy Mackal and his companions spotted a black object in Urquhart Bay, a sighting that added to the lore of Nessie with varying accounts from boaters that summer.

1971: Robert Rines and his wife saw a 20-foot-long hump in Urquhart Bay, which was later captured on film through a series of underwater explorations.

1979: Donald MacKinnon distinctly described a grey animal measuring about twenty-four feet long with visible legs, contributing to various descriptions throughout the decades.

1987: Barbara Grant and Mary Appleby reported a pillar-like object in the loch.

1990: A group of tourists reported seeing a large, dark shape moving across the loch while on a sightseeing cruise. Their description matched previous accounts of Nessie, reigniting interest among visitors that year.

1994: Gary Campbell, a Nessie enthusiast, reported a sighting of a large creature with long limbs in the waters of Loch Ness. He noted it was swimming, creating visible ripples.

2001: A photo taken by a group of campers showed a long-necked creature emerging from the water near Urquhart Castle. This photograph sparked media interest and analysis of alleged Nessie evidence.

2007: A local fisherman spotted a large, serpentine creature while fishing on the loch. His description included scales and a long tail, adding to the diversity of Nessie's sightings.

2012: A video uploaded to social media appeared to show a large animal surfacing and moving through the water. The clip quickly gained traction online, with many viewers speculating that it could be Nessie.

2015: Several tourists reported seeing a large creature with a long neck and three humps in the area of Fort Augustus. This sighting was notable for being observed by multiple witnesses, leading to renewed discussions about the monster in the media.

2018: Chie Kelly captured a video while walking along the shore, claiming to have seen a long, dark shape moving beneath the water's surface. Her footage became a point of discussion among Nessie enthusiasts, reigniting interest in the possibility of the creature's existence.

Nessie's Neighbours: Scotland is home to thousands of lochs and lochans, many of which are said to harbour mysterious creatures similar in description to Nessie. Various sightings have been reported, such as Wee Oichy in Loch Oich, last seen in 1998; Lizzie in Loch Lochy, spotted by Eric Robinson in 1960; and Lomie in Loch Lomond, observed in 2018. Other encounters include Beathach Mor in Loch Awe, seen by Sally Umbo in 2000; a grey beast in Loch Leven in 1934;

a creature identified by Mrs. B.F. Cox in Loch Linnhe during the 1940s; and a serpent-like creature in Loch Garry in 2018. The most dramatic account involves Morag in Loch Morar, encountered by Duncan McDonell and William Simpson in 1969, whose boat was attacked by the beast while they were fishing upon the loch. While the reasons for these creatures' presence in so many Scottish Lochs are unclear, they are thought to potentially be linked to migratory behaviour driven by the search for food and territory.

Beastly Evidence

Photography and Film:

Hugh Grey took the first photo of Nessie near Foyers on 12 November 1933. It shows a large body causing a disturbance in the water. Grey could not see the head, which was underwater.

The Surgeon's Photo: The Surgeon's photo, taken by Lt. Col. R. Kenneth Wilson in 1934, was initially believed to be authentic but later faced scepticism. Claims emerged in the 1990s that Christian Spurling and Marmaduke Wetherell faked the image using a toy submarine with a wooden head. The credibility of the hoax has been questioned, with critics arguing that Spurling was unable to be at the site or lacked knowledge about specific details. A lesser-known second photo exists but is not mentioned in Spurling's account.

Fraser Film: James Fraser recorded footage of Nessie using a 16mm movie camera with a telephoto lens in Urquhart Bay. This film was presented at the Linnaean Society of London's annual meeting, where members identified the creature as a seal, whale, or otter. Maurice Burton reviewed five stills from this now-lost film and estimated the object to be 12 feet long and around 150 yards from the shore.

Malcolm Irvine Film: On 12 December 1933, Malcolm Irvine filmed Nessie. The footage was brief due to the camera jamming during the shot and is now missing. (Photo!) On 22 September 1936, he filmed another creature in the loch near Urquhart Castle. This one-minute footage featured a grey, 16-foot animal with two humps moving quickly across the water. It was highlighted in cinemas across Britain as newsreel footage titled *The Loch Ness Monster: Proof at Last!* Long considered lost, the film was rediscovered in 2001 in the Scottish Screen Archive.

G.E. Taylor Film: On 29 May 1938, G.E. Taylor recorded the first colour film of Nessie near Foyers. The footage captured the creature's neck moving up and down, with a roundish body protruding about a foot above the water. Scientists from the National Institute of Oceanography (now the Southampton Oceanographic Centre) examined the three minutes of footage. They concluded the object was a dead horse or cow floating on the surface. Roy Mackal, however, believes it depicted a live animal feeding on fish.

Lachlan Stuart Humps: On 14 July 1951, Lachlan Stuart, a Forestry Commission worker, photographed Nessie at Whitefield. The image depicted three humps and was quickly published by the *Sunday Express* the following day. (Photo!) Later in the 1980s, author Richard Frere claimed that Stuart admitted the image was merely three hay bales partially submerged and covered with a tarp.

Peter McNab Photos: Bank manager Peter McNab captured two photos of an elongated creature off Urquhart Castle. To date, only one photo has survived. Some argue it shows the large humps of a creature resembling Nessie swimming near the castle, while others suggest it depicts a standing wave from a nearby boat.

Tim Dinsdale Film: On 23 April 1960, aeronautical engineer Tim Dinsdale filmed a zigzagging, mahogany-coloured object in Foyers Bay using a Bolex Camera. He later recorded a boat moving in the same direction for comparison. In 1966, the Royal Air Force Joint Air Reconnaissance Intelligence Centre (JARIC) analysed the film and confirmed it depicted an "animate object" between 12 and 16 feet long. In 1993, the Project Urquhart investigation enhanced the film, revealing a shadow behind and beneath the head, suggesting a body similar to a plesiosaur. Yet, some researchers contend the footage shows a fishing boat.

Peter O'Connor Photo: On 27 May 1960, Peter O'Connor captured a photo of Nessie while camping near Foyers. The image resembled an overturned boat with a short, cylindrical neck. A few weeks later, Maurice Burton discovered plastic sacks and string at the site, leading him to conclude the photo was a hoax.

The LNPIB (Loch Ness Phenomenon Investigation Bureau): Between 1962 and 1972, the Loch Ness Phenomenon Investigation Bureau (LNPIB) – founded by David James, Constance Whyte, Richard Fitter, and Sir Peter Scott, and overseen by Tim Dinsdale – monitored long-range surveillance cameras positioned at key locations along the loch. Although footage of several lengths was collected, the monitoring endeavour was deemed unsuccessful. On 6 June 1963, three separate films were captured by LNPIB observers; one appeared to show a water disturbance caused by ducks, while the others were harder to explain. One depicted a dark, cylindrical object, and the other highlighted a dome-shaped object rapidly moving through the water.

Dick Raynor Film: Dick Raynor filmed a brief sequence of 35mm, black-and-white footage showing a V-shaped wake emanating from Dores Bay. The movement stopped when the passenger boat *Scott II* entered the frame. JARIC analysed the film and identified a 7-foot object surfacing. However, Raynor now believes the footage captured a flock of birds.

Robert H. Rines - Flipper Photo: On 8 August 1972, underwater footage was recorded in Urquhart Bay near Temple Pier by a team led by Robert H. Rines from the Academy of Applied Science in Belmont, Massachusetts. This footage, taken from an underwater camera suspended from Rines's boat, the *Nan*, corresponded with Raytheon sonar tracking from another vessel, the *Narwhal*, which monitored a large object chasing fish. Two frames displayed a triangular (rhomboid) flipper or fin against a rough body, while a third captured two blobs. The flipper images only became distinctly visible after digital enhancement, leading to claims of retouching. However, dense peat particles in the water obscured significant details.

Sonar Evidence:

1954: The *Rival III*, a fishing vessel navigating near Urquhart Castle, recorded the first echo-sounder trace of an unidentified target in Loch Ness, detected at a depth of 480 feet.

1968: D. Gordon Tucker, utilizing advanced digital multibeam sonar equipment stationed at Temple Pier, detected two large targets in the loch. One target ascended from the loch floor at about one hundred feet per minute, while another moved horizontally and dove at 450 feet per minute. This rapid movement suggested that the targets were unlikely to be schools of fish. In the summer of 1969, a searchlight-sonar target was picked up by the Vickers Oceanics research submarine *Pisces*, approximately six hundred feet away from Urquhart Castle, about fifty feet from the bottom. As the submarine approached, the object evaded detection and was lost.

1969: Robert E. Love Jr. recorded an unmistakable searchlight sonar target while on the motorboat *Rangitea*. The target exhibited a looped movement at a depth of 220 feet northeast of Foyers, lasting more than three minutes, using a Honeywell Scanar II-F sonar mounted at the prow.

1972: The Robert Rines team aboard the *Narwhal* utilized a Raytheon echo sounder to identify two targets correlated with a simultaneous photograph (notably, the famous flipper photo). The targets were approximately 8 feet apart, with one interpreted as a large object featuring an appendage 9 feet long.

1976: Robert Rines and Charles Wyckoff of Klein Associates recorded large, moving objects using an EG&G Mark 1B side-scan sonar mounted at Temple Pier.

1978: Theo Brown suspended underwater speakers from a small inflatable boat southwest of Foyers, playing infrasound recordings designed to attract marine predators. During this time, sonar picked up a 30-50-foot animal ascending from the deep, which swiftly retreated when a large motorboat passed nearby.

1978: Tom Cummings and Garry Kozak of Klein Associates captured a side-scan sonar image of a moving object that left a turbulence wake.

1982: Adrian Shine's research yielded forty sonar contacts using three types of sonar apparatus from field boats, including several strong single targets.

1987: During Operation Deepscan, organized by Adrian Shine, a flotilla of nineteen motor cruisers equipped with echo-sounding sonar covered 60 per cent of Loch Ness. This operation uncovered two large, indistinct objects moving close to the surface and a submerged tree thought to be the gargoyle head photographed in 1975.

1993: In sonar tests conducted during Nicholas Witchell's Project Urquhart expedition, Colin Bean recorded an underwater storm caused by atmospheric conditions. The following day, he identified two large underwater targets, definitively not shoals of fish.

1997: Robert Rines and Charles Wyckoff returned to Loch Ness for a scientific documentary sponsored by the Nova television series. Contrary to the producers' original intention to debunk the Loch Ness legend, the two significant sonar contacts recorded during their expedition prompted further contemplation about the existence of Nessie.

2000: Sonic surveys conducted that year detected a series of unidentified underwater sounds, matching the frequency (747-751 hertz) only found in walrus (*Odobenus rosmarus*), elephant seal (*Mirounga angustirostris*), and killer whale (*Orcinus orca*) sounds—similar to a pig grunting or human snoring.

2001: On 1 July, the skipper of the *M.V. Nessie Hunter* noted an unusual target on the Furuno sonar display. The image captured depicted an elongated, sinuous object with two dorsal protuberances.

2002: An article in the *Inverness Courier* reported sonar readings captured by local researchers. The readings hint at large, unidentified shapes detected around fifteen fathoms deep in the loch, stirring renewed interest in the Loch Ness Monster.

2005: *The Scotsman* featured stories of tourists capturing sonar evidence using handheld devices during boat trips, with several reports describing large, moving targets on their screens.

2010: Sonar specialists from a university-led expedition published findings in the *Journal of Marine Research*, detailing several sonar contacts that suggested large creatures were present beneath the surface of Loch Ness, reigniting discussions among cryptozoologists.

2016: The *Daily Record* reported on a group of adventurers who, using state-of-the-art sonar technology, captured images of a large object at a depth of approximately 200 feet, claiming it could be the elusive Nessie.

2020: Local news outlets covered a series of sonar tests conducted by a team of marine biologists, which revealed multiple unexplained sonar readings and suggested the presence of creatures exceeding 20 feet in length.

2022: A documentary aired on a popular streaming service highlighting an expedition with advanced sonar technology, where researchers documented a significant underwater object while broadcasting live, capturing widespread attention.

2025: Reports from a recent expedition highlighted the discovery of unusual sonar activity in the northern part of Loch Ness. Experts suggested that these readings corresponded with migratory patterns of larger aquatic animals, further fuelling the Loch Ness mystery.

Physical Evidence: In 1978, truck driver Stanley Roberts rented his holiday cruiser to a family. While they were sailing, they unexpectedly collided with a large unknown object on Loch Ness near Urquhart Castle. The propeller stopped turning, and the family became worried as their elderly grandfather, who was on board, had a sudden heart attack. With their propeller disabled and no radio on board, they started firing distress flares to attract attention and were subsequently rescued and towed back to Fort Augustus, where their grandfather was rushed to a hospital and sadly pronounced dead upon arrival. Roberts, the owner of the cruiser, initially having only been told by the family that there had been an accident, decided to take it to a local boatyard for repairs. Only later, and too late, did he discover that the workers had found flesh and black skin an inch thick along the prop shaft and, once removed, had thrown it back into the water. Could this have been the only physical evidence of the Loch Ness monster ever discovered and, if yes, how close did we come in 1978 to discovering the identity of this 1500-year-old mystery?

Beastly Theories!

Boat Wakes: A boat wake describes the waves created by the movement of a vessel through the water. These wakes can manifest as a series of humps and can persist for 20 to 30 minutes after the boat has passed. They are caused by water disturbance, which generates ripples and waves that spread outward. A standing wave, often created when two opposing waves meet (an interference effect), can appear as a solid mass in the water from certain distances or angles, potentially leading to confusion with marine creatures. Additionally, the silhouette of a distant motorboat on the horizon can resemble that of a moving animal, contributing to misidentifications.

Grey Seal: The grey seal is the largest seal species found in the North Atlantic, with males growing up to 7 feet 6 inches (2.3 meters) in Canadian waters, while their eastern Atlantic counterparts tend to be smaller, averaging about 6.5 feet (2 meters). The largest populations are in the UK, particularly in the Hebrides, Orkneys, and Shetland Islands, where extensive rookeries are established. Grey seals occasionally enter freshwater lochs as they hunt for food. Documented sightings include Gordon Williamson's photograph of a harbour seal in Loch Ness in 1985 and Dick Raynor's video of a grey seal in Urquhart Bay in October 1999, highlighting their presence in the area.

Sturgeon: The sturgeon is a rare and ancient fish species found in British waters, capable of reaching lengths of up to 9 feet (2.7 meters). They are recognized for their distinctive dorsal scutes—bony plates along their back—quite different from the smooth, rounded shapes often associated with the Loch Ness Monster or Nessie. Sturgeons have a long history, dating back over 200 million years, and are primarily bottom feeders, foraging for invertebrates and small fish in river and estuarine environments.

Giant Eel: While tales of giant eels in Loch Ness have circulated, scientific evidence remains elusive. Claims from locals suggest an 18-foot-long eel was trapped in the intake of the Foyers hydroelectric station, yet this remains unproven. The European eel (*Anguilla anguilla*) typically reaches a maximum length of about 5 feet (1.5 meters). In contrast, the European conger (*Conger conger*), a large marine eel, can grow to about 10 feet (3 meters). Such measurements challenge the idea of a giant eel as a species capable of reaching a size sufficient to account for Nessie sightings.

Catfish: The Wels catfish is a massive freshwater fish in parts of Europe. Some individuals are reported to grow up to 13 feet (4 meters) long, although they can weigh over 300 pounds (136 kilograms). When spotted, their whisker-like barbels can give them a unique appearance in the water. Their sheer size and elongation may contribute to witnesses misidentifying them as a mythical creature like Nessie.

Cryptid Amphibian: The concept of a giant amphibian, first proposed by Malcolm Burr and Rupert T. Gould in 1934 and later by Roy

Mackal in 1976, surrounds the idea of colossal freshwater creatures reminiscent of ancient amphibians. Mackal speculated on the existence of an Elasmosaurus, an extinct family of amphibious reptiles with elongated, eel-like bodies that thrived during the Carboniferous period. They could have grown up to 15 feet (4.5 meters) in length, and their flipper-like limbs may have contributed to sightings attributed to Nessie.

Unknown Longneck Seal: Bernard Heuvelmans theorized the possibility of an unknown species of long-necked giant seal related to the marine longneck, which Antonie Cornelius Oudemans initially proposed in 1934. This hypothetical creature would be characterized by its lengthy neck and large body, giving it a distinctive appearance that could lead to misidentifications in Loch Ness. If it existed, such a species could add to the mystique surrounding sightings in the loch of the legendary creature.

A Prehistoric Survivor: The plesiosaur, a type of marine reptile, existed with paddle-like limbs varying in length from 6 to 46 feet. Some had long necks with upward-facing eyes, although neck movements were limited. For survival in Scotland's climate, it would need to be warm-blooded. Plesiosaurs swam like sea lions or turtles, with the long-necked types ambushing fish from below. Fossils date from the Middle Triassic to the end of the Cretaceous, with a slight extinction at the Jurassic's end reducing diversity. Some believe plesiosaurs could explain the Loch Ness Monster, suggesting it adapted to freshwater over time.

Basking Shark/Greenland Shark: The basking shark is unlikely due to its specific feeding habits and recognizable dorsal fin, which isn't reported in Nessie sightings. The Greenland shark also finds the loch unsuitable despite its depth, preferring cold waters. However, they have been found far inland in deep fjords, which some researchers believe could relate to the Loch Ness Monster myth. Their long lifespan (250-500 years) could theoretically explain numerous Nessie sightings if one lived in Loch Ness.

Historical Hippocampus: The hippocampus, a mythological sea creature from various cultures, may resemble descriptions of the Loch Ness Monster. Curiously, rounded horns on its head echo some eyewitness accounts. An archaeologist speculated it might be a gryphon's head, yet the connection to the Roman hippocampus is noteworthy, especially given similar descriptions in past sightings.

'Alpaca' Suitcase: A recent observation at Loch Ness left many spectators puzzled, as they believed they had seen the famous creature swimming close to the shore, only to realize that what they were actually looking at was the long, slender neck of an alpaca. The alpaca, one of several that had escaped from a nearby farm, sparked a flurry of online jokes about the true identity of Nessie being unveiled and also fuelled another conspiracy regarding the 1934 'surgeon's photo.' While this amusing incident was certainly entertaining, it's fair to conclude that swimming alpacas had no connection to Nessie's sightings from 90 years ago, nor even from 20 years ago, for that matter!

The Travelling Nessie Theory: It is the author's opinion that the creatures of Loch Ness inhabit both salt and freshwater environments and occasionally move between lochs, rivers, and the sea, under the cover of darkness, which is prevalent in this rural and dimly lit part of the British Isles. The reasons for their journeys are not well understood, just as little is known about the creatures themselves. However, it is reasonable to suspect that, like other known species, their transient behaviour is driven by factors such as food, biology, and ecology. Another possibility is that their movements could reflect a territorial roaming behaviour. This idea is supported by the fact that only a tiny percentage of sightings (just 2%) involve more than one animal. If this theory about the solitary nature of these creatures is accurate, then Scotland's 31,460 lochs and lochans, along with its abundant coastal waters, would provide ample territory for a solitary population of these animals to roam.

THE PATAGONIAN PLESIOSAUR

What's in a Name? The Spanish term "Little Nahuel" derives from the lake, also called the Patagonian plesiosaur. It translates to yaguarete (Jaguar), and is named after the largest big cat found in Argentina. It can be traced back to indigenous Patagon legends of water monsters that predate the conquest of America.

Monstrous Measurements: Length ranges from 15 to 20 feet, with a rough skin. It has a snake-like head and a neck that is 9 feet long. The creature has several humps and closely resembles paleontological depictions of a plesiosaur. Its long neck, similar to a swan's, stands high above the water.

Terrifying Tracks: While the tracks of the Patagonian have been observed, they have never been described in detail.

Beastly Behaviours: Surfaces only when the lake is calm. Makes distinctive breathing sounds. Nocturnal. Can travel on land.

Deadly Diet: It is commonly believed that these creatures primarily feed on aquatic life, such as fish, turtles, and otters. However, there have also been occasional reports of livestock, pets, and even humans falling victim to these animals, which are thought to be ambush predators.

Watery Abode: The Patagonian plesiosaur has been observed in Lago Nahuel Huapi in Neuquén Province, Argentina, and in the Lake region of Chubut Province, which features Lago Blanco. There have also been reports from nearby areas in Chile and along the river basins that flow into the Pacific Ocean. Many researchers think these creatures may reside in both fresh and saltwater environments.

Scary Sightings

Lago Nahuel Huapi:

1600s/1700s: The legend of Nahuelito is said to have originated around 1540, and was mentioned by conquistadors from local natives near Lake Nahuel Huapi. However, no printed references to the creature exist before the early 20th century. Additionally, early chroniclers, missionaries, and explorers seem not to have reported any sightings. Notably, even one of the greatest proponents of the Patagonian plesiosaur theory, Dr. Clemente Onelli, only mentioned unusual creatures in Patagonia dating back to the plesiosaur craze of the 1880s, but these sightings did not include Lake Nahuel Huapi. The first documented account of a strange water creature in Lake Nahuel Huapi would not be recorded for another four decades in the 1920s.

1896: During an expedition of an undisclosed location in Patagonia, Dr. Clemente Onelli recounted an intriguing experience. While camping, he received reports from local inhabitants about strange sounds reminiscent of a cart rumbling over rocks. When Onelli and his team went to investigate, they witnessed a massive dark shadow swimming away. The creature craned its neck several times in a swan-like fashion before vanishing from sight. While interviewing locals near the location, Onelli also discovered that prospectors, approximately two decades earlier, had found the skeleton of a colossal being near the Chilean border.

1910: George Garrett claimed to have spotted a large creature while managing a company on Lake Nahuel Huapi. He described the animal as 15 to 20 feet long and around six feet tall above the water. This sighting was made public in an article in the *Toronto Globe* on 6 April 1922, where Garrett recounted his experience of seeing the creature in a narrow inlet called Pass Coytrue. After observing it for a few minutes, the creature vanished. Garrett noted how residents mentioned that Indigenous people had often spoken of seeing large water animals.

1938: There was a reported sighting at Lake Gutierrez, which is located about 10 miles from Bariloche and is connected to Lake Nahuel Huapi via the Rio Gutiérrez.

1960: A story surfaced about the Argentine navy's pursuit of a significant submerged object, often mistakenly attributed to a Newsweek article. This article discusses the navy's search for an "unidentified undersea object," which was a Cold War espionage vessel operating near a naval base in the South Atlantic. It humorously speculates, "Could it be a whale? An amphibious UFO? Or the Loch Ness monster took a wrong turn?" However, the article does not mention Nahuelito.

1976: In February, near the Parque Hotel by Bariloche, Aquiles Lamfre reported seeing a whirlpool in the calm lake about a mile from the shore. Along with it was a large creature with a dark back and a lengthy neck topped with a snake-like head, which then disappeared beneath the water. Eleven years later, he claimed to have observed the creature's body rising from the lake again, although this time it was missing its head and neck.

1978: On 16 February, Coca and Vincent Trussle, living in a lake-view home, experienced strange occurrences that intensified every February. Coca recalled a particularly unusual event near Bariloche, which her friends Bill and Hilda Rumboll also witnessed. Hilda later described her sighting in the March 1978 issue of *Revista Siete Días* in an article titled *¿Monstruos prehistóricos en Bariloche?* She recounted a calm autumn afternoon when a creature swiftly crossed the lake, creating a significant wake. Through binoculars, Hilda observed what looked like a long neck, reminiscent of a swan, which transformed into the shape of a post before disappearing amid turbulent waters. She estimated the creature's length to be around 16 feet.

1979: In May, several people near the lake observed an object moving in the water 0.6 miles from the shoreline. They estimated its length to be around 16 feet. Some sceptics suggested it was a submerged tree trunk.

1986: In October, Ms. Stella Maris López encountered a large creature with a triangular head resembling that of a snake, along with a pair of humps covered in scales.

1986: In December, engineer Guillermo Varzi (or Barzi) was returning from a picnic at Bahia Lynch on the Quetrihué Peninsula when he noticed something moving at 15 to 18 miles per hour. His daughter, Martina, captured a photo of the mysterious object, which was later featured in *Diario Rio Negro*. Varzi initially believed it to be a submarine but soon discerned a serpent-like head and dark fins resembling those of a dolphin or shark trailing behind.

1987: In November, José Ulesia and 26 colleagues from the Centro Atómico Bariloche observed the shadowy outline of a creature in the lake near Playa Bonita.

1987: Alfredo Julio Passo, a former pilot with Austral Líneas Aéreas and captain of the tourist boat *Paisano*, reported witnessing a creature with a "head resembling that of a black snake."

1988: In January, the local newspaper *Rio Negro* reported a sighting near San Carlos de Bariloche. Witnesses, including telephone company workers, firefighters, and a Forest Department employee, observed a large creature in Lake Nahuel Huapi, describing it as leaving a frothy wake approximately 49 feet long. One witness mentioned seeing two humps and a dark shape moving swiftly through the water.

Eleven days later, a short video filmed by an unknown author showed something quickly moving across the lake, creating a wake with at least two dark objects. A witness at Playa Bonita described the creature as having an angular head resembling a giant snake and characteristics of an ancient animal.

1989: A group of tourists guided by Isabel Muller encountered a creature measuring about 66 feet long beneath the water's surface. One of the members, Jorge Brodo, managed to capture a photograph of it, describing the being as "resembling a submarine underwater, though its movements were notably more fluid."

1990: The Buenos Aires newspaper *Diario Popular* reported an unusual sighting near Isla Victoria, where witnesses described observing a peculiar hump resembling the back of an animal.

1994: On the evening of 1 January, Jessica Campbell and Paula Jacarbe were at the beach on the San Pedro Peninsula, enjoying a calm lake, when they spotted a large creature near the shore. It resembled a whale, featuring several humps and two small fins, and they even heard its breathing. However, like many other sightings, they never saw its head. The creature surfaced a couple of times, and when it approached Ms Campbell as she sat on a rock, she quickly fled. Two years later, Campbell had another encounter with the creature, seeing it twice in a single afternoon, including when it swam directly toward her while she was perched on the rocks.

1993: In September, a video was broadcast on Bariloche Cable TV's program *Buenos Muchachos*, highlighting an unusual moving wake in the Campanario Arm of the lake.

1998: In January, a creature appeared in Ragintuco, a stream located just north of Huemul Fjord. While fishing there, a couple named Graciela Carello and Rubén Ehara experienced something incredible. The previously tranquil surface of the water suddenly became disturbed, revealing a dark brown back that emerged from the foam. Startled, the creature quickly submerged again, generating large waves. The estimated length of its back was about 6.5 feet.

2000: At 7 AM on a calm, overcast summer day, Christian Muller was situated 6.8 miles from the heart of Bariloche when he noticed what he initially thought was a boat due to the wake it was leaving. However, the object's dark hue caught his attention, as none of the ships at the local nautical club was painted that colour. Abruptly, the large, dark figure vanished beneath the lake's surface.

2006: In April, three photographs allegedly depicting Nahuelito were mysteriously dropped off at the reception of the local newspaper *El Cordillerano*. However, there is a strong suspicion that these images are fraudulent.

2007: In November, a woman named Rosalba Painefil witnessed something remarkable near the mouth of the Ñirihuau River, east of Bariloche. She described it as a massive creature, unlike any cow or deer. It emerged onto the shore momentarily before retreating back into the lake, where it vanished from sight. Rosalba noted that while it had a head, it didn't resemble any known animal; its size alone was astonishing.

2008: In April, two distinct objects resembling "bus roofs" or "rectangular submarines" emerged near the downtown area of Bariloche, creating a significant number of bubbles. Their dimensions were approximately 26 by 13 feet and 20 by 10 feet. One of the objects protruded about 16 inches above the water and had an appearance likened to a "tortoise" or a "hamburger," both of which gleamed under the sunlight.

2008: In November, the Bariloche newspaper El Cordillerano published a photograph that was a hoax. The photographer claimed he spotted some huillínes swimming beneath the surface. However, the image resembled a floating log and was dismissed as a precise fake.

Lake Pueyrredón:

1910: Lake Pueyrredón, also known as Cochrane in Chile, with whom it shares a border, covers an area of 67 square miles and is situated at an elevation of 505 feet above sea level, draining into the Pacific Ocean. This scenic spot is near the famous unicorn paintings in Cueva del Indio and the Chilean National Preserve called "Los Tamangos." In an intriguing story from 1910, Dr. Clemente Onelli recounted an incident involving a local named Alfredo Sepúlveda. He claimed to have seen an animal he called a "saurius" while swimming in the lake.

Tamango River:

1898: The Tamango River, commonly called the Chacabuco River, is located approximately 6 miles north of Lake Pueyrredón, separated by a steep range of hills. This river flows into the South Pacific Ocean. In 1898, a topographer from the Argentine Border Commission named Juan Waag stumbled upon the fresh tracks of a large, unidentified creature along its banks.

Santa Cruz:

1913: A sighting of a creature was documented by an Englishman who observed the being in a lake at an undisclosed site within Santa Cruz territory. The creature was described as having an elongated neck and a robust body.

Lago Lácar:

1950s: This location was famous for several reports of the Patagonian plesiosaur. However, it is more widely recognized as the habitat of another creature, the Cuero. According to local indigenous people, this man-eating beast resembles a cowhide surrounded by sharp teeth and ensnares any unfortunate animal that ventures too close.

Lago Blanco/White Lake:

1897: Clemente Onelli, the director of the Jardin Zoologico in Buenos Aires, interviewed a Chilean farmer living near Lago Blanco (White Lake), a shallow body of water, nine miles long, near to the base of the Andean foothills. The farmer had reported hearing unusual nocturnal sounds resembling something heavy being dragged along the pebbly shore. He also claimed to have seen a long-necked creature in the lake, which would quickly dive whenever disturbed.

Laguna Negra/Black Lake:

1921: In October, American prospector Martin Sheffield discovered large animal tracks near a mountain lake west of Esquel, Argentina. Following these tracks, he claimed to have seen a creature resembling a plesiosaur, described as having a long neck like a swan and a crocodile-like body. Sheffield, a well-regarded gold prospector in the region, detailed his findings in a letter to Dr. Clemente Onelli, the director of Buenos Aires Zoo, emphasizing the creature's massive size and suggesting it could be hunted. This lake, Laguna Negra (or Laguna del Plesiosaurio), became the centre of attention after Sheffield's letter sparked public interest.

The revelation of Sheffield's sighting led to a media frenzy, prompting the organization of an expedition to search for the creature, which was dubbed the "plesiosaur" by the press. This event gained international coverage, predating the Loch Ness monster stories by over a decade. Sheffield's background as a hunter and his connection to notorious outlaws like Butch Cassidy and the Sundance Kid, along with mention of Sir Arthur Conan Doyle's *The Lost World*, suggests influences on his narrative of the creature, blurring the lines between myth and reality in the scenic Andes.

1922: On 23 March, Onelli organized an expedition led by Jose Cihagi and Emilio Frey to explore recent reports regarding a mysterious creature. Despite encountering some bureaucratic obstacles related to permits, the team arrived at the lake on 18 April, where Sheffield had previously spotted the animal. However, their search was unsuccessful, even after detonating dynamite in the water to stir up the area. With the approach of southern winter, the group had to leave and return to Buenos Aires on 26 April.

Lake Tagua-Tagua:

1995: It was at Lake Tagua-Tagua that Carlos Pinto reported encountering a strange creature while traveling upstream in his motorboat. He described it as having the head of a small foal, a shiny hide, and a short, stiff mane. The animal swam swiftly, nearly capsizing his boat. Additionally, Pinto's aunt, living nearby, witnessed a peculiar sight involving her pregnant mare. After appearing to give birth, a creature resembling a small foal emerged, walking like a duck with webbed feet. It began to shed its fur and then disappeared into the river leading to the lake, while the mare neighed as if calling for it. The woman initially believed it was her foal, but it could have been a predator that had captured and brought it to the lake.

Lake Vidal Gormaz:

Date Unknown: Tito Bahamonde and his wife Amandina Velázquez, residents near Lake Vidal Gormaz, shared their experience of encountering a "monster" rumoured to inhabit the lake. This expansive body of water, an extension of the South Pacific Ocean, spans 37 miles and winds through the Andes. It is fed by multiple mountain rivers, such as the Manso and Puelo rivers, which flow down from the western slopes. Is it possible that this lake also attracts an occasional unknown visitor from the ocean?

Strait of Magellan:

1900s: Reports of sea serpent sightings similar to Patagonia's Lake Monsters were documented in the Strait of Magellan. This lends credibility to the itinerant lake monster theory, suggesting that these creatures may alternate between inhabiting salt and fresh water at different times.

Cabra Corral:

1987: Lucio Temporetti and six other fishermen reported encountering a massive serpent with a prominent head that left a significant wake as it navigated through the water.

2011: In November, *El Tribuno* newspaper published a still photograph that allegedly depicted the head of a large creature. A witness named Leo Bonino, who was in the vicinity, also claimed to have seen a sizable reptilian.

2011: On Christmas Day, a fisherman named Sebastien Papetti captured video footage of a peculiar creature at Cabra Corral, a manmade lake in Argentina's Salta Province. Seeing a large reptilian figure with an oval-shaped head gracefully gliding through the water, Papetti was taken aback. He estimated the creature to be more than 49 feet long and noted that it briefly raised its head above the water before diving down. Papetti reported that several other fishermen had also encountered this unusual animal, which resembled a massive snake swimming while keeping its head visible. The local media labelled the creature "Cabralito," a name that pays homage to its habitat at Lake Cabra Corral and its famous cryptid counterpart, Nahuelito from Lago Nahuel Huapi.

Lago Huechulafquen:

1922: This glacial lake, stretching 18 miles in length and 3 miles in width, with depths reaching 1,640 feet, is famously believed to be home to a monster of the plesiosaur variety known as Huechelito. Modern sightings date back to 1922 when a local named Emilio Frey reported seeing a long-necked creature with a lizard-like head. Emilio claimed that the creature caused the water to boil when it submerged.

1980s: Border Patrol officers fired at a massive reptile that was sunbathing along the riverbank. The creature fled their pursuit, disappearing into the lake's murky depths.

2009: Jorge Salcedo captured photographs of a dark, multi-humped reptilian creature swimming about 500 feet away from his catamaran, moving with vertical undulations. The authenticity of Salcedo's images was verified and subsequently sent to the United States for analysis. Biologist Alejandro del Valle, who examined the photos, concluded that, although she could not identify the creature, it closely resembled a giant snake. The local community was so frightened by this sighting that the mayor established a special team to investigate the phenomenon.

Lago Puiman:

Unknown Date/s: The northern arm of Lake Huechulafquen is known as Lago Puiman, and is divided from the main lake by a narrow waterway. This adjoining body of water is also said to be home to a creature resembling a plesiosaur.

Beastly Evidence

Film & Photography:

Río Negro Photos: In 1988, images of Nahuelito were featured in a magazine by the Río Negro newspaper. Taken from a short distance with an analogue camera, the photos showed the enigmatic object near the coastline of Bariloche. An anonymous man who submitted the photos wrote in a letter, "This is not merely a log with strange shapes. It's not a wave. Nahuelito has revealed itself."

El Cordillerano Photos: On 17 April 2006, El Cordillerano, a local newspaper, published a story about an anonymous photographer who submitted two intriguing images claiming to show Nahuelito. The photographer left a note with the photographs stating: "This is not a twisted tree trunk, nor is it a wave. Nahuelito has revealed itself. Lake Nahuel Huapi, Saturday, 15 April, at 9 o'clock. I prefer to remain anonymous to avoid any future complications."

Physical Evidence:

Cryptid Carcass: Dr. Clemente Onelli was a key figure in the early research of Patagonian plesiosaurs, contributing significantly to our understanding of initial sightings. Around 1907, he learned from a Norwegian engineer named Vaag about a waterway he discovered while working on the Argentina-Chile border called the River Tamango. Vaag claimed to have found the remains of a large creature resembling a plesiosaur, although the fate of these remains unclear. In a different area, Ultima Esperanza, researchers reported discovering a large quadruped's preserved hide and bones, prompting speculation that it could be a recently deceased mammoth. These discoveries spurred numerous expeditions across Patagonia, fuelled by curiosity and the hope of uncovering a lost zoological world. However, despite some intriguing finds, no substantial evidence of extraordinary zoological phenomena was uncovered.

Fossil Features: Patagonia was once home to large prehistoric creatures, including mammals and reptiles. In 1911, Professor Frederic B. Loomis led an expedition in Chubut that uncovered significant fossils, including a skull of a pyrotherium. More recently, palaeontologist Fernando Novas and his team discovered a complete skeleton of a plesiosaur, a marine reptile, dating back about 65 million years. The skeleton was found in Argentino Lake, prompted by a tip from Kenneth Lacovara, who had previously excavated a massive dinosaur nearby.

The Hunt for a Specimen: The 1922 expedition led by Dr. Onelli was motivated by reports of a creature resembling a plesiosaurus in Patagonia. Despite scientific scepticism about the existence of such an animal, including criticisms of Onelli's report, there was significant interest within Argentina, prompting a proposal for an expedition to investigate the claims further. Dr Albarrin, the President of the Society for the Protection of Animals, voiced concerns regarding the potential capture or hunting of the creature under Argentine law, arguing that if it were indeed a plesiosaurus, it would be a unique scientific marvel that should be preserved rather than exploited.

The expedition began on 22 March and assembled a diverse team, including Emilio Frey and José María Cinaghi. After a brief stop in Bariloche, where they heard additional reports of similar creatures, the team reached Sheffield's cabin on 21 April. Unfortunately, Sheffield was not present, but they were able to gather insights from his family. Following the last known sighting, they explored the small lake where the creature was said to have appeared, finding it surprisingly shallow and devoid of fish. This raised questions about the creature's existence, yet residents continued to affirm its presence.

After an unsuccessful search that included using dynamite in the lake, the team expanded their search to nearby Lake Puelo via the Epuyén River but still found no evidence of the elusive creature. The expedition faced scientific scepticism, with experts such as Professor Brewster Loomis expressing doubts about the stories they heard. As winter approached and no significant findings emerged, Onelli postponed further exploration until the following summer. The expedition was officially called off on 23 April 1923 and, following Dr Onelli's untimely death in 1924, was never resumed, leaving the mysterious creature's fate unresolved.

Interestingly, despite Onelli's extensive discussions about plesiosaurs, on this expedition, he was primarily focused on searching for a mylodon —a large, prehistoric herbivorous mammal related to modern sloths—rather than a plesiosaur, despite his frequent references to the latter. To mislead potential competitors, he even created a narrative suggesting that Sheffield had sighted an exaggeratedly monstrous creature at the lake in Esquel rather than the smaller Black Lake where the expedition was taking place.

Onelli's secret instructions emphasized the goal of verifying the existence of a mylodon, which he believed could be closely related to the domestic Cryopterium; a belief based on evidence such as excrement and dry hides found at Mylodon Cave in 1896. While he expressed cautious belief in Sheffield's account of seeing tracks, he dismissed the significance of squashed grass near the lagoon, suggesting that it could have simply been a resting place for huemul, a stout, stocky deer known for its swimming ability and fondness for water.

A Musical Monster! *El Plesiosauro* is a tango composed in 1922 by Rafael D'Agostino, who was recognized for his contributions to the popular music scene, and Amílcar Morbidelli, noted for his poignant lyrics. This piece emerged during a wave of public fascination and media frenzy surrounding sensational reports of a plesiosaur discovered alive in Patagonia, which fuelled imaginations and inspired various forms of artistic expression. Although the existence of a living plesiosaur was never substantiated, the story captivated the public, reflecting a broader curiosity about prehistoric creatures and the mysteries of the natural world.

The original lyrics of *El Plesiosauro* are in Spanish, but here is a loose translation into English.

I'm a poor wanted animal
for the ungrateful and without conscience.
Because I'm weird and I'm curious too
(according to the people there).

Leave them alone here, enjoying themselves
In the solitude of this lake
What will you do with taking me out if it's in vain
Take me out of this place alive?

Don't the gentlemen know
that this is not picking flowers?
They intend to hunt me down and take me away
as if nothing were.

Damned! Don't name me.
I owe you nothing, Onelli.
Let me live with equal prerogatives
like you live there.

Beastly Theories!

Giant Otter: The Giant Otter (*Pteronura brasiliensis*) can grow up to 6 feet long, including its tail, and is primarily found in northern regions, though there are historical records in Uruguay. If present, its size may lead to mistaken sightings of Patagonian plesiosaurs, especially when seen from a distance, confusing observers who might mistake them for lake monsters like Nahuelito. However, a better explanation for some of these sightings is groups of Huillínes (Patagonian otters), which swim playfully and can resemble an extinct reptile when moving in a line. Their wet fur may also create the illusion of scales. Of course, calm conditions can lead to misinterpretations of disturbances on the water's surface caused even by smaller creatures or objects.

Prehistoric Survivor: Plesiosaurs were large aquatic reptiles that existed alongside dinosaurs. They were characterized by their broad bodies, short tails, and long necks. Plesiosaurs thrived in marine environments and had a global distribution, with fossils found in Patagonia. Despite their extinction 65 million years ago, an alleged sighting in early 20th-century Patagonia sparked interest and led to an expedition to capture what was dubbed "the plesiosaur."

The expedition garnered international media attention eleven years before the Loch Ness monster became famous. Sheffield, inspired by Sir Arthur Conan Doyle's *The Lost World*, described the creature in a way that aligned with plesiosaur characteristics. However, further examination revealed that plesiosaurs couldn't exhibit graceful movements or produce footprints as suggested.

In 1955, naturalist Alexander Laime claimed to have spotted small, reptilian creatures resembling plesiosaurs on Auyan-tepui, which could be a pygmy species. However, other experts speculated they might be long-necked otters or crocodiles. The narrative intertwines the allure of prehistoric survival and ongoing debates about the identity of these creatures in remote ecosystems.

Humongous Huemel or Monstrous Mylodon? In his "secret instructions" for the expedition, he aimed to mislead the public into believing that Sheffield had encountered an exaggerated monstrous creature at a location other than the small Black Lake, specifically at another lake in Esquel. He intended this to deter potential hunters from discovering the proper focus of his expedition.

He firmly believed that the creature was a Mylodon rather than a plesiosaur. His directives included a mission to investigate the potential existence of this prehistoric animal, which he suggested might be closely related to the domestic Cryopterium, based on remains found at Mylodon Cave in 1896.

While he had reservations about Sheffield's account, he dismissed the idea that the squashed grass by the lagoon was evidence of the creature, suggesting instead that it could have been a resting spot for the huemul, a stocky deer with coarse brown fur. Interestingly, despite its known swimming ability and abundance in the region, he didn't consider the huemul a source of the tracks reported by Sheffield.

Onelli's descriptions of the creature, emphasizing svelte necks and swan-like postures, seemed crafted to reinforce the idea of a plesiosaur, potentially as part of a strategy to mislead anyone attempting to capture the animal before he could act. Throughout this, he maintained his belief that the creature was related to the mylodon found in the Eberhard Cave.

Lost in Translation: Many sceptics believe that the sightings of the Patagonian plesiosaur were inspired by Sir Arthur Conan Doyle's book, *The Lost World*, which was serialized in Buenos Aires in 1914.

In his book, Doyle described plesiosaurs as creatures that moved their necks with "graceful, swan-like undulations," featuring a "barrel-shaped body and huge flippers behind their long, serpent-like necks." This description is quite reminiscent of the plesiosaur sightings frequently reported throughout Patagonia in the years following the book's publication.

However, palaeontologists now assert that it would have been physiologically impossible for a plesiosaur to adopt a "swan-like" pose or to lift its head and neck above the water's surface.

Glacial Lake-Lairs! Numerous reports of lake monsters often highlight a notable connection between sightings of these creatures and the characteristics of glacial lakes. This raises intriguing questions: Could these deep, cold bodies of water serve as the perfect habitat for the long-thought-extinct plesiosaurids? Alternatively, might glacial lakes worldwide share certain geological features that create patterns which resemble the physical manifestations of such mythical creatures? Could these lakes truly support the existence of extraordinary aquatic reptiles or do they merely give rise to optical illusions fuelled by local folklore and alien environmental conditions.

OGOPOGO

What's in a Name? "Ogopogo" originates from a British music hall hit, *The Ogopogo*, written in 1924 by Cumberland Clark, but it was Ronald Kenvyn of the *Vancouver Daily Province* who officially declared "Ogopogo" as the name of the monster on 24 August 1926. Apart from its western moniker the monster has several variant names within First Nations peoples, including Auck, Hayash-hayash kustskaka kupa lake (Chinook for "huge animal in the lake"), Naitaka, Ukuk masachi kupa lake (Chinook for "wicked one in the lake"), and Naitaka, (Salishan for "Lake Demon"). Additional variations of this most commonly used name occur such as Na-ha-ha-itkh, na-ha-ha-itque ("snake in the water"), N'ha-a-itk, N'ha-ha-itq, N'hatik, and N'haw-hetq.

Monstrous Measurements: This serpentine creature measures between 20 and 70 feet long and comes in black, dark green, grey, or dark blue. Its skin is smooth and shiny, with some barnacle-like calcium deposits beneath the surface. The head resembles a horse or goat, held at a right angle to the neck, which features horn-like protrusions; ears are rarely reported, and there may be whiskers or a beard. Its slim neck measures 5 to 10 feet long, and its body usually has two to six humps or arching coils, though reports have noted as few as one and as many as fourteen. The middle hump is typically the tallest, rising 2 to 3 feet above the water. Observations suggest the presence of jointed feet that assist in swimming, and the tail can be forked or formed by two flippers.

Terrifying Tracks: No tracks have been identified. However, several large unidentified 'slips' resembling those of a giant snake or alligator have occasionally been observed in the muddy or grassy areas surrounding the shoreline.

Beastly Behaviours: This creature stirs the water into a frenzy and is primarily active in the afternoon. Occasionally, it spouts water. It swims using vertical undulations, reaching up to 40 miles per hour. Two or three of these animals have been observed together occasionally.

Deadly Diet: The creature is assumed to consume fish or freshwater shrimp primarily. However, it was once observed snatching a seagull. In this area, it has access to larger animals like beavers or deer to prey on, but it has never been seen doing so.

Watery Abode: Okanagan Lake, located in British Columbia, is famous for the home of Ogopogo, but there are also similar stories found in lakes across Saskatchewan and Manitoba. The "Favourite Haunt" of Ogopogo is thought to be a deep cave beneath Squally Point, near Rattlesnake Island, an uninhabited, small rocky island situated directly east of Peachland, British Columbia. Over the years, numerous incidents of Ogopogo have been reported in the vicinity of Rattlesnake Island. This island is a popular destination for kayakers and canoers, many of whom hope to glimpse the elusive creature.

Interestingly, an attempt to commercialize Rattlesnake Island in the mid-1970s was halted. The island is part of Okanagan Mountain Park, a local recreational area. Local myth also suggests that in the middle of the lake, there is a cave where Ogopogo is believed to dwell.

Scary Sightings

1872: Susan Allison observed a 60-foot animal swimming against the wind off the western shore during a storm. The following year, in 1873, she became the first non-native to officially record a sighting of the creature when she again witnessed it near her home, now the site of Quail's Gate Winery in West Kelowna. Mrs. Allison said the beast she saw closely resembled the local Native legends she'd heard about N'ha-a-itk.

1923: On 21 July, Lydia Hodgson, who lived in Okanagan Landing, saw Ogopogo while she was horseback riding along the shore. Initially, she mistook it for an upturned boat, but as she approached, she discerned three humps and a head. The creature moved its head from side to side, and she could see its eyes. When Hodgson called out to her son, Ogopogo quickly dove below the surface and swam toward the lake's centre.

1926: On 19 July, John L. Logie, his wife, and their driver, P.J. Dodwell, encountered a 20-foot-long creature while driving by the lake north of Peachland. The animal raced beside their car, causing a foot-high wave in the water. Later that same year, around 30 vehicles parked along an Okanagan Mission beach reported sightings of "Ogopogo."

1926: On 18 November, Ogopogo was spotted between Gellatly Point and Westbank during a baptism ceremony that attracted around sixty people to the shore. Witnesses reported seeing a head resembling a sheep about 2 feet above the water and several coils comparable in size to automobile tyres.

1935: On 6 October, Edward Grahame, Jim Ripley, and Charles B. Grahame were fishing at the lake's northern end when they spotted Ogopogo surfacing approximately 200 feet away from their rowboat. The creature's undulating humps were about a foot above the water's surface.

1947: Several boaters observed the creature simultaneously. One witness, Mr Kray, provided a detailed account: "It had a long, serpentine body approximately 30 feet long, featuring about five undulating sections separated by two-foot gaps, where part of the body was submerged. It had a forked tail, though only half would emerge above the water. Occasionally, the creature would dive underwater and then resurface."

1948: On 26 February, bus driver Don Nourse saw four small animals 50 feet from the shore.

1949: On the evening of 2 July, the families of Leslie L. Kerry and W.F. Watson Jr. observed Ogopogo near Kelowna. The creature measured 30 feet in length, had a sinuous shape and comprised five distinct undulations. They also noted a forked tail.

1950: On 12 August, Rev. W.S. Beames observed Ogopogo near Naramata. He noticed a disturbance resembling a thrashing firehose caused by several humps that emerged and created a significant wake.

1959: Mr and Mrs R.H. Miller and Mr and Mrs Pat Marten reported seeing a tremendous creature with a snake-like head and a blunt nose swimming approximately 250 feet behind their motorboat. The group observed the unknown animal for over three minutes before it submerged.

1964: A member of the Parmenter family managed to capture a photograph of something they encountered in the lake. At an unspecified time, Geoffrey Tozer, the son-in-law of W.A.C. Bennett, who served as the Premier of British Columbia from 1953 to 1972, claimed to have spotted the "creature."

1974: In July, Barbra Clark was swimming toward a diving platform off the lake's southern shore when she felt something large and heavy bump against her legs. After reaching the platform, she saw a serpentine creature moving through the clear water. She also saw a tail that resembled a fluke, measuring 4 to 6 feet in width.

1976: Ed Fletcher, a resident of North Vancouver, claimed to have captured a photograph of an intriguing sight he observed in Lake Okanagan.

1978: In October, Bill Steciuk was driving across a bridge over Okanagan Lake on his way to Kelowna when he noticed something moving in the water. He stopped his car, causing the traffic behind him also to halt. Soon, around 20 other people gathered by the railing to see what he was looking at. Together, they observed a head with three black humps about 60 meters away, rising from the water. Bill and the onlookers watched the creature swimming for a minute before it sank beneath the surface, creating a noticeable wake. This experience convinced Bill of the creature's existence, and he promised to search for Ogopogo one day.

1980: A group of vacationers spotted what they believed to be Ogopogo, with one member, Larry Thal, capturing the sighting on a home movie film. Arlene Gaal, an author and researcher on the subject, later analysed this footage. She noted that Larry's film illustrated the creature's swimming motions, highlighting its speed and the significant waves it generated. Additionally, it showed an appendage that occasionally surfaced. Notably, the creature in Larry's film and another shot by Art Folden seemed to be of similar dimensions, with Larry's footage revealing a creature measuring forty to sixty feet in length.

1981: A member of the Wachlin family captured a photo during Regatta time on 24 July around 1:00 PM They were on a rented ski boat, navigating the west side of the lake near Peachland, just northwest of Rattlesnake Island. A water-skier had just sped past them in the opposite direction when a creature appeared right in front of their boat, facing northeast. They noticed no visible head, leading them to suspect it might lie beneath the surface. Initially, they thought it was the wake from the other boat, but then they realized it was going in different directions. As they approached, the creature began to move quickly in a sinuous manner. They steered their boat directly towards it, but as they got closer, the beast submerged, creating a large swirling pool. Turning their boat around, they managed to spot the creature a couple of feet beneath the water, moving at an impressive speed across the lake before it dove deeper out of sight. The creature was around 50 feet in length and was either a very dark green or black.

1986: In late July, while canoeing near Ellison Provincial Park with his two daughters, the author encountered a mysterious rounded object about 100 meters from the beach. Initially thinking it was a toy, they paddled closer and were struck by a strong fishy smell. The object measured approximately 1 foot wide by 4 feet long, with dark green scales, and shortly after, they noticed a large head resembling that of a horse, complete with horn-like structures. Realizing they might be witnessing the Ogopogo, the author's daughters became frightened, prompting them to return to shore. The creature, which moved slowly and appeared to have a long neck, eventually submerged after about two minutes. Despite having a camera, the author was too shocked to use it, and they have not seen anything like it since.

1989: Hunting guide Ernie Giroux and his wife reported seeing a "bizarre animal" emerging from the calm waters. Giroux described the creature as about 15 feet long, swimming gracefully and quickly. He mentioned the animal had a round head resembling a football, and at one point, several feet of its neck and body surfaced above the water.

1989: In July, 42-year-old Ken Chaplin filmed a creature in Okanagan Lake after his father, 78-year-old Clem Chaplin, claimed he saw Ogopogo. The footage shows a hairless, greenish creature, about 15 feet long, which the Chaplins believe could be Ogopogo. Their video gained media attention, including coverage from *Time Magazine*, but opinions remain divided on its authenticity, with some suggesting it could be an otter or beaver.

1989: On 30 July, John Kirk, along with his son and two members of the British Columbia Scientific Cryptozoology Club, Jim and Barbara

Clark, had frequent sightings of a 35ft. humped animal at Peach Orchard Beach, where one large hump was visible through a 40X telescope. Just a couple of days later, on 1 August 1989, John Kirk observed the same size animal, this time noted to have three to six humps, thrashing frenziedly near Green Bay.

1990: On 24 July, Mike Guzzi noticed a peculiar image at a depth of 350 feet on his fish-finding sonar near Bear Creek. He led Japanese reporter Masayuki Tamaki on a search for Ogopogo for Nippon TV. The sonar image showed a creature with a head, a tail, and a 30-foot-long body, with bubbles rising from its head.

1993: In July, near Forman Hill, six miles north of Penticton, John Moore observed an animal with a horse's head protruding about six feet from the water, creating a wake. It moved in a straight line for approximately thirty minutes.

2000: A businessman from Penticton and his wife observed the head and neck of a large creature swimming through the water for several minutes while boating off Rattlesnake Island near Peachland.

2000: In August, James Ivany claimed to have seen a mysterious creature while on vacation at Okanagan Lake Provincial Park. He described being on the beach with a girl when, at around 5:30 AM, he spotted what looked like a submarine surfacing near Rattlesnake Island. Approximately 100 feet long and moving quickly, it disappeared south towards Penticton within 30 seconds. The lake was calm that morning, and the creature, which created a noticeable wake but made no sound, was faster than any speedboat Ivany had seen that week.

2000: Six adults, including four security guards, spotted a strange-looking creature at the end of Bernard Avenue. The beast, measuring four meters (12 feet) long, had four flippers—two at each end—and moved forward like a caterpillar.

2000: A minister and his wife were walking in Kalamoir Park, located on the west side of Okanagan Lake near Kelowna, when they noticed an unusual creature swimming on the lake's surface and captured its image.

2000: Visitors from Prince George, British Columbia, were walking in Bertram Creek Park, located south of Kelowna, when they noticed a disturbance in the lake about 300 feet out. What looked like a huge log was moving parallel to the shore, despite the waves. They estimated that it was 40 feet long and observed it for about 45 seconds before it disappeared.

2000: Daryl Ellis was swimming across a lake to raise money for cancer research when he encountered two large creatures, identified as Ogopogo, beneath him near Rattlesnake Island. One of the creatures was estimated to be between 20 and 30 feet long, while the other was smaller. As he approached the Okanagan Lake Bridge, a greyish animal leapt from the water nearby, revealing an eye the size of a grapefruit. This creature swam as close as 9 meters to Daryl, observing him closely before they both vanished. Mr. Ellis's sighting was later captured by a local artist trained in police sketch artistry.

2001-2002: Dan Basaraba from Peachland witnessed the unusual phenomenon on two separate occasions and captured photographs each time. The first occurrence was on 19 July 2001, and precisely a year later in 2002, he managed to take a second image.

2002: While filming a documentary about Ogopogo, a crew of 14 people, including Bill Steciuk, witnessed two or three humps moving in and out of the water. This sighting occurred at the exact location where Bill had first spotted what he believed to be Ogopogo over 24 years earlier.

2003: In August, between 12:30 PM and 1:00 PM on a bright, clear day, two elderly residents were out on their boat when they suddenly spotted a long black object with humps swimming past them. It moved so rapidly that their ship began to rock significantly. They were alarmed and attempted to leave the area but noticed two creatures following them. The creatures swam so close that they even bumped into the boat before finally swimming away. The elderly couple was not alone in this experience; five others on the ship also witnessed the unusual creatures.

2003: On 5 August, Steve Lavallee, a DJ, shared an experience from his 25th birthday celebration with friends on a rented boat near Bear Creek Park. While swimming in the lake, he noticed unusual zig-zagging waves that looked like humps, resembling water flowing over a boulder. Jokingly calling it "Ogopogo," the group soon became intrigued as they spotted multiple similar waves and decided to chase them. Despite their efforts in an 8-man Larson bowrider, the waves, which Steve later described as originating from a large object just below the surface, were challenging to follow. He estimated the humps to be about 2.5 feet high and 3 feet wide, leaving the group puzzled about the nature of the phenomenon they witnessed.

2003: In September, Scott Tait reported a sighting near Peachland, British Columbia, shortly after forest fires in Kelowna. While travelling back to Vancouver, he and his wife observed two objects approximately 20 feet from the swimming area, moving slowly south. Initially resembling waves, the objects remained unaffected by a wave that washed over them. They were about 17-20 feet long and separated by 5-6 feet, moving in unison. Tait noted that his first impression was of a wave with something rolling inside it, and he expressed uncertainty about the nature of what he saw, seeking an explanation for the event.

2003: On 11 November, Steve Tarjan and his wife observed a large, greenish object in the lake while visiting a new development in Kalamoir Park. They noticed puffs of condensation above the water and a significant disturbance below. The object, which was about three school buses long, moved smoothly towards them, turned, and then dove, changing colours before disappearing. The experience left them excited, feeling the creature seemed alive and massive.

2004: On 9 August, John Casorso and his family were on a houseboat on Lake Okanagan when they experienced a violent rocking that woke them. Upon investigation, John spotted a large creature swimming away and captured approximately 15 minutes of video footage. He estimated the creature to be about 15 meters long and noted that it was around 125 meters away, with a long dark hump rising out from the water. John believed there could be more than one creature, consistent with other reported sightings, and felt it could not have been a wave due to its stable presence.

2006: In June, Jill Jellett from Peachland reported a sighting while dining at Shawnesey's Bay Marina Restaurant in Summerland. She observed a golden retriever fetching an object in the water when something unusual caught her attention. Initially thinking the dog was returning, she was surprised to see a smooth, seal-like creature rise about 5 feet from the lake. It had a rounded shape, submerging silently, not pointed like a seal. Jill estimated the creature's thickness to be about 14 inches, distinct from any fish she had seen before, like a sturgeon. She regretted not having her camera to capture the sighting.

2006: On 7 September, Michelle and Gilles Beliveau from Westbank took a photo of an object just below the water south of the Kelowna Mission area on the east side of Okanagan Lake. The image was captured from their boat at 2:30 PM They estimated the object to be about 25 feet long and approximately 50 feet from their boat.

2014: In March, Jeff Cottam from Ontario reported seeing an unusual aquatic creature while visiting Peachland with his son. Photographing the lake, he observed an animal about 20 to 30 feet from shore, which had a head resembling a sea lion or snake and a long, shiny black body at least ten to twelve feet long. He managed to take two photographs, the second showing more of the body and two Canada Geese in the frame. The creature moved swiftly before diving underwater and did not reappear. After sharing his experience with his son, he learned about the legend of Ogopogo, but Cottam insisted that what he saw was very real and not mythical.

2015: On 24 May, at approximately 6:00 PM, Bill Steciuk took photos from his balcony at his condo in Kelowna, which overlooks Lake Okanagan—about 200 meters from the shore, an object surfaced from the water. Bill quickly grabbed his camera and captured images of the scene. The object remained in the same spot for a minute, rotating its head as if surveying its surroundings. Shortly after, it "leapt" out from the water, revealing its head and part of its "neck," before diving back down and disappearing beneath the surface.

2017: On 24 June, a family on Lake Okanagan experienced an unusual sighting while boating. Around 1:30 PM, they noticed a jet ski creating large waves, but as they neared, they discovered it was not a jet ski but an object generating three distinct, symmetrical waves. The family, consisting of a husband, wife, and son, was surprised to find that none of them had their phones to record the event, which is unusual for them. They observed the waves rolling away from the object towards the west, with no other boats around on a calm day. After waiting about 15 minutes in the area, nothing reappeared, leaving them puzzled and unable to find a logical explanation for what they saw.

2018: On 24 August, Tracey W., a long-time resident of Kelowna, reported an intriguing sighting while crossing a bridge to Westbank for dinner. As she approached the end of the bridge, she noticed something long swimming in the water, creating waves as it moved. Excited, she urged her husband to slow down, but he only saw the waves. Unable to pull over due to traffic, Tracey, who has lived in Kelowna for 30 years, was thrilled to see something unusual in the lake finally. Shortly after, she learned that two gentlemen had also spotted something similar and captured it on video from Bear Creek Provincial Park, highlighting the rarity of such sightings.

2018: On 9 September, Andrew, a local photographer, reported a remarkable sighting at Bluebird Bay. While capturing images of the lake, he observed a large object suddenly emerge from the water, moving swiftly from left to right. Although a boat was visible in the distance toward Squally Point, it was not large enough to create such a significant wake, and there were no recorded tremors in the Okanagan that day to explain the disturbance.

2018: On 7 September, David Halbauer and his brother Keith reported witnessing a large, snake-like creature at Bear Creek Provincial Park, estimated to be about 15 meters (50 feet) long. Halbauer described it as rolling in and out of the water and noted a disturbance behind it despite the remaining lake being calm. He attempted to film the creature, but the glare made it difficult to see. Halbauer compared the creature to a dinosaur, while Keith expressed amazement at the sight.

2018: On 18 September, a contractor named Martin reported an Ogopogo sighting while working on the 22nd floor of a high-rise condo in Kelowna. Observing calm water with few boats, he noticed something resembling a giant snake breaching the surface, creating significant waves. His co-worker also witnessed the anomaly, which lasted about 2-3 minutes before vanishing. Martin attempted to capture the sighting on his phone, but the disturbance had disappeared by the time he got it out. This incident was part of a series of reported sightings in the area.

2018: On 30 September, at around 4:00 PM, Katrina T. from Peachland, British Columbia, reported witnessing an unusual creature swimming in the middle of the lake, making large splashes before disappearing at the shore. Although her phone battery was low and she couldn't record a video, she took several pictures of the area and nearby caves. Shortly after her sighting, five boats arrived to investigate the situation.

2019: In February, Wendy Steciuk, a resident of a beachfront condo near Mission Creek, observed something unusual on the lake from her living room window around 4:45 PM on 9 February. Noticing the movement, she grabbed her camera—used for previous "Ogopogo" sightings—and took several pictures from her balcony, noting that the object was about 130 meters away.

2019: On 2 September, Kennedy H. reported a story. At around 6:40 AM, they noticed unusual movement in the water while crossing the bridge into Kelowna. They pulled over for a closer look but could not capture a photo of what they saw. It looked like multiple scale-like humps emerging from the water while slowly rotating. Surrounding these humps were larger waves, which left them wondering if varying water temperatures caused the phenomenon or if they had encountered the legendary Ogopogo.

2019: 8 September, anonymous report: "I was kayaking with my friend on Okanagan Lake towards James Grant Island when we suddenly noticed a large wave approaching us. The lake was incredibly calm, smooth, and mirror-like; there were no boats nearby or any disturbances in the water. Out of nowhere, we both saw this long wave come toward us. Although we didn't see any source for the wave, my friend felt a bump under her kayak as it passed. After it moved past us, the wave just disappeared. Our husbands were at the Fintry community beach and witnessed the event. My husband described it as a peculiar wave moving across the lake, as if something large was beneath the surface."

2021: Andrew Stark, an avid photographer living in a lakeside condo complex south of the Eldorado Marina off Lakeshore Road, took several photos from his patio around 4:15 PM on 6 April 2021, which overlooks the lake. Andrew estimated that the object he photographed was about 300 meters to the southwest and remained visible for approximately two minutes.

2021: 10th May, a woman walked along a service road in Summerland, approximately 300 feet above the lake, at around 8:15 AM She noticed a disturbance in the water, with fish jumping and a large black object thrashing in the middle of the lake. Numerous seagulls were also flying over this specific area. This activity lasted for about a minute before the black object submerged and reappeared, moving quickly across the surface toward the lake's centre. The event lasted approximately three minutes before submerging out of sight.

Meet the Pogos!

Manipogo: Manipogo is a lake monster that was reported to inhabit Lake Manitoba, Canada, with sightings dating back to approximately 1908. Named in 1960 by Tom Locke, the creature is described as serpentine, ranging from 10 to 50 feet in length, and characterized by a brownish-black body and a flat, diamond-shaped head. Accounts of the monster highlight its distinctive humps and a bellows-like sound resembling a train whistle. The name Manipogo is sometimes used interchangeably with Winnipogo in other Manitoban lakes, and significant sightings include a group of witnesses in 1960 who reported seeing three of these creatures swimming together, as well as a notable sighting in 1962 by fishermen who observed a large serpent-like being several yards from their boat.

Throughout the years, numerous reports of the Manipogo have emerged. In 1948, a creature was claimed to have risen six feet out the water, emitting what was described as a "prehistoric type of dinosaur cry." Other prominent sightings include encounters across decades, such as in 1935 when Timber inspector C. F. Ross reported seeing a creature resembling a dinosaur with a single horn. In addition, the Manipogo has appeared in popular culture, including features in documentaries like *Northern Mysteries*. The folklore surrounding this creature persists, contributing to the mystique of the lakes in Manitoba and the surrounding regions.

Winnipogo: This is the legendary lake monster of Lake Winnipegosis in Manitoba, Canada, first reported in 1909. Investigated by Dr James McLeod from the University of Manitoba, sightings describe a serpentine creature over twenty feet long with a small, flat head. In the 1930s, Oscar Frederickson discovered a large bone believed to be a spinal vertebra, which was later shown to McLeod and resembled a vertebra of an extinct whale-like creature. Significant sightings include a large creature pushing ice in 1918, a dinosaur-like animal with a horn in 1935, and two incidents in the 1980s where a boat collided with a serpentine creature. The name "Winnipogo" is obviously derived from its more famous cousin, "Ogopogo."

Igipogo: Another legendary freshwater monster said to inhabit Lake Simcoe in Ontario, Canada, drawing comparisons to the Loch Ness monster. Its name, coined in the 1950s, is inspired by the Ogopogo from Lake Okanagan, British Columbia, and the slogan "I Go Pogo" from the 1952 comic strip by Walt Kelly. The creature is described as a seal-like animal measuring 12 to 70 feet long, with a charcoal-grey body, a dog or horse-like face, prominent eyes, and several dorsal fins. It is often reported basking in the sun, suggesting it can breathe air, and sightings primarily occur in Kempenfelt Bay, known for the lake's deepest waters.

Significant sightings of Igopogo include the first alleged encounter by David Soules in 1823 and notable reports in the 1950s and 1980s, with a sonar detection by William W. Skrypetz in 1983 and a videotape in 1991 showing a large creature surfacing. Eyewitness accounts describe various features, including antennae and legs, although many sightings tend to highlight a consistent seal-like appearance. Reports of Igopogo date back to the 1880s, and interest in the creature has persisted over the decades, with residents giving it various monikers such as Beaverton Bessie and Kempenfelt Kelly.

Beastly Evidence

Sonar Strikes! On 24 July 1990, Mike Guzzi observed an image at a depth of 350 feet on his fish-finding sonar while conducting an Ogopogo search near Bear Creek with Japanese reporter Masayuki Tamaki for Nippon TV. The image appeared to consist of a head, tail, and a 30-foot body, with bubbles rising from the head.

Film & Photography:

1968: Arthur Folden captured one minute of 8-millimeter footage showing a 70-foot creature 200 to 300 yards from Rattlesnake Island.

The film depicts the object surfacing and diving three times; unfortunately, Folden paused the camera each time it submerged. A preliminary review by Kerry Voth in 2000 indicated that the object appeared solid, featuring one vertical protrusion and two lateral protrusions, surfacing at a rolling angle, contributing to the Ogopogo's unique characteristics.

1976: Edward R. Fletcher took five photographs of Ogopogo in the lake near the Westbank Yacht Club. The creature seemed to measure about 40 feet in length while coiled and extended to 70–75 feet when relaxed, providing significant evidence of the creature's presence.

1979: On 28 May, Arlene Gaal captured an image of a long, dark hump creating a wake near Kinsmen Beach.

1979: A tourist from Alberta filmed three minutes of Ogopogo playing in the water at Peachland Hill. The animal disturbed the water and produced loud thumping noises. The current whereabouts of this film is unknown.

1980: Larry Thal, a tourist from Vancouver, recorded eight to ten seconds of Super 8 footage of an animal observed for forty-five minutes off Monteo Beach by approximately fifty other tourists. The 50-60-foot creature submerged and resurfaced, swimming back and forth from Okanagan Lake Bridge. Arlene Gaal claimed she could see a head with jaws in an enhanced version of the footage.

1982: Eugene Boiselle filmed video footage of Ogopogo, or potentially an unusual disturbance in the water, from Knox Mountain Park.

1987: John Kirk videotaped one minute of a 40-foot Ogopogo gliding through the lake from the top of Mountain Hill.

1989: On 17 July, Ken Chaplin recorded a black, 15-foot creature in the lake near Bear Creek's mouth. It raised its head, slapped its tail on the water, and submerged. In 1989, Chapman employed advanced video camera technology to document his observations. Experts analysed Ken Chaplin's footage, and regional wildlife biologist Robert Lincoln believed the recording was authentic, speculating that it showcased a live animal, likely a river otter or beaver, noting similarities between a frame from Ken's video and a photo of a beaver preparing to slap its tail on the water; the two were almost identical. However, Ken Chaplin argued that the creature he saw was too large to be a beaver. Gaal suspected it could have been a miniature Ogopogo.

1989: On 22 July, accompanying Chaplin to the site, Arlene Gaal saw the head and back of a dark animal 15-20 feet long moving from the creek into the lake. She succeeded in taking two photos of the creature while Chaplin recorded more footage. Many analysts concluded that the video depicted nothing more than a beaver. John Kirk successfully filmed Ogopogo again near Peachland, with his footage lasting about 25 minutes and featuring a large hump in the distance.

1992: Paul DeMara recorded an animal causing a disturbance in the lake from a cottage near Okanagan Centre. His wife, mother, and friends witnessed a water skier crossing its path and falling into the water. Over the next five to ten minutes, DeMara filmed two more sequences of unidentified objects in the lake. The final clip showed a head, neck, and part of a back rising from the water.

1996: Michael Zaiser took five photographs of a 40-foot long-necked creature creating a disturbance in the water off Okanagan Mountain Park.

2000: On 18 April, while staging a recreation of a 1978 Ogopogo sighting, a film crew recorded 90 seconds of footage capturing three humps undulating in the water approximately 200 yards away. Fourteen observers, including the original witness, Bill Steciuk, saw the black, shiny creature.

Expedition/s: Many monster hunters have searched for Ogopogo over the years, and the lake has been the setting for numerous film crews hoping to capture a glimpse of the creature on camera, forever immortalized on film. However, one individual stands out among these enthusiasts for sheer dedication and love of the chase. A classic citizen scientist whose fascination with the legend of Ogopogo is noteworthy: Bill Steciuk. Bill became captivated by the legend after his first sighting in 1978. Still, it wasn't until years later that he organized expeditions to search for the creature using his renovated houseboat, with assistance from expert Len Melnyk and a remotely operated vehicle (ROV). The first expedition took place on 12 August 2000, utilizing advanced sonar technology and focusing on Rattlesnake Island. The two men were excited to detect a large, moving object at a depth of 7.5 meters. This discovery motivated a second expedition on 12 August 2001, which explored nearby areas with reported sightings. Although the results of the second expedition were less conclusive, they still indicated the presence of something unusual.

A Cryptid Cadaver: In 2009, a peculiar specimen was discovered along the shores of Okanagan Lake, sparking intrigue among residents and scientists alike. Dan Poppoff found the creature while kayaking and chose to preserve its carcass, measuring over one meter, in his freezer. He reached out to legendary lake monster hunter Arlene Gaal, a local authority on the mysterious Ogopogo, who helped facilitate the examination and analysis of the specimen. The sample was later sent for DNA testing, revealing it as a previously unclassified freshwater fish species.

Music Tameth the Beast! Like all good monsters, the Ogopogo also has its own theme tune! In "Ogopogo: The True Story of the Okanagan Lake Million Dollar Monster," author Arlene Gaal recounts the tale of a Vancouver Province reporter named Ronald Kenvyn, who crafted a parody of a popular British song, which included this whimsical stanza:

His mother was an earwig;
His father was a whale.
A little bit of head and hardly any tail—
And Ogopogo was his name.

Thus, Ogopogo captured the imagination and eventually replaced the original Native name, N'ha-a-itk, becoming a well-loved part of local legend.

Stamp of Approval! Not many know that Ogopogo has an official stamp published in 2004 by Canada Post. This unique stamp features an artistic representation of the legendary creature, providing a fascinating nod to the folklore surrounding it. Although not proof of the creature's existence, it represents a cultural acknowledgement of the significance of this legend. The stamp's illustration of Ogopogo also reflects a common chimeric interpretation of these many water monsters, much like the Japanese Zuiyo Maru postage stamp, which was issued in 1983 and depicted a skeletal plesiosaur. Similarly, the Royal Mint's recent release celebrating the Loch Ness Monster highlights its iconic form, further cementing the intertwining of myth and culture in numismatic commemorations. Each of these stamps captures an image and the imagination and intrigue accompanying legendary creatures from folklore.

Beastly Theories

Sturgeon: The White Sturgeon is the largest freshwater fish in North America, with some individuals growing up to 20 feet in length. It is found in the Fraser/Nechako, Columbia, and Kootenay River systems in British Columbia, though it has not been recorded in the Okanagan area. Unlike most fish, the White Sturgeon has a body covered in large bony scutes rather than scales.

Ancient Fossil Fiend: The legend of Ogopogo may have originated from fossil bones, particularly a notable vertebra discovered by Oscar Frederickson in the 1930s. This vertebra was studied by zoologist James A. McLeod in 1960. Some cryptozoologists believe Ogopogo resembles the prehistoric Basilosaurus, which is known for its long, log-like body and head that resembles a horse or goat. Witnesses often describe Ogopogo as looking like a floating log, and they note its quick movements and behaviours, such as feeding on aquatic plants or fish. Some observations also mention the presence of fins or feet.

Surviving Plesiosaur: More than a hundred species of plesiosaurs have been documented in fossil records, raising the intriguing possibility that creatures like Ogopogo could be surviving remnants of these ancient reptiles. The characteristics of Okanagan Lake resemble those of Loch Ness, which has led to comparisons between Ogopogo and the Loch Ness Monster, also known as Nessie. However, unlike Nessie, Ogopogo is described as a "many-humped" lake monster and may have connections to primitive whales.

Probing Pinniped: Historical accounts support the theory that some Ogopogo sightings could be attributed to seals venturing into Okanagan Lake. For example, a local fisherman described a large, seal-like creature in 1968. Seals are known to explore new territories for food, and Okanagan Lake's ecosystem could attract them. As interest in Ogopogo grew, the connection between seal sightings and the legend became more accepted, highlighting the intriguing relationship between wildlife and local folklore.

THE SKRIMSL

What's in a Name? The Skrimsl, meaning Water Monster, is also known as Lagarfljotsormurinn ("The Serpent of Lagarfljot"), as well as Haf-skills and Okind.

Monstrous Measurements: The creature measures 46 feet in length. Its head and neck together are 6 feet long, the body measures 22 feet, and the tail is 18 feet long. The creature has a pale colour, whiskers on its face, and features a prominent hump.

Terrifying Tracks: A Skrimsl allegedly came ashore in 1819, leaving behind tracks. However, the specific form of these tracks was never described.

Beastly Behaviours: This creature swims with a graceful undulation but can also move side to side in a snake-like manner. It actively hunts salmon and other fish among the fast-moving ice flows of the river, often ambushing its prey in bottlenecks where the current is strongest. In the past, it was commonly observed "rocking on the surface of the water, like a large boat floating keel up," and there were claims that it would attack and sink boats.

Deadly Diet: These waters are rich in salmon, eel, lamprey, and char, among various other fish species, which are believed to be primary components of the creature's diet. Additionally, these aquatic animals were said to hunt seals.

Watery Abode: Primarily seen in Logurin Lake, Iceland, and its outflow, the Lagarfljot River, but has also been observed in Skorodalsvatn and other lakes and coastal fjords, indicating that the animal frequents both saltwater and freshwater.

Scary Sightings

1345: A large, humped creature was reported in the lake.

1595: In his posthumous work, *Reise Igiennem Island* (1772), Icelandic patriot Eggert Ólafsson documented reports of large aquatic animals in the western regions of Iceland.

1749-1750: Several sightings were documented during this period, but their details are now lost to time.

1819: The Grímsey Skrimsl was noted for often coming ashore and leaving tracks behind. Local fishermen also reported this creature was aggressive and sometimes attacked and sank their boats. The beast was frequently seen rocking on the water like an upturned vessel.

1840: A Skrimsl was also reportedly sighted along the Grímsey coast.

1862: Reverend Sabine Baring-Gould travelled through Iceland and recorded anecdotal accounts of the Skrimsl in his book *Iceland: Its Scenes and Sagas* (1863). His accounts were based on testimonies from friends investigating similar stories at Skorradalsvatn.

1967: Employees at the Hallormsstaður forestry station witnessed a serpent swimming in the lake. They tracked it by car to the forest's edge, where it vanished near the Klifá River.

_1998:_ A class of children and their teacher from Hallormsstadadarskoli observed a pale streak undulating through the water near Geitagerdi Farm for about twenty-five minutes. One student photographed the sighting, but the photo's location is currently unknown.

_2012:_ In February, a man named Hjörtur E. Kjerúlf first spotted the creature from his kitchen window while drinking coffee. Hjörtur managed to record footage of the beast, which, upon closer inspection, appeared to resemble a long, serpentine figure moving against the current.

_2012:_ On 8 March, Hjörtur Kjerúlf had a second encounter with the elusive lake monster, capturing the sighting on film again. The beast remains primarily submerged in this new footage, skilfully navigating through the water while avoiding drifting ice flows. Similar to his first video, this clip contains several cuts, and the consistent visibility of the same shoreline throughout caused many sceptics to question whether the creature travelled any significant distance during the sighting. However, how the beast manoeuvres around the ice raises intriguing possibilities. Its evasive actions would be challenging to replicate if someone were trying to create a hoax, adding an element of authenticity to the footage. This sighting continues to fuel interest and argument surrounding the existence of the lake monster.

Beastly Evidence

Film and Photography: As previously mentioned, the most convincing evidence for the Skrimsl's existence was recorded by eyewitness Hjörtur E. Kjerúlf during two incidents several months apart in early 2012. The first video features a long, snake-like creature gliding gracefully across the surface of a calm lake. The second video captures a large, elongated creature swimming in a fluid, undulating motion, skillfully manoeuvring around ice flows in a strong current and occasionally breaking through the water's surface.

Official Status: Following the release of videos of the Lagarfljot Worm, the Icelandic government conducted a comprehensive investigation, deeming the footage authentic; however, concerns about the investigation's impartiality arose due to the potential for increased tourism. This official proclamation was announced in 2014 after two years of analysis by Iceland's Truth Committee, which concluded that "the Worm is likely real," with seven out of thirteen members believing the animate object in the video was, in fact, proof of the existence of the Skrimsl. Their findings lent credibility to the search for the beast, igniting excitement among Lake Monster researchers that official participation in the hunt for cryptids was achievable; leading to ongoing discussions about the creature's existence and how to capture more concrete evidence.

A Serpentine Song! What is it about lake monsters that inspires people to write songs and poems about them? I am unaware of any other type of cryptid with such a rich collection of musical compositions and poetic works dedicated to them. One notable example is this piece, which has been loosely translated from the Compilation of Folklore by Jón Árnason.

> Once upon a time, a woman lived on a farm in Hérað by Lagarfljót Lake. She had a grown daughter, to whom she gave a golden ring. The girl said: "How can I profit the most from this gold, mother?" "Put it under a heath-worm (lyngormur)," the mother replied. The girl picked up a heath worm, put the gold under the worm and put the worm into a coffer.
>
> The worm lay in the coffer for a couple of days. But when the girl checked on her coffer, the worm had grown in size, and the coffer had started to fall apart. The girl became frightened, grabbed the coffer and threw it into the lake.
>
> After a long while, people noticed the worm (serpent) in the lake. The worm started destroying people and animals, crossing the lake. Sometimes, it would stretch onto the banks

> of the lake and spout terrible poison. The people in this area didn't know how to solve this awful predicament. Two Finns were called in. They were supposed to kill the worm and get the gold.
>
> They jumped into the lake but reappeared soon. The Finns said that this was a being of superior strength, and the worm could not be killed and the gold retrieved. They told of another worm under the gold and that that worm was far worse than the first one. They then tied the worm with two ropes, one behind the flippers and the other around its tail.
>
> Since then, the worm has not been able to destroy people or animals, but from time to time, it raises its hump, and when that happens, it is a premonition of some big event.

Beastly Theories!

Unexpected Ungulates!? The possibility that horses, cows, or even deer could be mistaken for monstrous creatures while swimming in a lake raises fascinating questions about perception and the human imagination. This theory often surfaces to explain various Lake Monster sightings reported throughout history. Many enthusiasts and sceptics alike have pondered the likelihood of such commonplace animals being misconstrued as extraordinary beings lurking beneath the water's surface.

Supporters of this idea point to the visual distortions caused by water, particularly when viewed from a distance or in poor lighting conditions. They argue that the shapes and movements of these animals, especially when partially submerged, can create illusions that lead witnesses to believe they have seen something far more fantastical. However, despite its appeal, this theory fails to provide a convincing match for the extraordinary creatures individuals claim to have encountered in these mysterious waters.

Eyewitness descriptions often include details that describe long necks, massive size, or even unusual behaviours, aspects that straying horses or cows do not cover. Additionally, many reported sightings occur in remote areas where the likelihood of encountering these ungulates is far less, leading to further scrutiny of this explanation.

Out of Place Anaconda: Ironically, this theory is less likely than that of a surviving plesiosaur. While estimates of the size of the rumoured Lagarfljot Monster might be exaggerated, and a full-grown constrictor, such as an Anaconda or a Reticulated Python, could indeed serve as a plausible monster imposter for Iceland's ancient serpent, it is fundamentally biologically impossible for either of these species to thrive in this environment.

Iceland is in a temperate zone, but experiences harsh, frigid winters that challenge even the hardiest species. The geographical and climate conditions are not conducive to the survival of tropical reptiles. Additionally, the waters of Lake Lagarfljot are often ice-covered during the cold months and maintain an average temperature just above freezing in winter. These factors collectively create an environment entirely inhospitable to any currently known reptile species, particularly those requiring warmer temperatures and more stable climates for sustenance and reproduction.

Furthermore, the ice and extreme weather conditions would inhibit a large snake's hunting practices and habitat needs. All these points reinforce the unlikelihood of encountering an Anaconda or similar species in Iceland, making it a fascinating but improbable candidate for the legendary monster of Lake Lagarfljot. Rather than an ancient serpent or mythical creature, the lore surrounding the lake may be more accurately attributed to local folklore and imagination, fuelled by sightings of familiar but misunderstood creatures.

Folkloric Fable: Folklore may explain the numerous legends that share similarities across different nations, particularly between countries and their former colonies. In our work as cryptozoologists, we often come across nations reporting sightings of the same creatures. It is fascinating to see cultural descendants living in colonial territories thousands of miles away from their ancestral nations who continue to have encounters with similarly described beings. Whether these reports stem from a shared descriptive tradition to explain common animals or inherited cultural memories warrants further investigation; nevertheless, this topic certainly deserves continued exploration. Below, we examine the creation myth behind the origin of this particular monster; those familiar with such myths will recognize a recurring pattern.

Super Otter: Some cryptozoologists have posited that the animal depicted resembles a mammal similar to seals or otters, leading them to conclude that its neck is too short to align with the characteristics of a typical long-necked lake monster. This observation has sparked intriguing discussions about the creature's potential identity. Instead, they propose that this enigmatic being might represent a freshwater version of the super-otter, scientifically categorized under the hypothetical genus *Hyperhydra*. This imagined creature is described as having a seal-like head, a pointed tail, and a body characterized by multiple bends, which sets it apart from more familiar aquatic mammals.

Renowned cryptozoologist Bernard Heuvelmans theorized that the super-otter could have evolved as a giant "walking whale" related to lesser-known prehistoric families such as *Ambulocetidae*, *Remingtonocetidae*, or *Protocetidae*. These families are significant in studying cetacean evolution, highlighting the transition of mammals from land-dwelling to fully aquatic lifestyles. Furthermore, Michael Woodley presented an alternative theory that the creature might be a giant sea otter, drawing potential links to the legendary freshwater dobhar-chú, which is steeped in folklore and is said to inhabit lakes in Ireland.

ALTAMAHA-HA

What's in a Name? The Altamaha-ha, often called "Altie," is named after the Altamaha River in Georgia. Contrary to a common belief that its name means "path to Tama," "Altamaha" originally referred to a prehistoric chiefdom near the Oconee River visited by Hernando de Soto in 1540. The legend of Altamaha-ha predates British colonization and is associated with the Lower Muskogee Creek Tribe.

Monstrous Measurements: The Altamaha-ha is a bizarre cryptid. Its length ranges from 10 to 25 feet and has a diameter of 10 to 12 inches. It has smooth, grey-brown skin, a small head, and a long neck, often described as having two or three humps. Its body resembles a sturgeon's and features a bony ridge along its back. It swims similarly to a dolphin with front flippers and no hind limbs. The creature has a crocodile-like snout, large protruding eyes, and sharp teeth. Its colouring is typically grey or green, with a whitish-yellow underbelly. Reports suggest that the Altamaha-ha typically measures between 20 to 30 feet long. However, some witnesses have claimed to see smaller or larger variations, indicating that it may not be the only one of its kind.

Terrifying Tracks: Often leaves a trail that looks like a cross between a large crocodile slide and a two-flippered turtle, observable on sandbanks and riverbanks within territory said to be frequented by the creature.

Beastly Behaviours: This creature moves through the water by undulating its body. It has been reported lounging on the shore or casually swimming along the river. This creature will react defensively in the presence of boaters, emitting a loud hissing noise like a giant viper.

Deadly Diet: The Altamaha River, recognized as one of "America's Last Great Places," boasts a rich biodiversity. This area is home to many species, including salamanders, frogs, toads, lizards, turtles, snakes, and, notably, the American alligator, which has the fourth-largest population in Georgia. Additionally, the river hosts river otters, beavers, feral pigs, and the West Indian manatee, as well as a variety of fish species such as bass, catfish, sturgeon, and gar. However, whether the Altamaha River creature preys on any of these species remains unclear, as feeding has not been observed.

Watery Abode: Believed to inhabit the marshes and channels at the mouth of the Altamaha River in Georgia, particularly around Darien and Butler Island. It's a significant part of coastal Georgia folklore and is one of North America's most frequently sighted monsters. The Altamaha River, one of Georgia's largest rivers, stretches approximately 137 miles and has a vast basin, second only to the Mississippi River. The surrounding area features islands, marshes, canals, and old rice fields, creating a habitat for the mysterious creature.

Scary Sightings

1830: In April, a correspondent for the *Savannah Georgian* reported multiple sightings of a sea monster along the Georgia coast. The principal eyewitness, Captain Delano of the schooner *Eagle*, described the creature as approximately 70 feet long, with a circumference similar to a barrel and an alligator-like head. Five other crew members also reported seeing the monster near St. Simons Island, and the sightings attracted attention over several weeks.

1920s: Timbermen riding the river see a large, snakelike water monster.

1935: A group of hunters embarked on a journey that would become the stuff of legends. As they navigated the winding river, their keen eyes caught sight of something extraordinary—a massive serpent gliding gracefully through the water. They couldn't believe their eyes; describing what they saw as something akin to a "giant snake."

1940s: A group of adventurous Boy Scouts on a wilderness excursion had an extraordinary sighting of the mysterious creature.

1950s: Two officials from Reidsville State Prison had a frightening encounter with the creature, which they observed disporting itself in the river.

1969: Two brothers fishing at Clark's Bluff on the Altamaha River shared their encounter with the press. They described the creature they saw as having an alligator-like snout, a horizontal tail, a triangular ridge along its back, and sharp pointed teeth. Initially, they thought it was a sturgeon but changed their minds after looking closer. They estimated the creature's length to be around 10 to 12 feet and noted its gunmetal grey colour.

1970s: As newspapers nationwide reported the sightings, more witnesses started to step forward. One of these witnesses was Harvey Blackman from Brunswick, who claimed he saw the creature at "Two Way" on the Altamaha River. He described it as having a snake-like head measuring 15 to 20 feet long. Another witness, Frank Culpepper, reported seeing its wake in the same vicinity, noting that it created such a significant disturbance in the water that nearby boats were rocked about. One of the men with him grabbed a rifle, but the creature disappeared before he could take a shot.

1980: Multiple sightings of a creature known as the Altamaha-ha were reported.

The first encounter involved two men stranded on a mud bank near Cathead Creek. They observed the creature lying half in the water, thrashing to free itself. Described as dark-coloured, with rough skin and approximately 20 feet long, the beast eventually broke free, submerged, and vanished from sight.

Later that year, another man reported seeing the Altamaha-ha at Smith Lake. He described the creature as between 15 to 20 feet long, snake-like in shape, with two brown humps protruding from the water, creating a wake similar to that of a speedboat. In December, another sighting provided a similar description, reaffirming the creature's characteristics.

Additionally, a local crabber mentioned that the Altamaha-ha came close to his boat, where he had an excellent view and remarked that it looked like "the world's biggest eel." Another crab fisherman echoed this description in a separate report, again comparing the creature to "the world's biggest eel."

Lastly, a man in a boat near Brunswick saw something over 20 feet long and 6 feet wide break the water's surface, adding to the growing intrigue surrounding this mysterious creature.

1983: On 16 January, Tim Sanders observed a creature measuring 20 to 25 feet from the Champney River Bridge. Its massive form glided silently through the water, leaving him shocked and amazed by the experience.

1997: On 6 July, Jim and Mary Marshall were boating on the river when they saw an animal that was 10 to 12 feet long with three humps.

2002: A man pulling a boat up the river near Brunswick reported seeing something over 20 feet long and 6 feet wide break the water's surface.

Beastly Evidence

Artistic License? Jacques Le Moyne was a French artist who documented the natural history of present-day Georgia and Florida during his mid-16th-century expedition. His work included sketches and paintings of the region's flora, fauna, and Indigenous peoples, providing some of the earliest European representations of North American wildlife. His illustrations, especially his exaggerated depictions of alligators, contributed to a fantastical interpretation of the area's creatures, blending reality with myth.

The Altamaha River region, where Le Moyne explored, is linked to local legends such as the Altamaha-ha, a creature reminiscent of the Loch Ness Monster. The similarities between Le Moyne's imaginative alligator sketches and descriptions of the Altamaha-ha highlight how natural history and folklore intertwine in Southern culture, keeping alive the fascination with the region's mysterious wildlife and the stories surrounding it.

Captured on Camera: In 2010, an amateur photographer captured a video of something strange swimming in the channel off Fort King George Historic Site in Darien, Georgia. The footage quickly garnered attention due to the mysterious nature of the creature, which had an elongated body and was not identifiable as any known marine species in the area.

Fort King George, established in 1721, is located near the Altamaha River, a region rich in biodiversity. The channel where the creature was spotted is known for its brackish waters, which serve as a habitat for wildlife, including fish, manatees, and dolphins.

Several marine biologists and amateur cryptozoologists analysed the video and proposed varying theories about the creature's identity. Some suggested it might be a large fish or a misunderstood native species, while others posited more outlandish ideas, claiming it could be a sea serpent or an undiscovered creature.

The sighting sparked interest in local folklore about mysterious creatures reported in the waters of the Georgia coast, reminiscent of legends that have circulated for centuries. Despite the various interpretations and ongoing discussions, the creature's true identity remains a mystery, adding to the intrigue surrounding the footage.

A Papier Mache Piast! In 2018, decomposing remains were found on a beach in the Wolf Island National Wildlife Refuge, located off the coast of Georgia. These remains sparked speculation that they could be the body of an Altamaha-ha, a legendary creature said to inhabit the Altamaha River in Georgia. However, anonymous performance artist Zardulu later claimed responsibility for the remains, revealing that they were created from a stuffed shark and papier-mâché, highlighting the blending of art and folklore in contemporary culture. This revelation pointed to the ongoing interest in mythical creatures and the role of modern artists in shaping narratives around them.

Beastly Theories!

Freshwater Seal: Some researchers speculate that the Altamaha-ha could be a large, undiscovered freshwater seal species. Believers in this theory describe an impressive creature stretching up to 30 feet long, with characteristic flippers akin to seals. Freshwater seals are known to inhabit rivers and lakes, suggesting that such a creature could go unnoticed in the vast waterways of the Altamaha River region.

Gargantuan Gar: The alligator gar, a large freshwater fish native to North America, has been proposed as an identity for recent sightings attributed to the Altamaha-ha. Known for its long, torpedo-shaped body and sharp teeth, the alligator gar can grow up to 10 feet in length, which may account for the descriptions of a large creature in the river. With its prehistoric appearance, this fish captures the imagination of both sceptics and believers regarding the legend of the Altamaha-ha.

Colonial Transplant: The region where the Altamaha-ha is often sighted is a beautiful, mysterious estuary known for its extensive marshes, intricate river channels, and remnants of 18th and 19th-century rice fields and canals. The connection to a town founded by Scottish Highlanders from the shores of Loch Ness adds a layer of intrigue. Darien, initially called New Inverness, was established in 1735 and carries the folklore of the Loch Ness Monster. Traditional accounts suggest that the Tama Indians, who lived along the Altamaha River, had legends of a large, snake-like creature inhabiting these waters. While no concrete documentation exists, early explorers noted that Creek Indians shared tales of giant snakes within their territories, linking the legend to Muscogee traditions.

Tama Indian Tales: Numerous accounts of a serpent-like creature have emerged from Southeastern Georgia since at least the 18th century. The Tama Tribe has passed down legends of a giant, snake-like inhabitant of the Altamaha River, which predates European settlement. If proven true, this would indicate that these stories originate from the land's original inhabitants rather than adaptations of European tales such as Scotland's Loch Ness Monster. Additionally, sightings have continued today, with visitors recounting stories of a mysterious creature swimming in the Altamaha River. Despite a lack of physical evidence, the narratives have persisted for centuries, with descriptions of a giant beast that hisses and bellows echoing through time.

19th Century Sensationalism: The concept of sea serpents in the Darien area was already ingrained in the local lexicon long before 1830. Notably, in 1826, a sloop sailing from the local wharves bore the name *Sea Serpent*. This raises the question of whether the name was a tribute to the Altamaha-ha legend. Sightings of the creature date back to the early 1800s, confirming that residents have long reported encountering something unusual in the waters near the mouth of the Altamaha River.

CANAVAR

What's in a Name? In Turkish folklore, the Lake Van Monster (Turkish: Van Gölü Canavarı; Kurdish: Cinawirê Gola Wanê; Armenian: Vana lchi hresh) is a legendary creature believed to dwell in Lake Van in eastern Turkey.

Monstrous Measurements: Its length ranges from 24 to 50 feet, with a width of 3 to 6 feet. It is usually white or copper brown in colour and features a long stripe along its back. The creature has a hairy beaked head adorned with horns and three upright spines or fins. It has two large eyes and what are either nostrils or a breathing hole on its head. Witnesses often liken it to bygone marine reptiles like the plesiosaur.

Terrifying Tracks: Although no tracks have been reported, there are reports of the creature being spotted lying on the shingle near the water's edge, stretched out like a gigantic serpent, as to whether the beast is legless or possessing small discreet fins has not been observed.

Beastly Behaviours: This elusive beast is often described as shy and reclusive. It chooses to live in the shadows and is mostly active at dusk and dawn. Although there's a chilling tale from the late 1800s involving a predatory encounter with a group of men, modern sightings tell a different story in which this creature prefers to keep its distance from humans.

Deadly Diet: The creature is believed to subsist on the only fish that inhabits the brackish waters of Lake Van — the *Chalcalburnus tarichi*, commonly known as the Pearl Mullet. This Cyprinid fish is related to chub and dace and is found in large numbers within the lake. The Pearl Mullet primarily feeds on the abundant phytoplankton, which consists of 103 species, and zooplankton, comprising 36 species, which thrive in this ecosystem due to the lake's high alkaline content.

Watery Abode: Lake Van, located in Van Province, Turkey, is a unique monster habitat and one of the largest endorheic lakes globally. It covers 1,457 square miles and holds 38% of Turkey's surface water. Formed by a volcanic eruption that blocked its outlet, the lake features high salinity, which prevents it from freezing in winter. It has alkaline water rich in sodium carbonate and sulphate and measures 73 miles at its widest point, with an average depth of 561 feet and a maximum depth of 1,479 feet.

Scary Sightings

1889: In 2010, a newspaper article dating back to 1889 was discovered featuring an account of a significant creature sighting at Lake Van. This article, published in *Saadet News* during the Ottoman era, describes the experience of three men who were travelling from Tatvan to Ahlat. While camping by the lake, they decided to wash their hands in the water. Suddenly, a large creature emerged and attacked them, seizing one man by the leg in an attempt to drag him into the lake. The other two men tried to save their friend, but they could not overpower the creature's strength. In a desperate attempt, they grabbed some burning material from their camp and used it to fend off the beast. Upon contact with the fire, the creature emitted a terrible scream and retreated into the lake's depths, taking the captured man with it. He was never seen again.

1995: On 2 November, the *Daily Telegraph* reported that the Turkish provincial deputy governor claimed to have seen a mysterious, dinosaur-like creature in the country's largest lake. This sighting prompted Turkish authorities to launch a full search, with a parliamentary commission organizing a dedicated search party in pursuit of what many hoped would be Turkey's version of the Loch Ness Monster.

1997: On 12 June, Unal Kozak, a 26-year-old lecturer at a local university, first captured the elusive Lake Van monster on videotape. The brief footage revealed a black and brown creature with a prominent hump and a visible eye, which Kozak estimated to be over 20 meters long. This encounter sparked a surge of interest in the beast, and scientists later verified the authenticity of Kozak's photographs, leading to numerous subsequent sightings.

Intrigued by the legend of the Lake Van monster, Kozak dedicated himself to investigating the creature. He interviewed eyewitnesses, set up cameras in areas where the monster was rumoured to frequent, and compiled around 1,000 witness reports. He claims to have filmed the creature on three occasions.

The most notable of these videos, which aired on CNN, shows an object moving in the water with a beaked head poking above the surface, revealing a breathing hole and two eyes. This sighting and others fuelled the growing curiosity and debate about the creature's existence, making the Lake Van monster a focal point for cryptozoologists and enthusiasts alike.

The pictures were sent to Cambridge University for examination, and Jacques Cousteau, the world-famous marine biologist, was expected to visit and study the lake. Unfortunately, he passed away just two weeks after the event.

Following each sighting, professional camera crews rented boats and staked out the lake in an attempt to capture clear footage of the alleged beast, but each time they were unsuccessful.

Beastly Evidence

Ancient Authentication:

A Cryptid Chronicle: Ancient Armenian traditions claim that the Van Monster inhabits Lake Van, as noted by chroniclers Movses Khorenatsi and Ananiya Shirakatsi, who documented vishaps—water dragons believed to be so large they could devour the world. The god Vahagn, known as vishapakagh ("reaper of vishaps"), was said to dive into the lake to capture these monsters. This legend may reflect an adaptation of Urartian myths about the god Teisheba fighting the water monster Ullikummi. Researchers have observed that locals refer to storms over the lake as vishap kami (dragon wind) but believe modern lake monster tales are more influenced by Western folklore than Armenian traditions.

Sacred Stonework: Akdamar Island, the largest island in Lake Van, is home to an Armenian church known as Akdamar Church, which was constructed in AD 915. The outer walls of the church are embellished with intricately carved stone images. Among these depictions, one prominently features a creature resembling a sea monster beneath a ship. Many observers interpret this image as a reference to the Lake Van Monster. If this interpretation is accurate, it suggests that the existence of this legend has been acknowledged for over a millennium. Nevertheless, considering the representation of a man being cast into the sea and subsequently devoured by a sea monster, it is more likely that this relief illustrates the biblical narrative of Jonah and the Whale.

Film & Photography: Unal Kozak's video footage of a creature in Lake Van, filmed on 10 June 1997, sparked worldwide interest. The dark object appears to move through the water and has been described as a dark-brown hump with an eye. Some analysts claim bubbles suggest an animate creature breathing beneath the surface. In late 1997, the film aired on CNN, fuelling cryptozoological debates. Turkish biologist Orhan Erman stated that no beast of that size could survive in Lake Van, a soda lake. The video has been analysed and remains contentious, with ideas ranging from a clever hoax to a giant squid or floating debris.

A Dinosaurian Deception: A 4-meter-high statue has been constructed in the eastern province of Van, Turkey, to honour reported sightings of the creature. While some sceptics suggest that the region might benefit from an influx of tourists and question the statue's authenticity, it's hard to overlook the lack of creativity in its design. The statue draws inspiration more from a random selection of plastic dinosaur toys than from a genuine depiction of the creature, leaving many to wonder about the effort put into this tribute.

Expedition/s:

Shosetsu Tendai Expedition: In 2006, the magazine *Shosetsu Tendai* organized a Japanese expedition. The expedition claimed to have captured footage of a large creature swimming beneath the surface of Lake Van. This expedition sparked interest in the possibility of undiscovered marine life in the lake, which is known for its unique ecosystem.

Media Monster Hunts: In 2009, the TV show *Destination Truth*, hosted by Josh Gates, investigated the Van Lake Monster. The crew explored the lake using scuba divers and even spent the night on Akdamar Island searching for evidence. Unfortunately, their expedition yielded little in the way of conclusive findings. The Van Lake Monster has also been featured on the Australian cryptozoology show *Animal X*, reflecting ongoing intrigue and fascination with the creature.

Van Yüzüncü Yıl University Expedition: In 2019, a team of researchers from Turkey's Van Yüzüncü Yıl University embarked on an expedition to search for the elusive lake monster of Lake Van. Instead of locating the creature, they made a remarkable discovery: a well-preserved, 3,000-year-old castle submerged at the bottom of the lake. This castle, which has an approximate circumference of 1 mile, is attributed to the Urartu civilization, which thrived between the 9th and 6th centuries BC.

Additionally, the team uncovered a sunken Russian ship that had disappeared in 1948, an extensive underwater formation of stalagmites known as the "Fairy Chimneys," and an ancient graveyard from the Seljuk Era. Although they did not find the monster they were seeking, these discoveries highlight that Lake Van is rich in historical and geological mysteries, raising further questions about its depths and the legends surrounding it.

A Prime Poet! Bülent Ecevit, the former Prime Minister of Turkey and a celebrated poet wrote *Van Gölü Canavarı*, or *Lake Van Monster*. This poem captures the enchanting and mythical tales surrounding Lake Van, blending folklore and history surrounding the monster's legend.

Beastly Theories!

A Living Mosasaur: Mosasaurus was an enormous marine reptile from the late Cretaceous period, reaching lengths of up to 50 feet (15 meters) and characterized by its streamlined body, powerful tail, and paddle-like limbs, which made it an efficient swimmer and formidable predator. Closely related to modern lizards and snakes, Mosasaurs evolved from terrestrial reptiles that adapted to aquatic life, thriving in ancient seas as they hunted for fish and cephalopods. Some theories surrounding the Lake Van Monster suggest it could be a modern-day descendant of ancient creatures like Mosasaurs, although these propositions lack scientific confirmation. The idea is fuelled by regional folklore and the possibility of undiscovered species in deep lakes, but the connection remains speculative.

Mosasaurs went extinct around 66 million years ago during the mass extinction event at the end of the Cretaceous period, due to dramatic environmental changes.

When a Hoax Gets Out of Hand: The identity and origin of the Lake Van Monster continues to puzzle the Turkish scientific community, who assert that no creature resembling the monster could survive in the lake, instead suggesting that local beliefs about lake monsters were likely influenced by Western culture rather than traditional folklore. Many interviewed locals also viewed the lake monster story as a "commercial ploy," believing that the 1997 footage shot by Ünal Kozak, which claims to show the creature, was part of a local government hoax designed to boost tourism.

ISSIE

What's in a Name? Issie (Isshī) is a legendary creature thought to dwell in Lake Ikeda on Kyushu Island in Japan. It is frequently described as bearing a resemblance to a lizard. The naming convention is akin to "Nessie," which denotes the Loch Ness Monster. Locals often affectionately call it Issie-kun!

Monstrous Measurements: The creature is described as being anywhere between 16 and 90 feet long and has a dark body with patterns or stripes. Its most noticeable features are two large humps, each about 5 meters (16 feet) long, which give it a strong appearance. Some eyewitnesses described it as a giant eel with flippers gliding smoothly through the water.

Beastly Behaviours: Often spotted gliding through the lake with its two prominent humps, the creature occasionally lifts its elongated neck above the water to survey its environment. When it comes up for air, the water becomes turbulent. As it submerges, it creates a whirlpool effect due to its significant weight and the disruption caused by its disappearing beneath the surface like a heavy rock. Unlike other lake monsters, this creature is not always spotted alone and can often be seen travelling in groups of two or more!

Deadly Diet: Nobody knows precisely what Issie prefers to eat, but Lake Ikeda has no food shortage. The lake is home to a large population of giant mottled eels, which are a protected species designated by Ibusuki City. Each eel weighs about 20 kg and can grow up to six feet long.

Watery Abode: This creature's home, Lake Ikeda, is in Kagoshima Prefecture on Kyushu Island, Japan. With a maximum depth of about 764 feet and a circumference of approximately 9.3 miles, it is the largest lake in Kyushu. As a caldera lake, it does not have direct access to the ocean and primarily relies on rainfall to maintain its water levels.

Scary Sightings

1978: The creature was photographed by a man named "Mr. Matsubara." On December 16, 1978, Toshiaki Matsubara saw a strange whirlpool in Lake Ikeda and took a series of photos of an animal with humps. This marked the first photograph of Issie, the legendary creature of Lake Ikeda. One afternoon, while standing near the shore with a camera, Matsubara saw something rise out of the lake—a snake-like creature with dark skin and humps on its back, appearing to be at least 45 feet long. Additionally, that year twenty other people reported sightings of the beast swimming in the lake, describing it as black and about 16.4 feet long.

1991: Another visitor to the lake captured footage of a bizarre-looking creature estimated to be 98.4 feet long. On January 4, 1991, Hideaki Tomiyasu recorded a nine-minute video of a long, dark object with two humps, which submerged when a motorboat passed by.

Do Beasts of a 'Flipper' Swim Together? In Japan, various lake monsters are reported across different regions, each known by a 'unique' Nessie-like name.

Notable sightings include:

Kusshi: Interestingly, Issie has a cousin - Kusshi, who resides in northern Japan, specifically in Hokkaido. This creature has a captivating history, having been spotted multiple times in the 1970s at Lake Kussharo, with over thirty eyewitness accounts affirming its presence. Like Issie, Kusshi has become a local mascot and a beloved regional symbol.

Lake Kussharo is particularly striking during winter when its expansive surface becomes completely frozen solid, transforming it into a picturesque wonderland. This has left many researchers questioning where the creature goes during winter or whether it may, in fact, hibernate.

Like so many others, Kussie (Kusshī) is the elusive Japanese lake monster. Like Nessie, Kussie is often compared to Nessie, and in the tradition of the usual lazy and lacklustre naming convention, it doesn't hesitate to draw inspiration from Scotland's iconic cash cow!

Hassie: was first observed in 1986 in the Nagara River near Haneda, Gifu, when two schoolteachers saw a shadowy triangular shape measuring about 6.5 feet long and 3.3 feet wide, with a dark brown or black back.

Assie: Filmed in Lake Akan, Hokkaido, appearing as a large shadow approximately 32.8 feet long.

Assie no. 2: Sighted in Lake Ashi, commune of Hakone, district of Ashigara, Honshu in 1940; it is described as a streamlined entity around 32.8 feet long with a long neck.

Matsudodon: A 6.5-foot entity resembling a sea lion seen near Tokyo's Edogawa River from the early to mid-1970s. Uniquely, this creature was bipedal, emerging from the water to climb a tree.

Missy: A 10-foot reptilian creature spotted in Mizumoto Park near Tokyo that differs from known species like alligators.

Namitarô: First seen in the Takanami pond near Itoigawa in 1966, it is identified as a large unidentified fish with suggestions of a dorsal fin.

Takitarô: This 11.5-foot fish of the salmon family was first reported in Ootori Pond in 1982. Its roots are in Japanese legends dating back to the 9th century.

Beastly Evidence

Film & photography: In 1978, a photograph of a mysterious creature in Lake Ikeda emerged, capturing the attention of both locals and tourists. In 1991, resident Toshiaki Matsuhara encountered the beast and managed to film footage showing the creatures swimming on the lake's surface. Matsuhara also took a picture, which was later promoted by the local tourism board as a genuine photograph of the legendary creature known as "Issie." Since these remarkable events, the regional tourism authorities have actively promoted the Issie story to attract visitors, boosting interest in the lake and its potential secrets.

An Efficacious Effigy: The local tourism office erected a statue of Issie, the mythical monster of Lake Ikeda, in an attempt to attract visitors to the lake. The statue, affectionately named "Issie-kun," a name that has since been pasted onto the beast that inspired its creation, has become a much-loved regional mascot, generating toys, t-shirts, mugs, etc. for tourists to purchase as a keepsake.

The Legend of the Lake: Deep within the enchanting surroundings of Lake Ikeda on Kyushu Island lies an intriguing legend about a white mare and her beloved foal. Once upon a time, this gentle mare roamed the lakeside, nurturing her young. Tragedy struck when a wandering samurai snatched her foal, leaving the mare heartbroken and desperate.

In a fit of sorrow, the mare leapt off a cliff into the shimmering waters below, her anguish so profound that it transformed her into a colossal creature known as Issie. Now, this mysterious lake monster, with its two prominent humps, occasionally rises to the surface, searching for the lost child it once treasured so dearly.

The tale has captivated many, not only for its adventure elements but also for its enigmatic twist. While the original mare is described as female, Issie is often portrayed as male. This fascinating contradiction adds yet another layer of intrigue to the legend. Even to this day, many people travel to the lake, hoping to see Issie, the guardian of lost hopes, as she endlessly searches for her foal in the lake's deep waters.

A Sacred Site: People viewed Lake Ikeda as a holy place before the monster sightings began. Shinto priests believed the lake's circular shape, formed by volcanic activity, was the starting point of humanity. Today, locals still see the lake as sacred and visit the nearby Okudari Shrine to pray. Lake Ikeda holds a vital place in the local Shinto stories and traditions, which regard it as the origin of humankind.

Beastly Theories!

A Prehistoric Survivor: Plesiosaurs were marine reptiles that thrived from the late Triassic to the end of the Cretaceous period, characterized by their long necks, large bodies, and flipper-like limbs. They are divided into long-necked and short-necked varieties, with their efficient swimming abilities making them effective predators of their time. The notion of Issie, a creature residing in Lake Ikeda, draws parallels to plesiosaurs due to eyewitness accounts describing it as having a long neck, large body, and flipper-like appendages, which fuels speculation about its identity as a living descendant of these ancient reptiles.

Various factors contribute to the belief that Issie could be a plesiosaur. Local folklore and cryptozoological interests reinforce the idea, as stories depict Issie in a manner reminiscent of legendary sea monsters like the Loch Ness Monster. Moreover, the mystery surrounding the depths of Lake Ikeda and the possibility of undiscovered species in isolated ecosystems keep the legend alive, inviting speculation that a creature akin to plesiosaurs might still inhabit our waters.

Giant Eel: Lake Ikeda is home to some of the most enormous eels in the world, growing up to 6.5 feet long. Approximately 5,000 years ago, a volcanic eruption created this caldera, making it Kyushu's largest lake and Japan's fourth largest and cutting it off from the sea. However, in the Meiji era, an irrigation canal was built to connect the lake to the ocean, allowing saltwater fish to enter and thrive. It is believed that this is when the giant mottled eel, now designated as a protected species in Ibusuki, entered the lake, later becoming trapped yet thriving in its new home and attaining enormous dimensions. Could this sizeable, unidentified creature we know as "Issie" be an oversized descendant of this giant eel?

A Tourist Trap? The story of Issie had transformed into a tourist attraction since 1978 when twenty witnesses at a local ceremony claimed to have spotted a black creature with two humps moving in the water. The regional tourism office, seeing an undeniable opportunity and spurred on by the success of Scotland's Loch Ness, quickly erected a statue of Issie (nicknaming it "Issie-kun"), instantaneously transforming the beast into a local mascot, with merchandise ranging from stuffed animals to kindergarten playgrounds themed around the creature and being available everywhere around the lake. But could there be more to this legend than a clever marketing ploy to separate curious tourists from their Yen, or is the mercantile nature of humankind a natural reaction to having a living dinosaur on one's doorstep?

GUAI WU

What's in a Name? The term originates from Mandarin Chinese, specifically from the Sino-Tibetan language family, and translates to "strange beast." The phrase "guài wù" carries a broader connotation and can also refer to a monster, an oddity, or an eccentric individual. In Chinese culture, this moniker is not only used to evoke images of mythical creatures but can also apply to unique people who stand out from the ordinary.

Monstrous Measurements: This creature is as large as an ox, featuring a black coat and a white underbelly. It has a large head that resembles a seal's, with a long neck that measures about 5 feet. Recent reports indicate that some observers have seen a human-like head on this neck. A distinct white ring encircles the base of its neck, while the rest of its skin is smooth and muted grey. Some sightings have likened it to a buffalo, contributing to its mysterious nature.

Beastly Behaviours: These creatures engage in social behaviours and are playful. As they frolic in the water, chasing each other and diving, they create ripples and whirlpools on the surface. They appear highly agile, swimming with great speed and alacrity before diving and disappearing. Sometimes, they raise their long necks, adorned with petite, seal-like heads, above the water in a periscoping fashion. They are known to sink suddenly below the surface if disturbed by the noise of approaching boats.

Deadly Diet: Lake Tianchi is home to 26 fish species, including several introduced since the 1960s, such as trout (now referred to as Tianchi trout), carp, and mosquito fish. Any of these species could provide ample food for various creatures to thrive comfortably in the lake.

Watery Abode: The creatures are believed to inhabit Chon-Ji Lake (commonly called Tianchi, Changbai, or Dragon Lake) in Jilin Province, China. This body of water is so high that the Shanghai Office of the Guinness Book of Records documented it as the highest volcanic lake in the world.

Scary Sightings

1906: This was the first documented sighting of a monster emerging from the murky depths of this far-from-heavenly lake, although the beast had been known for centuries according to local records compiled for an article in the *Sydney Morning Herald*. During this incident, a large animal resembling a buffalo lunged out of the water with a deafening roar and attempted to assault three bystanders until one of them fired at it. It was struck six times in the belly before bellowing again and disappearing beneath the surface.

1962: From August 21 to 23, a person using a telescope observed two monsters chasing each other in the water. Over a hundred individuals reported sightings during this period. A subsequent account, unfortunately undated, described a creature with a human-like head featuring large round eyes and a protruding mouth. The beast was said to have smooth, grey skin and a white ring separating its 4 to 5-foot-long neck from its body.

1980: In August, a team of meteorologists reported encountering a large creature with a 3-foot neck, a cow-like head, and a duck-like beak. On 18 September, the *Yanbian Daily* published an eye-catching headline: *Changbai Mountain Found Strange Animals, Relevant Departments Are Closely Watching.*

On 22 August, at 8:40 AM, several staff members from the Changbai Mountain Tianchi Meteorological Station observed two unusual creatures near the summit of Tiantian Peak. The creatures swam rapidly, covering over 30 feet in the blink of an eye. One creature's visible head resembled a water snake tilting upward, with smooth grey fur observed beneath its jaws, although its mouth, eyes, and nose were unclear.

When the staff shouted, the creatures submerged. Approximately ten minutes later, one resurfaced about 130 feet from the shore. Its strange appearance included a head the size of a human's, with chestnut-sized eyes and a protruding mouth. Its neck measured about 4 inches in diameter and 4 to 5 feet in length, featuring white rings connecting it to its body. The fur was smooth and greyish-white, reminiscent of a seal. Besides its head, part of its back was visible above the water, leading to speculation it was as large as a cow.

1987: In early January, fifty tourists were astonished when a lake monster emerged near the eastern shore. One eyewitness, Shen Ruder, described it as roaring like a locomotive while spraying water from its nostrils.

1994: On September 2, photos and videos of a dragon-like creature were captured. Some images and footage showcased a large being swimming in the lake and claimed the video depicted a creature creating waves 6 feet high; unfortunately, this footage has been lost.

1996: Over 200 people witnessed four black animals playing in the lake, an event that was allegedly captured on film by a photographer named Wang Ling. However, like other footage, this recording also became lost.

2003: On July 11, several government officials spotted a shoal of mysterious creatures swimming through the volcanic waters. Provincial

Forestry Bureau Vice-Director Zhang Lufeng said that the monsters had been seen more than five times within 50 minutes, with the number of visible creatures often varying—sometimes only one was spotted. At other times, there were as many as twenty. They observed the creatures from about 1.2 to 1.9 miles away, appearing only as black or white dots. However, the ripples they created led the officials to conclude that the objects were 'living beings.' Four days later, the Lake Tianchi Monster resurfaced, witnessed by twelve military servicemen. They described it as having a back covered in scales and 4-inch-long horns on its black head. The monster swam around the lake for about two minutes before disappearing again below the surface.

2004: Approximately 500 people witnessed a serpentine creature with black scales and a horse-like head emerge from the water at Lake Tianchi.

2005: Soldiers from the People's Liberation Army sighted a similar blackish-green serpent. The same year, the *China Daily* reported that Zheng Changchun, a tourist in Jilin Province, spotted the Lake Tianchi Monster, describing a strange black object rising from the water. He recorded a video where a black creature can be seen surfacing and plunging into the lake three times.

2007: Chinese TV reporter Zhuo Yongsheng claimed to have filmed six unidentified creatures in the volcanic lake on September 6. He sent still photos to Xinhua's Jilin bureau, showing the creatures swimming in pairs, creating circular ripples. Zhuo observed these seal-like, finned beings for 90 minutes before they vanished around 7:00 AM. He noted they swam as fast as yachts and moved in perfect unison, giving the impression of coordinated behaviour.

Zhuo had climbed to the southern slope of Mount Changbaishan with two local guides at 5:05 AM, initially hoping to photograph the sunrise. They spotted the black figures in the lake when the view became clear at 5:26 AM. Zhuo initially doubted lake monster legends but changed his mind after witnessing the creatures. The rumours about a monster in the volcanic lake have persisted for over a century, although scientists argue that the cold conditions of the lake are unsuitable for large creatures.

2013: In July, a worker named Wu Chengzhi at a volcano monitoring station had an extraordinary experience measuring the lake's temperature with a colleague. He noticed a V-shaped ripple in the water, followed by a dark figure that was moving swiftly through the lake. Wu managed to capture several photographs, one shared with the media, depicting a fawn-like head and neck emerging from the water.

2020: The *Daily Mail* reported an incident involving a park ranger named Xiao Yu at a Chinese national park on Mount Paektu. He spotted a large creature estimated to be around 7 feet wide in the lake and posted footage online. This lake, known as Tian Chi or 'Heaven Lake,' is often associated with legends of a mysterious beast similar to the Loch Ness Monster.

Xiao Yu filmed a black circular object that seemed to hover on the lake's surface while patrolling the area. The footage from a viewing platform 1,640 feet above the lake showed the object remaining stationary for several minutes. Xiao noted that while the shape appeared small in the video, it was pretty substantial. He explained that he had seen similar things, usually fishing boats, but this was unlike anything he could identify as a vessel.

Beastly Evidence

Film & Photography: In 2007, Zhuo Yongsheng, a Chinese TV reporter, reported capturing a 20-minute video of six unidentified creatures in a volcanic lake on September 6. He submitted still photos to Xinhua's Jilin provincial bureau. According to news reports, one image depicted the six creatures swimming in parallel formations arranged in three pairs. At the same time, another photo showed them closer together, creating circular ripples on the lake's surface. Zhuo noted that he observed the six seal-like creatures, which had fins, swimming and interacting in the lake for an hour and a half before disappearing around 7:00 AM. He described their swimming speed as comparable to yachts and mentioned that they were sometimes submerged. Zhuo remarked on their synchronized movements, suggesting they were coordinated by an unseen force, and added that their fins or wings were longer than their bodies.

The Loongtan Pool: Historical accounts of "the presence of monsters" in Changbai Mountain Tianchi can be found in various sources, including *Fengtian Tongzhi*, *Fusong County Chronicles*, and *Changbai Jianggang Chronicles*. Liu Jianfeng, the county magistrate of Antu County, documented his experiences in his 1908 work *Changbai Mountain Jianggang Zhilue*. He recounted an incident involving four hunters who visited Diaoaotai a decade prior, discovering a pool below the peak at Zhipan that contained water of a striking golden-yellow colour. The creature described by the hunters had a head the size of a small bird, with a square-shaped top, horns, and numerous whiskers on its neck. As it moved, it created a disturbance that caused fear among the observers. While climbing partway up the slope, a sudden rumble prompted them to believe they had spotted dragons, which led to the area being named Longtan.

Beastly Theories!

Freshwater Seals: The concept of a freshwater seal species is a subject of interest, although there have been rare instances of marine seal species being found in freshwater habitats. For example, harbour seals have been observed in rivers and estuaries, such as the Columbia River in the United States, away from their usual ocean habitat.

Seals can sometimes travel notable distances upstream, either in search of food or during migration, highlighting their adaptability. There have also been reports of grey seals entering brackish waters, indicating their capability to exist in various environments.

However, these sightings are isolated and do not suggest the presence of established populations in freshwater. A self-sustaining population of seals in a confined freshwater lake is considered unlikely, primarily because their biological requirements, such as access to saline water and specific prey, are not fulfilled in these environments.

Tianchi Super Trout! A senior researcher from North Korea claimed that the "Tianchi monster," recently filmed by a Chinese photographer, is a mutated descendant of trout introduced to Tianchi Lake by North Korean scientists 40 years ago.

In an interview, 77-year-old Kim Li-tae revealed he was part of the team that released nine trout and other fish species into the lake on July 30, 1960. Despite its volcanic origin, researchers found that fish can thrive in the lake by feeding on insects carried by winds. According to Kim, these fish have since mutated and evolved into a distinct variety known as "Tianchi trout. "

In 2000, researchers recorded a "Tianchi trout" reaching 2.8 feet and weighing 17 pounds, but they haven't tested deeper waters yet. The "Tianchi monster," filmed by Chinese photographer Zhuo Yongsheng, may represent one of these trout from the lake's depths.

LUKWATA

What's in a Name? It has been suggested that the name "Lukwata" originated from the exclamation "Look at the water!" spoken in imperfect English. However, a more plausible explanation is that "lu" means "giant", and "lukumbi" refers to "an enormous animal" in the Bantu language. Therefore, Lukwata is a generic term for a monstrous animal. It is also known as Lokwata or Luquata.

Monstrous Measurements: The creature's length ranges from 20 to 30 feet. Its body is dark in colour with a white underside and features a round or ovoid head. The neck measures approximately 4 feet in length, and it has a long, spiny fin extending along its dolphin-like body. Traditionally, it is noted for its square-shaped head. Some researchers claim its description is closer to that of a type of unknown elongate plesiosaur.

Terrifying Tracks: Unknown

Beastly Behaviours: The creature exhibits aggressive tendencies and is often observed swimming with its head and neck above the water. It propels itself through vertical undulations and can create whirlpools in its vicinity. It is known for its loud, bellowing vocalizations and has been reported to attempt to seize fishermen in boats or canoes. Accounts suggest that it battles with crocodiles, which are described as its primary competitor. Locally, it is believed to have a long neck and a small head.

Deadly Diet: This highly carnivorous and aggressive creature preys on humans and other land-based animals that venture too close to the water's edge. It is also believed to hunt catfish and other fish species and will kill and feed on any crocodiles that enter its territory, as they are its main competitors.

Watery Abode: The Lukwata is found across Lake Victoria and its tributary rivers in Uganda, Tanzania, and Kenya. From Uganda to Kenya's Kavirondo (Winam) Gulf, communities on both lake shores have legends and tales of encountering this fearsome serpent.

Scary Sightings

1898: The Lukwata was first referenced by Church Missionary Society missionary Martin John Hall in 1898 and again by William Arthur Crabtree in 1902. However, it was not fully described until 1904 by Sir Harry Johnston, the discoverer of the okapi. In his work *The Uganda Protectorate*, Johnston noted persistent rumours of a monster called the Lukwata in Lake Victoria, which he believed resembled a small cetacean, a large manatee, or a giant fish. Locals associated the Lukwata with dangerous whirlpools. In 1905, traveller John Cathcart Wason depicted the Lukwata as a long-necked creature, claiming it appeared with its head and neck at least ten feet above the lake's surface.

1900: The most renowned sighting of the Lukwata occurred when English diplomat Sir Clement Lloyd Hill experienced an encounter during his tour of British East Africa as Superintendent of African Protectorates. While Hill never published a first-hand account, four third-party sources—Harry Johnston, Charles William Hobley, Sir

Hector Duff, and Sir Henry Hesketh Bell—all provided differing accounts, influenced by their interpretations. Johnston's was the earliest and shortest, suggesting that Hill's boat was nearly capsized by a monstrous water creature with a large, square-shaped, fish-like head while crossing Lake Nyanza.

1905: Charles William Hobley, a British East African administrator interested in cryptids, offered a slightly modified account of Hill's sighting in 1913, which Bernard Heuvelmans considered the most credible. Hobley claimed that while travelling from Kisumu to Entebbe, Hill observed a creature attempting to seize a native at the bow, its head visible, roundish in shape, and dark in colour, which Hill was sure was not a crocodile.

1913: Hobley recorded that the Lukwata was known on the shores of Uganda and Kenya, with reports of it sometimes attacking canoes. Captain William Hichens and Edward James Wayland of the Uganda Geological Survey gathered accounts from Kenya, where locals noted that crocodiles occasionally tore the Lukwata apart. They also claimed that parts of its body were retrieved for use as amulets. Wayland reported hearing the lukwata's roar and claimed to have seen a fragment of its bone.

1928: Naturalist Arthur Blayney Percival mentioned in his writings that several people on Lake Victoria, including experienced steamer crews, had reported sightings of the Lukwata.

1957: Constance Whyte, in *More Than a Legend*, referenced descriptions of a creature similar to the lau in Lake Victoria, recalled by soldiers who had served in British East Africa during and after World War II. The lau was described as having a humped body up to 100 feet in length, a brownish top and light-yellow underside, with a long neck and a snake-like head featuring two "tentacles."

1959: Major A. J. Ward from the King's African Rifles reported a sighting of a creature, referred to as Lukwata, which was described to him by the director of Macalder's Mine and his wife. They claimed to have observed a humped animal measuring between 20 to 30 feet long from the shore of Muhuru Bay. The witnesses saw the serpent in Lake Victoria around 4:30 PM at the end of 1959. As they approached a small jetty, the wife described seeing an unusual object emerging from the papyrus swamp at the lake's edge, moving promptly vertically. She characterized the head as snake-like and noted that it appeared black. The creature was estimated to be very long and thick, comparable in circumference to an average thigh or two thighs. It raced, partly submerged in the water, heading toward the lake's centre. The couple believed it was resting in the papyrus when they disturbed it, as the road was adjacent to the swamp.

Beastly Evidence

A Local Legend: Although there is currently no evidence supporting the existence of a creature like the Lukwata in Lake Victoria, Africa, a Baganda folktale tells of the friendship between a Lukwata and a monkey. It came to pass that the King of the Balukwata took ill, and his wizard told him to eat a monkey's heart as a cure. The King offered great rewards to any Balukwata who would bring him the heart of a monkey. So, the Lukwata went to the home of his friend the monkey and hailed him. "How are you? You should come visit me; my wife and sons want to see you." "But I cannot swim," said the monkey. "I'll carry you on my back," said the Lukwata, and they were off. Halfway across the lake, the Lukwata, having a crisis of conscience, decided to tell the monkey the truth. "I'm really sorry, but our King is sick and needs your heart." The monkey thought fast. "You silly thing," he told the Lukwata, "I don't have my heart with me. I leave it behind so I can jump through the trees. Take me back, and I'll fetch my heart from the branch where I left it." Of course, the unsuspecting Lukwata swam back, and the monkey escaped to safety in the trees – but not before mocking his erstwhile friend's intelligence.

Beastly Theories!

Cryptid Catfish: A large, unidentified species of catfish from the family *Siluridae* has been proposed as a candidate for the Lukwata due to its unique barbels, which support this theory. A voracious catfish could pull a person from a canoe, further reinforcing this idea. Additionally, some suggest that an oversized marbled lungfish, whose smaller relatives are common in Lake Victoria, might also be a contender for the Lukwata.

Certain features of the Lukwata, such as its deep rumbling sound and the use of its bones as amulets, resemble descriptions of another cryptid known as the Lau, believed to inhabit the White Nile. Some theorists suggest that the Lau, like the Lukwata, could be a superstitious amalgamation of different serpentine fish, including a giant catfish.

An African Rock Python: It has been suggested that the term "Lukwata" is associated with various large aquatic creatures in Lake Victoria, such as giant African rock pythons (*Python sebae*). If these pythons were to grow to immense sizes, their long, serpentine bodies and striking patterns could easily lead to misidentifications as lake monsters. Their ability to swim and hunt in water could create an illusion of an unknown creature lurking beneath the surface, especially during fleeting encounters with onlookers from a distance.

A Large Freshwater Turtle: It has been proposed that these sightings refer to the large African softshell turtle (*Trionyx triunguis*). Should these turtles reach significant sizes, their broad, flattened bodies and soft, leathery shells could easily be mistaken for monstrous creatures when partially submerged in water. Their unique, alien appearance and how they can swiftly manoeuvre in their freshwater habitats might give onlookers the impression of a mysterious lake monster gliding just beneath the surface.

SEA SERPENTS

Def.

Sea serpents are large, snake-like creatures reported in oceans around the world. Descriptions of them vary widely, often combining traits of known and unknown marine animals with cultural legends and folklore. Their peculiar features often connected with regional religions, superstitions, and myths, making their identification somewhat complex.

YELLOW BELLY

What's in a Name? Yellow-Belly is named for its pale-yellow colour. It was first categorized and named by the father of cryptozoology, Bernard Heuvelmans.

Monstrous Measurements: This creature resembles a tadpole and measures between 60 and 100 feet long. Its colouration is a pale yellow, featuring a prominent, large, flat head. A single black stripe runs longitudinally along its spine, while bold transverse black bands adorn its sides. Its immense, cylindrical tail gracefully tapers toward the end and has no visible fins or flippers.

Beastly Behaviours: Typically observed from May to September, this creature swims using a unique method characterized by vertical undulations. It often shows curiosity toward ships, sometimes circling them, but does not appear to have any predatory interest in their occupants.

Deadly Diet: Unknown

Watery Abode: This species thrives in warm, tropical waters, and is found in the Indian and Pacific Oceans.

Scary Sightings

1876: On September 11, Captain John K. Webster and surgeon James Anderson were aboard the steamer *Nestor* when they encountered a massive, unidentified creature in the Strait of Malacca, near Malaysia. The pair observed the remarkable being for almost half an hour as it circled the vessel.

This enigmatic creature, measuring 60 to 100 feet long, exhibited a form reminiscent of a large tadpole. It featured a broad, flat head connected directly to its body, lacking any visible neck, fins, or flippers. The creature's skin bore a yellow hue, accented by a prominent black stripe extending along its spine and smaller stripes that spiralled around its sides. Its long, cylindrical tail tapered gracefully to a rounded tip. The sighting left a lasting impression on the two men, who meticulously recorded the details of this extraordinary event.

1885: On October 4, almost nine years after the sighting near the *Nestor*, a creature resembling a sea monster was reported off the north coast of KwaZulu Natal in South Africa. Multiple witnesses described the creature as having yellow skin with black stripes and approximately 90 feet long. This time, witnesses noted that the beast had fins on each side, occasionally breaking the surface and slapping against the water as it submerged. The monster was seen off the Dolphin Coast, near to Umhlali in KwaZulu Province, and was characterized by its yellow appearance, dark dorsal stripe, and impressive size.

1964: One of the most famous sightings of the Yellow Belly occurred on December 12th in Stonehaven Bay, near Hook Island, Queensland. Robert Le Serrec, his family, and their family friend, Henk de Jong, were spending three months on Hook Island after their boat was wrecked on the Great Barrier Reef.

While crossing the bay one day, Robert's wife spotted a massive, tadpole-like creature resting on the sandy bottom. It was reported to measure 80 feet long. Initially thought to be dead due to a large white wound on its body—from a ship propeller—the creature eventually opened its mouth and began to move toward their small motorboat.

The creature appeared covered in smooth, dark skin with brown stripes wrapping around it. It had no visible fins and seemed to lack teeth. Its eyes were positioned on top of its head, with slit-shaped pupils. Concerned that the creature might become aggressive, the family quickly made their way out of the bay. As they headed toward the shore, the large creature left the bay and returned to the open ocean, never to be seen again.

Beastly Evidence

Le Serrec's Serpent: The identity of the Yellow-Belly or Hook Island Sea Monster, mentioned in cryptozoological discussions, has been the subject of various theories, including a deflated balloon, discarded plastic, or a tightly bunched fish shoal. The most famous documentation comes from Robert Le Serrec, who, while on holiday in December 1964, captured photographs of the creature resembling a giant, tadpole-like figure approximately 24 meters long resting in Stonehaven Bay, Queensland. Initially shared in the March 1965 issue of *Everyone* magazine, the story was investigated by renowned cryptozoologists Bernard Heuvelmans and Ivan T. Sanderson, both expressing scepticism about its authenticity.

While some speculated that the photos could depict a real animal, both experts believed it was a hoax, involving a plastic bag used by the US Navy or some other inanimate object. Heuvelmans reported doubts about Le Serrec's credibility, noting his previous claims of going away to profit from an encounter with a sea serpent and possible legal troubles. Despite this scepticism, Sanderson and Heuvelmans occasionally entertained the notion of the creature being real, suggesting it could be a giant swamp eel or a previously undiscovered shark species. However, both favoured the idea that the beast was likely plastic sheeting weighed down by sand.

Beastly Theories!

The Hoax Island Sea Monster: The Hook Island Monster case is a calculated hoax aimed at financial gain. In 1959, eyewitness Le Serrec sought to assemble an expedition that he claimed would be "financially fruitful," hinting at an ulterior motive tied to the sea serpent phenomenon. He later presented dubious photographic evidence of a creature resembling a giant tadpole, coincidentally matching descriptions emerging from cryptozoological discussions, particularly those by Heuvelmans. However, the likelihood that Le Serrec was inspired by Heuvelmans' later published ideas about the "yellow belly" monster raises questions about the authenticity of the photographs and the legitimacy of his claims.

Moreover, the aftermath of the Hook Island Monster sighting presents further evidence of a hoax. After years of speculation, reports surfaced in 2003 that Le Serrec had been located and was living in Asia, with plans for an interview regarding the case. This development, combined with the lack of credible evidence supporting the creature's existence and Le Serrec's past intentions to profit from the idea, suggests that the entire episode was little more than an elaborate scheme to capitalize on public intrigue surrounding sea serpents. The failure of the film to reveal any concrete evidence reinforces the notion that the Hook Island Monster was a well-coordinated attempt to deceive the public for monetary benefit.

The Super Eel: Super-eels are a type of sea serpent often categorized within a broader classification, including reports of giant eels and serpentine sharks. Some cryptozoologists propose the term "snark" to refer to these creatures. This classification is based on numerous sightings of marine animals, some confirmed, and others considered probable or possible.

Reports of these sea serpents come from diverse locations worldwide, with a distinct mottled variety noted in the Mediterranean Sea. Many cryptozoologists suggest that these entities could be deep-sea creatures. In some classifications, the super-eel is combined with other sea serpent types, while others recognize multiple eel-like varieties that don't have a direct equivalent. Additionally, some cryptozoologists separate the super-eel into two subtypes based on size: the megaconger and titanoconger.

CHESSIE

What's in a Name? Chessie is affectionately nicknamed after its home in Chesapeake Bay.

Monstrous Measurements: Primarily described as a large, serpent-like creature, Chessie has become a significant part of local folklore due to numerous sightings. Witnesses often report seeing this creature with a long, slender body, measuring up to 40 feet in length, adorned with small humps along its back. Its head resembles that of a horse or snake, and the creature is typically described as dark brown or black.

Terrifying Tracks: Unknown

Beastly Behaviours: The creature moves through the water with a side-to-side serpentine motion, creating visible waves on the surface. Its evenly spaced triangular humps can often be seen as it moves. The creature appears harmless and does not display any threatening or predatory behaviour towards humans or boats in its environment. It shows very little interest in humans at all.

Deadly Diet: The specific diet of Chessie, the legendary creature of the Chesapeake Bay, remains a mystery. However, the bay provides a rich environment filled with diverse prey. With over 300 fish species, including striped bass and American eel, as well as various shellfish like eastern oysters and blue crabs, Chessie has plenty of potential food sources. The bay is also home to more significant marine life, such as sharks, stingrays, bottlenose dolphins, and even occasional sightings of whales. This rich ecosystem overflows with prey, some of which could fall victim to an animal of Chessie's enormous size.

Watery Abode: This location can be found throughout the Chesapeake Bay estuary and its tributaries, which border the states of Maryland, Virginia, and Delaware along the Atlantic Coast of the USA.

Scary Sightings

1936: The earliest documented sighting of Chessie occurred when crew members of a military helicopter flying over Bush River claimed to have observed a large, reptilian creature in the water. This report has faced scepticism due to discrepancies in the helicopter technology available at that time. A military pilot described witnessing something substantial and serpentine writhing in a restricted area of the Bush River.

1980: In July, visitors at Ulmstead Estate Dock on the Magothy River spotted "three smooth, slightly triangular, dark humps" evenly spaced across the water. In August of the same year, Rosamond Hayes from Alexandria reported seeing an unfamiliar creature in the Prospect Bay area of Eastern Bay. Then, in September, a peculiar being was sighted near the Bay Bridge Tunnel at Virginia Beach, which was determined to be "certainly no manatee."

1982: The first sighting to gain widespread media attention occurred when Robert and Karen Frew recorded video footage of what they asserted was Chessie near Kent Island. The footage depicted a brownish entity moving laterally like an aquatic serpent, igniting considerable media curiosity. On a clear evening in May 1982, while hosting friends at their Bay-area home, Robert noticed something floating against the tide around 7:30 PM. The object was about 30 feet long. Enthralled, Robert and his friends rushed to document the encounter. Five minutes later, he successfully filmed Chessie, the Chesapeake Bay monster. Although this grainy video circulated on television, it was neither the creature's first nor last sighting. Later, in July, a sea creature was observed a short distance from Cloverland Beach. This period marked a surge of new and past accounts from Navy personnel, Coast Guard members, commercial fishermen, and even FBI and CIA agents, all describing Chessie as a snake-like entity with small humps and a greenish-brown hue.

1997: A sighting occurred close to the shore near Fort Smallwood Park, further fueling interest in the legend of Chessie.

2014: The latest significant sighting was reported on April 5, when two friends claimed to have encountered Chessie less than 5 feet from their car near the Magothy River.

Beastly Evidence

An Environmental Activist: Chessie, the legendary creature of the Chesapeake Bay, has evolved into an environmental icon representing the region's ecological health. The U.S. Fish and Wildlife Service published an educational colouring book in 1986 titled *Chessie: A Chesapeake Bay Story* to promote awareness of the Bay and its resources. A follow-up book, *Chessie Returns*, was released in 1991, solidifying Chessie's status as a symbol of environmental advocacy in Maryland. The friendly illustrations of this sea monster helped raise awareness about pollution in the Bay.

Cryptids like Chessie can be influential icons for tourism, trade, and environmentalism. They draw visitors to local attractions and generate economic interest while fostering a sense of environmental stewardship. By connecting folklore with ecological messaging, such symbols can champion conservation efforts and promote sustainable practices in their respective regions.

Beastly Theories!

A Manatee Misunderstood? In the summer of 1994, a massive Florida manatee named Chessie, weighing 1,100 pounds, gained attention when he was spotted in the Chesapeake Bay. As temperatures dropped in October, wildlife veterinarian Cindy Driscoll, with help from the U.S. Coast Guard, transported Chessie back to Florida for safety. His journey raised awareness for manatee conservation.

While Chessie's identity is clear as a manatee, the possibility of him being misidentified as a sea serpent is fascinating. The shifting waters of the Chesapeake could easily confuse sailors of the past, leading to tales of sea monsters. Manatees have often inspired myths; their large, graceful forms could evoke the extraordinary.

Chessie's presence reminds us of the rich cultural heritage of the Chesapeake Bay. His visits from 1994 to 2011 brought joy and highlighted the importance of preserving nature and the legends it inspires. Whether as a manatee or a myth, Chessie embodies the spirit of these waters, encouraging us to protect the unique ecosystem of the Chesapeake Bay.

The Many Humped Sea Serpent: The many-humped sea serpent, sometimes called the multi-humped sea serpent, is a well-known type of sea serpent whose history goes back as far as the longnecked variety.

Cryptozoologists theorize that the many-humped sea serpent could be a descendant of ancient marine mammals like zeuglodons or basilosaurids, while others suggest it may resemble a giant sea otter. It is prominently featured in various classification systems, with many reports worldwide taking place over centuries.

Some researchers believe that Chessie matches the description of the many-humped sea serpent which, like the longneck, is also thought to inhabit freshwater environments. This may explain similar creatures observed in freshwater environments.

OLD NED

What's in a Name? Locally referred to as "Old Ned," it's unclear why this particular name was chosen. While the First Nations people in the region knew this creature, it lacked a specific name in their traditions. Similar creatures are referred to as "Apotamkin" by the local tribes.

Monstrous Measurements: This elusive creature is described as bulky, measuring between 30 and 100 feet in length. It has a large head reminiscent of an alligator or horse and is coloured from reddish-brown to dark red, featuring a single pair of fins. Old Ned enjoys basking in the sun and is characterized as gentle rather than aggressive. Unlike traditional perceptions of lake monsters, which often depict them as dinosaurs with flippers, Old Ned is more serpentine and amphibious in appearance. Its lungs allow it to breathe air and remain submerged for extended periods. Descriptions of Old Ned vary, with some suggesting it may have an eel-like or even cetacean appearance, with length estimates exceeding 40 feet.

Terrifying Tracks: The creature leaves deep furrows in the sand yet does not seem to leave any footprints or tracks resembling flippers.

Beastly Behaviours: The creature often enjoys basking in the sun and is known to migrate down river systems in August. Equipped with lungs, it can breathe air and remain submerged for extended periods. While local legends include tales of a monster chasing a canoe and unusual incidents of the creature surfacing through the lake's ice, most sightings depict a docile being that prefers lounging and lolling in the late summer sun or floating peacefully in the evening calm waters. "It loves to bask. It loves to come up on a day like this and roll in the water," researchers say. "It's never vicious either. It doesn't attack people. It's one of those 'It's more afraid of you than you are of it.'" The serpent returns to Lake Utopia every 3 to 5 years from the Atlantic Ocean, to rear its young. Locals speculate that the reason Old Ned travels between Lake Utopia and the Atlantic Ocean periodically is for breeding or feeding purposes, noting that the creature is said to break holes through the surface of the frozen lake during winter.

Deadly Diet: The beast's dietary habits are unknown; however, the lake contains plentiful stocks of fish species such as smallmouth bass, trout, perch, and river eels. Some researchers hypothesize that this animal might be a herbivore.

Watery Abode: It primarily inhabits the Atlantic Ocean and Lake Utopia in New Brunswick, as well as its coastal waters, where it periodically breeds every 3 to 5 years.

Scary Sightings

1856: The first report surfaced, noted by loggers from St. George.

1867: Sawmill workers on the north shore of the lake reported seeing a creature 30 feet long and 10 feet wide thrashing in the water. On August 6, an "Old Ned" specimen was killed off Passamaquoddy Bay. It was described as a serpentine creature with a whale-like head, dorsal fin, and horizontal tail—features unique to mammals. Covered in short, shaggy fur resembling a buffalo robe, 13 sawmill workers observed it thrashing in the water from a raft approximately 100 yards away.

1868: A *Saint Croix Courier* reporter claimed he and fellow witnesses saw the monster. Later that year, an explosion executed under the water with 25 pounds of dynamite brought an animal to the surface, but despite four shots fired at it, it escaped. On August 3, a 28-foot creature was killed 200 feet from the shore of Passamaquoddy Bay and displayed in a travelling exhibit, with promotional material claiming it had a girth of 13 feet, legs measuring 5 feet 4 inches, and a mouth stretching 5 feet 6 inches wide.

1872: A *Dominion Gazette* article reported that those living by the lake unanimously believed in a colossal fish or serpent residing in Utopia, with sightings of it basking on the water's surface, looking like a pine log. Several witnesses described the monster with a large head that pursued their canoes, snapping its jaws. The *Canadian Illustrated News* noted a hunting party set out to capture the creature, but they returned empty-handed.

1891: A lumberman witnessed the creature, saying it was dark red, about 20 feet long above the water, and as wide as a small hogshead, resembling a large, broad eel.

1969: The *Saint John Evening Times Globe* featured an interview with Mrs. Fred McKillop from St. George, who stated she witnessed an enormous creature 18 years prior. "It looked like a huge black rock... It moved up and down the lake, boiling and churning the water, creating large waves," she recounted.

1982: On July 9, Sherman Hart and three others observed an animal surface about half a mile away, measuring 10-15 feet long and rising 1-2 feet above the water. Sherman Hatt described seeing a 10-foot-long hump emerge from the lake that resembled a submarine, with spray coming from both sides, commenting, "it was huge—huge!"

1996: Roger and Lois Wilcox, canoeing on the lake, reported seeing ripples break the glass-like surface about 300 feet away, moving towards Cannonball Island. Stewart Wilcox, a retired military airman, described an undulating creature measuring 40 to 50 feet long with a visible hump rising five feet from the water. He stated, "I just don't know what it was."

Beastly Evidence

Slime Time! Historical accounts from 1840 include a report of a slimy trail in the region, leading many researchers to conclude that the monster may travel overland, particularly in the Breadalbane area of St. George. This area represents the flattest route between the sea and the lake.

Death of a Monster! In 1868, many believed the Lake Utopia Monster had been killed. *Harper's Weekly* published an article reporting that a mysterious sea serpent had been found dead in Passamaquoddy Bay. The creature was described as having a dorsal fin and a flat tail similar to a shark. An accompanying artist's drawing depicted a basking shark, and it was suggested that the hind limbs shown in the illustration were claspers from a male basking shark. It was thought the creature was attempting to cross land to reach Lake Utopia.

Beastly Theories!

A Hybrid Hydra: The origins are steeped in cultural significance, particularly among the Passamaquoddy people, for whom Lake Utopia holds sacred status. Historical accounts suggest that legends surrounding this lake monster predate European colonization. Still, there is a compelling argument that these tales may have absorbed influences from European narratives about similar creatures, such as the fabled Loch Ness Monster.

As European colonizers shared their own lake monster folklore, these stories merged with Indigenous beliefs, creating a hybrid mythos that reflects both the rich heritage of the Passamaquoddy and the colonial transplant of European monster legends. Many observers insist that

Old Ned is more inclined to shy away from humans than to pose any threat, reinforcing the notion that, rather than being a fearsome predator, this celebrated creature embodies a unique blend of local tradition and borrowed lore from afar.

Enormous Eels! The American Eel (*Anguilla rostrata*) was once plentiful in the lake, reaching lengths of up to 5 feet. Some speculate that sightings of a giant eel could be attributed to large eels surfacing when food is scarce or during breeding. Sceptics suggest that sightings may be of eels hibernating in tightly packed groups, known to float to the surface in spring.

Eels are catadromous, spending years in freshwater before migrating to the ocean to breed and die shortly after. They can stay in freshwater systems for over a decade before returning to sea, which does not support the theory of "Old Ned" migrating every 3-5 years.

If a giant eel entered Lake Utopia through underground tunnels, sightings might increase, but eels don't need to surface often, reducing detection chances. They can overwinter in mud and remain active at times, which could explain reports of a large eel-like creature breaking through ice in the 1800s.

Conger eels, which can exceed 3 meters and weigh 140 kg, are aggressive and have been linked to such sightings due to their size and appearance. Although conger eels typically inhabit saltwater, they may struggle to survive if they access freshwater via underwater connections. Their unique swimming behaviour, where they undulate on their sides, fits some eyewitness descriptions.

Natal Navigation: Researchers propose that the mysterious Lake Utopia Monster, often described as a serpent-like creature, has been making rare appearances every three to five years. They suggest that it could return to its birthplace to spawn, which might explain the intermittent sightings of similar creatures in lakes with access to the sea across the globe.

Lake Utopia is connected to the Atlantic Ocean through the Magaguadavic River and a network of underground tunnels from The Gorge. This subterranean passage could serve as a migration route for the creature, allowing it to travel between freshwater and saltwater environments.

The researchers draw parallels between Lake Utopia and Loch Ness, noting that both lie within a geographical belt that correlates with numerous sea monster sightings. Some theories even suggest that the creature may traverse overland through the flattest ocean and lake routes.

While the existence of the Lake Utopia Monster remains unproven, speculation about its identity ranges from known aquatic animals to mythical sea creatures. Theories about its migratory patterns and potential breeding grounds imply it could be an amphibious creature capable of navigating freshwater and marine habitats.

Way-Out Whales! The theory that sightings of "Old Ned" could be misidentified whales entering the Magaguadavic River aligns with Occam's Razor, which states that more straightforward explanations are often the most likely. Misidentifying whales as "Old Ned" offers a straightforward rationale grounded in existing marine life habits and historical context, as large animals like whales can be mistaken for mythical creatures due to human perception biases. Given the variety of whale species and their natural behaviours, such sightings can easily be attributed to common animals rather than extraordinary claims; cutting through the complexity of folklore and focusing instead on what we understand about wildlife habits in this area.

CADDY

What's in a Name? Name popularized if not coined October 11, 1933, by *Victoria (B.C.) Daily Times* editor Archie H. Wills after repeated sightings in Cadboro Bay, British Columbia. Short form of *Cadborosaurus*, coined at the same time. Variant names: Amy, *Cadborosaurus*, Edizgiganteus (after Ediz Hook Light, Washington), Haietluk, Klamahsosaurus (on Texada Island), and Penda (after Pender Island). Scientific name: *Cadborosaurus willsi*, proposed by Edward L. Bousfield and Paul H. LeBlond in 1995.

Monstrous Measurements: A serpentine body that forms many humps or loops. Length: 16–100 feet. Diameter: 2 feet 6 inches–8 feet. Light brown to black. The small head resembles a sheep, horse, giraffe, or camel. Eyes in the front of the head. Small ears or horns. Pointed tongue. Two rows of fishlike teeth. Mane or fur is sometimes reported. The neck is 3-12 feet long, about as thick as an arm. It has one pair of front flippers, and its flat tail is fluked or formed from fused back flippers. Its back sometimes appears serrated, occasionally smooth.

Terrifying Tracks: Although Caddy has been observed lying on shore, no description of its tracks has been given. Although it has been described as "slithering back into the water, when disturbed."

Beastly Behaviours: Does not appear to undulate when it swims. Fast swimming speed, clocked at 40 knots. Breathes in short pants. Makes whale-like grunts and hisses.

Deadly Diet: Feeds on herring, salmon, and ducks.

Watery Abode: British Columbia seacoast, especially around Cadboro Bay and the Strait of Georgia.

Scary Sightings

1791: A crew member of the ship *Columbia* under American fur trader Capt. Robert Gray was the first to report a Caddy sighting in 1791.

1897: Osmond Fergusson watched a 25-foot animal with a long neck near the Queen Charlotte Islands, British Columbia, on June 26.

1905/1906: In September, Philip H. Welch saw a brown animal with a 6- to 8-foot neck from 100 yards away in Johnstone Strait. It had two bumps on its head that were 5 inches high and rounded on top.

1932: F. W. Kemp and his wife and son watched an 80-foot manned animal while they were sitting on Chatham Island beach, British Columbia, on August 10.

1933: On September 23, Dorothea Hooper and a neighbour observed a serpentine animal with a serrated back cavorting in Cadboro Bay about 400 yards distant. It created a commotion in the water as it swam out to sea.

1933: Maj. W. H. Langley and his wife sailed in Haro Strait on October 1, when they heard a loud grunt off Chatham Island. They saw the back of a vast, dark-green creature with serrated markings on the top and sides.

1933: Charles F. Eagles sketched a 60-foot animal that he saw in Oak Bay on October 14. It had crocodile-like spines on its neck.

1933: On December 3, Justice of the Peace G. F. Parkyn of Bedwell Harbour was one of twelve people watching from Pender Island as an animal with a large, horse-like head and neck gulped down a duck that Cyril Andrews had just shot.

1936: E. J. Stephenson and his wife and son watched a yellow-and-bluish, 90-foot-long, 3-foot-thick animal crawling over a reef into a lagoon on Saturna Island.

1937: A 10- to 12-foot carcass of a young Caddy was removed from the stomach of a sperm whale, photographed and displayed for a while at Naden Harbour whaling station. The photo shows it stretched out across packing cases. It was about 10 feet long, with a camel-like head, traces of flippers, and a paddling tail. The carcass was allegedly shipped off to the Field Museum in Chicago, but there is no record of its arrival.

1939: Captain Paul Sowerby reported what may have been one of the closest sightings of the creature known as Caddy. He recalled, "we were heading north, about thirty miles offshore, when we saw something standing about four feet out of the water. I steered the boat toward it to get a better look. At first, I thought it resembled a polar bear with ruffled fur. When we got close—thanks to the crystal-clear water—I saw a long column rising at least forty feet high, and it had enormous eyes. My mate, an old Newfoundlander, asked, 'Do you see its eyes?' I don't remember if it had a mouth or nose, but those big eyes stood out. They seemed to open from top to bottom."

1950: A Canadian naval officer was fishing in an open boat off Esquimalt Harbour in November when a 30-foot Caddy appeared and created a heavy wash. It swam with an undulating motion using large flippers on either side. It snapped its teeth together once before it dived after twenty-five seconds.

<u>1953:</u> On February 12, R. D. Cockburn, C. P. Crawford, and Ron Loach saw an animal with three humps off Qualicum Beach for five minutes. Two other men got into a boat and rowed within 20 feet, but it submerged and reappeared 100 yards away. Its head was dog-shaped and had two horns.

<u>1959:</u> In late November, David Miller and Alfred Webb came within 30 feet of an animal with a 10-foot neck sticking straight up out from the water off Discovery Island. It had coarse brown fur, red eyes, and small ears.

<u>1968:</u> A 16-inch-long juvenile Caddy was caught in a net by William Hagelund off De Courcy Island, but it was thrown back. It had spiny teeth, a saw-toothed ridge of plates along its backbone, and a bilobate tail.

<u>1984:</u> Mechanical engineer Jim M. Thompson was fishing off Spanish Banks, Vancouver, in January, when an 18- to 22-foot serpentine animal surfaced about 100 feet away. It had a giraffe-like head with small stubby horns and floppy ears. Soft, yellow fuzz covered its undersides.

<u>1991:</u> In July, Phyllis Harsh claimed to have caught a small, 2-foot baby caddy and returned it to the water near Johns Island (San Juan Islands).

<u>1992:</u> In May, music professor John Celona saw a multihumped animal about 25 feet long while sailing.

<u>1994:</u> Two students sighted Caddy swimming about in a bay.

Beastly Evidence

<u>A Collection of Cryptid Carcasses</u>

<u>1930:</u> On November 10, a skeleton measuring 24 feet was discovered in

ice at Glacier Island near Valdez. Some remains were preserved in Cordova for scientific study and were thought to be of a whale.

1934: In November, badly decomposed remains about 30 feet long were found on Henry Island near Prince Rupert. A Dr Neal Carter examined the remains, identifying the creature as a basking shark.

1937: A Cadborosaurus carcass was retrieved from the stomach of a sperm whale in Naden Harbour and photographed. A sample sent to the BC Provincial Museum was tentatively identified as a fetal baleen whale by museum director Francis Kermode.

1941: "Sarah the Sea Hag" was found on Kitsilano Beach. However, W.A. Clemens and Ian McTaggart-Cowan later identified it as a shark; its exact species remains undetermined.

1947: In December, a 45-foot creature was discovered at Vernon Bay, Barkley Sound, Vancouver Island. Further analysis confirmed it was a shark.

1950: A creature with four tails and thick hair was found in Delake, Oregon. It was identified as a whale shark.

1956: Near Dry Harbour south of Yakutat, Alaska, a carcass measuring 100 feet long was discovered. It had 2-inch-long hair, and Trevor Kincaid remarked that its description fits no known creature. W.A. Clemens identified it as a Baird's beaked whale.

1962: In April, a 14-foot carcass with an elephant-like head was found near Ucluelet. Dragged ashore by Simon Peter, it was later considered to be an elephant seal.

1963: In September, a carcass found near Oak Harbor on Whidbey Island had a head resembling that of a horse. A. D. Welander from Fisheries speculated it was a basking shark.

Catch & Release!

1968: William Hagelund caught a 16-inch juvenile Caddy in a net off De Courcy Island, but it was released. This creature had spiny teeth, a saw-toothed ridge of plates along its backbone, and a bilobate tail.

1991: Phyllis Harsh claimed to have caught a small, 2-foot baby Caddy, which she returned to the water near Johns Island in the San Juan Islands.

Captured on Camera:

2009: Fisherman Kelly Nash filmed several minutes of footage featuring ten to fifteen creatures in Nushagak Bay. A brief segment of this footage aired in 2011 on the Discovery TV show *Hilstranded*, where the Hilstrand brothers viewed Nash's recording but failed to find one of the creatures.

2009: Local man Jason Walton captured an image of Caddy on his sonar device while fishing near Discovery Island. The sonar displayed a large object with a curved shape and several protrusions, estimated to be about 25 feet long and 3 feet wide.

Beastly Theories!

A Beastly Basilosaurus: Cryptozoologists believe this type of archaic whale could grow up to 80 feet long and lived approximately 42 million years ago during the Late Eocene. Despite its serpentine shape and tail fluke, the creature's head resembles that of a camel or horse, which differs from the snake-like head characteristic of Basilosaurus. While some sightings of creatures like Ogopogo suggest a Basilosaurus origin, descriptions do not match the features attributed to Caddy.

A Prehistoric First: Researchers propose that long-necked marine reptiles known as plesiosaurs, which swam using paddle-like limbs, could be involved in sightings. Fossils of these creatures, ranging in size from 6 to 46 feet, date from the Middle Triassic to the Late Cretaceous. Although plesiosaurs share some characteristics with Caddy, no fossil record of any species aligns with Caddy's physiological description.

A Decaying Basking Shark: The 1937 carcass found in Naden Harbour might be explained as a highly decomposed basking shark, which can take on a plesiosaur-like appearance due to the differential decomposition of features like gill slits and a lower tail fluke. A 30-foot specimen discovered in November 1934 on Henry Island also turned out to be a basking shark, suggesting that numerous sea serpent carcasses could be distorted remains of sharks or whales. By 1996, reports of mysterious creatures increasingly pointed to the likelihood of simply being collections of sea-divulged debris that unknown individuals may have arranged.

STRONSAY BEAST

What's in a Name? Later, the Scottish anatomist John Barclay assigned the scientific nomenclature *Halsydrus pontoppidani* (Pontoppidan's sea snake) in honour of Erik Pontopiddan, a Danish bishop and historian, who chronicled sea serpents in his renowned work, *The Natural History of Norway*, published in 1752.

Monstrous Measurements: The creature measures 55 feet in length and 4 feet in width, although it is suspected to be longer due to a missing segment of its tail. The exact full length remains unconfirmed.

Beastly Behaviours: Although believed to inhabit deeper waters, this enigmatic being has also been observed in shallower regions and coastal coves. It has exhibited predatory behaviours, particularly toward children. It may possess the capability to breathe underwater, potentially through an unknown mechanism related to its long filiform mane.

Deadly Diet: This creature's dietary habits remain unknown, but it displays opportunistic predatory feeding behaviour.

Watery Abode: Similar creatures have been spotted in the seas and coastal regions around the Orkney Isles, including the Pentland Firth to the south and the North Sea to the east. These diverse habitats and the nearby waters of the Atlantic Ocean may serve as homes for these mysterious beings.

Scary Sightings

1808: On the island of Stronsay in the Orkney archipelago, a remarkable event was witnessed by farmer John Peace while he was fishing east of Rothiesholm Point. He spotted the carcass of a whale surrounded by circling seabirds. Upon closer examination of his boat, he realized it was an unusual creature that did not resemble anything he knew. George Sherar, another farmer watching from the shore, confirmed Peace's observations, and approximately ten days later, he could inspect the creature when it washed ashore. Sherar took measurements and reported that the animal was 55 feet long, possessing a serpentine, eel-like body with a 15-foot neck, a small head, and a long mane. It exhibited three pairs of limbs, each with five or six toes, contributing to its bizarre appearance. Sherar salvaged some vertebrae and the skull, leading to the creature being dubbed the Stronsay Beast.

This extraordinary creature had a head resembling that of a sheep and large eyes akin to those of a seal. Its skin was grey, smooth like velvet when stroked from head to tail but rough in the opposite direction, and it was covered in a layer of fatty tallow. The animal's bristly hair glowed silvery when wet. Due to a missing part of its tail, its total length was longer than the measured 55 feet, but precise figures remain a mystery.

1890s: The tale of the Stronsay Beast has sparked heated debate, yet the Orkney Islands boast a long history of sea serpent encounters. Among the most notable is the incident involving a boy named Alec Groundwater, who, while spending a day in Orphir, experienced a harrowing encounter. Perched on rocks with his legs overhanging the water, he witnessed turbulence beneath him as a creature with a broad, flat head and tusk-like teeth lunged at his legs, narrowly missing. As it retreated, he saw it rise above the surface, shaking its head and mane, sending water cascading down its body.

1900: A frightening near miss occurred when a brother and sister gathering whelks noticed a large creature with a horse-like head and long neck staring at them from the shallow water. The loud splashing prompted panic, and they fled in terror, scrambling across the seaweed beds until they reached safety.

1942: The Stronsay Beast was not the only mysterious marine creature reported in the Orkney Islands; in 1942 two additional carcasses were discovered and washed ashore along the mainland, one week apart. The first, found at Holm, measured 24 feet long, while the second, nicknamed Scapasaurus, was 28 feet long, discovered at Scapa. Experts declared both to be decomposing basking sharks, yet scepticism persisted. Even prominent figures like James Marwick, the Provost of the Education Board and a lecturer from Durham University, argued that the reptilian features suggested they could be some aquatic reptile. Marwick even went as far as to proclaim the Scapa carcass as evidence of the Loch Ness Monster and other sea serpents.

Beastly Evidence

Mysterious Remains: When the Stronsay Beast was discovered, some of its remains—including a skull, a 'paw,' and fibres from its mane—were sent to London but were lost during a German bombing raid in World War II. However, some biological samples, including bone fragments, survived. These remnants, part of Lord Byron's collection now at the National Library of Scotland, were discussed by Patrick Neill at a meeting of Edinburgh's Wernerian Natural History Society on November 19, 1808. At the following meeting on January 14, 1809, Neill formally named it 'Halsydrus pontoppidani', meaning 'Pontoppidan's water snake of the sea,' after an 18th-century Norwegian bishop noted for his sea serpent accounts.

Scottish anatomist Dr John Barclay presented a paper on the beast's remains, detailing its vertebrae, skull, and leg, which were fins. His findings, published in 1811, noted that the vertebrae resembled cotton reels and featured unique star-shaped calcification. This intrigued Sir Everard Home, a naturalist studying basking sharks, who identified a strong resemblance between the Stronsay Beast's features and those of a basking shark, the world's second-largest shark species.

Request Denied: In 2008, geneticist Dr Yvonne Simpson requested permission to conduct DNA analysis on the remains of the Stronsay Beast, but the National Library denied her request. A follow-up review in 2012 did not yield any new developments; as of now, the remains have not been analysed.

Cryptid Carcass: The remains of the Stronsay beast, though primarily lost, include three vertebrae currently housed in Edinburgh's Royal Museum of Scotland. When these remains were first discovered, the Natural History Society of Edinburgh could not identify them, which may have contributed to the theory of it being a new species of sea serpent—a reflection of the cultural biases of the 19th century before Darwin's work. Eyewitnesses reported that the Stronsay Beast was significantly longer than the largest known basking shark, which measures around 40 feet. Dr Simpson proposed that it could have been an unknown shark species due to its unusual size, yet no further evidence has surfaced. It seems like a missed opportunity not to have tested the remains with modern DNA technology, as it could have provided invaluable insights into this mysterious creature.

Beastly Theories!

Decaying Basking Shark: Some researchers question whether the 55-foot Stronsay Beast was truly a basking shark, speculating it might be a giant, unknown relative. The megamouth shark, *Megachasma pelagios*, was only discovered in 1976, highlighting that undiscovered large shark species may still exist. Alternatively, could the Stronsay Beast be an enormous basking shark?

Researchers suggest that larger fish were more common in the past, before the impact of pollution and industrial fishing. The Stronsay Beast was one of the last of its kind.

The confusion arises from the appearance of decomposing basking shark carcasses. As they decay, their gills and jaws detach, leaving a small cranium and a long backbone that resembles a neck. The triangular dorsal fin also rots away, and the muscle fibres can create a mane-like look. A decomposed tail fluke and distorted fins can further suggest the appearance of legs. This misleading form could be likened to a plesiosaur—a phenomenon frequently termed by sceptics and scientists alike pseudo-plesiosaur.

However, a key point often overlooked is that eyewitness descriptions depict the creature as a living entity, not a rotting corpse. Its distinct features—a sheep-like head, long neck, six limbs, and a bristly mane that shined in the dark—do not match those of a decomposed basking shark. Moreover, at 55 feet long, even without its tail, it far exceeds any recorded basking shark, dismissing the argument that it was simply one of these sharks.

A Frightening Theory! Some researchers have speculated that a particular species of plesiosaur, which many believe to be extinct, could still exist today. If this were the case, these creatures might have developed several unique adaptations to survive in contemporary aquatic environments. One intriguing possibility is the ability to extract oxygen from water, similar to adaptations observed in some existing species.

For instance, the Hawkesbury River turtle utilizes cloacal bursae—a specialized structure in its cloaca—to extract oxygen directly from water, allowing it to stay submerged for up to three days without surfacing for air. Similarly, the Lake Titicaca frog has developed baggy sacs of skin that enable it to absorb oxygen from its aquatic habitat, allowing it to thrive in an entirely aquatic lifestyle.

Additionally, there have been descriptions of the "strange beast," a creature reminiscent of plesiosaurs, characterized by a glowing gelatinous mane that extends along its spine to the tip of its tail. Researchers have speculated that this bioluminescent feature could serve a dual purpose: not only could it help the creature remain hidden from potential threats, such as humans, but it might also play a role in luring prey close to the water's edge.

The concept of bioluminescence in aquatic environments is well-documented, with various species using light displays for communication, camouflage, or predation. If these hypothetical plesiosaurs possess similar traits, they could leverage their glow to navigate their environments or hunt effectively.

Such adaptations highlight the incredible potential for undiscovered species to possess unique physiological traits that enable them to thrive in their particular habitats, emphasizing the importance of continued exploration and research in our oceans and waterways. While the existence of modern plesiosaurs remains speculative, these theories demonstrate a fascinating intersection of biology, evolution, and the mysteries of the natural world.

GAMBO

What's in a Name? The name 'Gambo' is believed to have been coined by Karl Shuker after the country, The Gambia. However, Shuker claims that the name was first introduced by *Fortean Times* magazine. A variant name for Gambo is Kunthum belein, a Mandinka word for dolphin that translates to "cutting jaws."

Monstrous Measurements: Gambo is a smooth-skinned creature measuring approximately 15 feet in length and 5 feet in width. It has a dark brown colouration on its upper side and white underneath. The beast features a dolphin-like head with small brown eyes and an 18-inch-long jaw filled with eighty sharp, uniform teeth. Notably, it lacks a blowhole and has nostrils at its snout's tip. Gambo has a short neck, no dorsal fin, and four paddle-shaped flippers, each measuring 18 inches long. Its pointed tail measures 5 feet. The creature's jaws are long and thin, tightly closed, and its forehead is slightly domed.

Terrifying Tracks: While specific tracks of Gambo have not been reported due to its oceanic nature, the physiognomy of the carcass found on the beach in Senegal implies that any tracks would be flipper-shaped and similar in appearance to those of an enormous sea turtle.

Beastly Behaviours: Little is known about Gambo's behaviour due to its limited sightings and the circumstances of its discovery involving a beached carcass. However, given its characteristics, one could speculate that it behaved similarly to modern marine reptiles, employing hunting strategies that used its conical teeth to grasp slippery prey. It may have occasionally ventured onto land to hide a clutch of eggs or clumsily make its way across a semi-submerged sandbank.

Deadly Diet: Gambo's diet remains unknown, but one might hypothesise that it could have preyed on fish and smaller marine animals similar to modern-day marine predators. Conical teeth suggest a diet requiring grasping and slicing flesh, indicating it was a carnivore.

Watery Abode: Gambo was discovered near Kotu, The Gambia, particularly on the beach at Bungalow Beach, where its carcass washed ashore on 12 June 1983. This indicates that its habitat was coastal waters, akin to areas frequented by sea serpents or large marine reptiles.

Scary Sightings

1983: Wildlife enthusiast Owen Burnham and his family discovered a giant sea creature's carcass on Bungalow Beach in The Gambia. Having lived in Senegal and being familiar with the region's wildlife, Owen meticulously sketched and measured the beast, which he described as being 15-16 feet long with a 10-foot body and a long, thin head featuring around eighty uniform teeth resembling those of a barracuda. The creature was brown above and white below, with evidence of gas distension making it streamlined, but it had no visible dorsal fin or blowhole. Despite the foul smell, the skin remained smooth, and Owen noted that the animal appeared to have died recently based on its visible eyes.

The local fishermen, who identified it with the Mandinka name kunthum belein, referred to the animal as "cutting jaws," a term typically used for dolphins. However, despite Owen's detailed descriptions, the fishermen claimed to have never seen such a creature. While some authorities suggested it might be a dolphin with missing appendages, Owen found this explanation unsatisfactory, given the creature's unique features. He has not encountered anything like it during his many visits to the coast since then.

Beastly Evidence

Owen Burnham Witness Report: The primary evidence for Gambo's existence comes from the sketch and measurements Owen Burnham took upon discovering its carcass. Unfortunately, as local fishermen were cutting up the creature, more extensive scientific analysis may have been hindered.

BBC Documentary: In May 1986, *BBC Wildlife*, a British monthly magazine, published a short account by Owen describing his discovery and included versions of his original sketches.

Beastly Theories

A Giant Marine Crocodile: Some might argue that Gambo could be a giant marine crocodile, as supported by historical accounts of large reptiles. The features of the carcass align with those of large crocodilians, such as their conical teeth and body shape. However, the lack of scale-covered skin and the specifics of its jaw structure raise questions about this possibility.

An Unknown Cryptid Lizard: Another theory is that Gambo represents a previously unknown species of marine lizard. Cryptozoologists often speculate that there are undiscovered species in the ocean, especially in remote coastal areas like The Gambia. To validate this, further evidence and sightings would be required.

A Prehistoric Survivor: A more sensational hypothesis suggests Gambo could be a living remnant of prehistoric marine reptiles like

Pliosaurus or mosasaurs. The presence of flippers and the overall morphology support this idea. Some researchers have pointed out that the reproductive habits of such creatures would make them visible if they were indeed surviving today, leading to ongoing debates about the plausibility of such creatures still existing.

THE DAEDALUS SEA SERPENT

What's in a Name? It's difficult to dismiss a sea serpent sighting when a naval captain and several crew members report witnessing it. This situation unfolded in August 1848 when the *HMS Daedalus*, a Royal Navy vessel, navigated towards St. Helena in the South Atlantic. The ship's captain, Captain McQuhae, and various crew members claimed to have seen a sea serpent approximately 60 feet long, with 4 feet of its head raised above the water's surface.

Monstrous Measurements: The creature was described as approximately 60 feet long, with its head elevated about 4 feet above the water.

Terrifying Tracks

Beastly Behaviours: The creature was noted to glide swiftly past the ship, close enough for Captain McQuhae to assert he would have recognized it had it been a familiar person.

Deadly Diet

Watery Abode: The sighting occurred off the coast of Africa, south of St. Helena Island in the South Atlantic.

Scary Sightings

1848: A captivating account of a sea serpent comes from the *HMS Daedalus* in 1848. When sailing 300 miles from present-day Namibia, the ship's officers and crew observed an enormous serpent swimming alongside them. Its head remained 4 feet above the water, while the body extended another 60 feet into the ocean. Seven crew members confirmed the sighting, stating that the creature remained visible for around twenty minutes.

Beastly Evidence

Naval Testimony! Captain McQuae described the creature's head as flat and snake-like, characterized by dark colouring and what resembled a "mane of a horse" or seaweed. A sketch published in British newspapers illustrated a giant snake, although this image garnered widespread attention despite the actual sightings.

Beastly Theories!

Outsized Oarfish: In January 1860, a notable animal washed ashore on Hungary Bay in Bermuda, further igniting the fascination with sea serpents. An observer named W.D. Munro provided a drawing, capturing the appearance of the oarfish or ribbonfish more accurately than the accounts from the Daedalus. Typically recognized as the longest bony fish, the giant oarfish can reach about 30 feet, with some reports suggesting individuals are even longer. Their unique characteristics might explain historic sightings of sea serpents. Oarfish are deep-water dwellers usually found in warm seas, coming to the surface mostly when dying or dead. Their hair-like filaments and oar-shaped sensory organs contribute to their serpentine appearance, leading to associations with mythical sea serpents.

Skimming Sei Whale: Sei whales, which can grow to 60 feet, are baleen whales known for skim feeding at the surface. Their upper jaws can protrude above the water, matching the reported appearance of the Daedalus serpent's white underside. The placement of their dorsal fin closely aligns with Lt. Drummond's sketch from the Daedalus sighting, suggesting that the creature reported might have been a sei whale. Despite their size, sei whales remain among the lesser understood of the baleen whales, with significant gaps in knowledge about their distribution and behaviour. They are overlooked on whale-watching tours due to their offshore habits, although they can occasionally be seen alongside more commonly pursued species.

Long-Necked Seal: Some theorize that the mysterious sea serpent could have been a long-necked seal from an unknown species. This theory aligns with historical records of unusual marine sightings, although definitive identification remains elusive.

Giant Sea Snake Theory: The giant sea snake theory suggests that accounts of large serpent-like creatures might arise from sightings of large marine reptiles or extinct creatures like the mosasaur, a fierce predator that once roamed the Earth's oceans during the Late Cretaceous period. Recent studies indicate that sizable snakes, such as the green anaconda, can also reach substantial lengths in the water. Coastal regions, often fraught with myths of sea monsters, might have further fuelled the imagination surrounding large snakes as sea serpents. Reports from various cultures throughout history, alongside rare encounters with unknown snake species in deep waters, may have contributed to the folklore surrounding sea serpents, giving birth to enduring legends of these fearsome creatures.

CON RIT

What's in a Name? This Vietnamese name refers to a millipede known for its toxic bite, but it has also been applied to a mysterious sea creature due to its perceived resemblance. Commonly called the 'sea millipede' or 'sea centipede,' this enigmatic creature piques the curiosity of marine enthusiasts.

Monstrous Measurements: The formidable sea millipede can grow up to 60 feet long, with a dark brown upper body and lighter yellow underside. Its body consists of armoured segments, each measuring approximately 2 feet long and 3 feet wide. Each segment features a pair of slender appendages extending around 2 feet 4 inches. Whiskers frame the creature's nostrils at the front, its reinforced skin resembles scales, and its spine bears a small saw-edged crest.

Terrifying Tracks: Currently, there is no information available regarding its tracks.

Beastly Behaviours: This extraordinary creature emits a loud blowing noise. Its flat body manoeuvres awkwardly, requiring it to lean to one side to turn. It primarily moves upward and downward, supported by numerous fins occasionally breaking the surface. Typically a coastal dweller, it exhibits a distinctive brown colour with spots.

Deadly Diet: Unknown.

Watery Abode: The sea millipede thrives in the warm waters of Halong Bay, Vietnam, and the China Sea. It is commonly found in tropical waters but occasionally ventures into warm temperate areas, favouring rocky and coral shallows.

Scary Sightings

1833: A Vietnamese man touched a beached Con Rit that had washed ashore at Hong Gai, Vietnam. The man, Tran Van Con, said of the beast, "it was 60 ft long and 3 ft wide and was composed of numerous identical segments - so hard in texture that they rang like sheet metal when one of the locals hit them with a stick. Each segment was dark-brown dorsally, light-yellow ventrally, measured 2 ft long and 3 ft wide, and bore a pair of 2 ft 4 in lateral spines. The terminal segment bore two additional spines, directed backwards like spiny tails. The head was gone. The stench from the decomposing carcass was so intense that the locals soon towed it out to sea, where it sank." Tran also mentioned that the locals called the creature Con Rit - the Vietnamese word for a millipede.

1899: While navigating near Cape Falcon, Algeria, the *HMS Narcissus* encountered what several sailors described as a sea monster. They estimated its length to be 135 feet and noted its remarkable speed, which allowed it to keep pace with the ship. The crew observed the creature for 30 minutes before it submerged and vanished from sight.

One signalman sailor vividly recounted the experience, stating:

> The creature appeared to be powered by an incredible number of fins, which we could see propelling it alongside us. Fins covered both sides of its body and seemed to be rotating continuously. They extended to the tail. Another intriguing

feature was its ability to spout water like a whale, but these sprays were small and emitted from various parts of its body.

Beastly Evidence

Lost to Science! The Sea Millipede is a mysterious organism with a huge headless body, representing a species unknown to science. Tran Van Con and local residents discovered it washed ashore at Hong Gai, Vietnam. This finding highlights a pattern of near misses or significant losses in the field of zoology. In many undeveloped areas and traditional cultures, such species often carry an ethno-known or sometimes superstitious status. This can lead to trophy hunting, veneration, and then a hasty sale or abandonment of the cursed carcass, as locals fear it may bring misfortune upon their community. I often wonder how many scientific breakthroughs we have missed due to this archaic way of thinking, which persists worldwide.

Beastly Theories!

A Prehistoric Stowaway! The Eurypterida, commonly called sea scorpions, represent a prominent group of arthropods that flourished between 500 and 250 million years ago. These organisms are characterised by their 12-segmented abdomen, which lacks appendages, distinguishing them from many contemporary arthropods. Contrary to popular belief, sea scorpions inhabited brackish or freshwater environments rather than exclusively marine ecosystems. The largest known species, 'Pterygotus', attained lengths of up to 9 feet. Notably, Norwegian palaeontologist Professor Johan Kiaer, upon recounting the discovery of a 3-foot 'Mixopterus' specimen, vividly describes the moment when his group turned over a large slab and saw one of these huge animals, saying that it was "lifelike and gleaming in the stone as if it might rise and crawl away."

A Cryptid Crustacean: Recent findings have unearthed the remains of a substantial, unidentified crustacean, preserving only the exoskeleton and limbs. In comparison, the largest extant crustacean, the Japanese spider crab, exhibits a claw span ranging from 10 to 12 feet yet has a body size of slightly over 1 foot, rendering it significantly smaller than the enigmatic creature under investigation.

<u>In the Wake of Sea Serpents:</u> Dr. Bernard Heuvelmans contributed to the discourse surrounding cryptozoology with his seminal work, *In the Wake of the Sea-Serpents* (1968), wherein he categorised sea serpent sightings into nine distinct types. However, the legitimacy of certain classifications has faced scrutiny. The most disputed is the so-called many-finned sea serpent, *Cetioscolopendra aeliani*, which was initially hypothesised to be associated with armoured prehistoric whales. Subsequent paleontological research discredited this association, revealing that the scales initially attributed to these specimens belonged to various other organisms.

Heuvelmans briefly explored the notion of sea scorpions and crustaceans before favouring a conjectural evolved armoured archdiocese, which he termed the many-finned sea serpent. While numerous eyewitness accounts describe elongated entities with lateral fins, contemporary understanding suggests that the concept of armoured archaeocetes is fundamentally flawed. Instead, the many fins may represent locomotory appendages rather than rigid spines, thereby challenging the hypothesis that these entities are mammals. This perspective aligns with the anatomical characteristics of crustaceans, which possess multiple limbs and robust exoskeletons that endure post-mortem decomposition, frequently leaving only the skeletal structure intact.

MORGAWR

What's in a Name? The sea serpent affectionately called 'Morgawr,' which means "Sea Giant" in the Cornish language, is one of the most famous worldwide. Noel Wain of the *Falmouth Packet* popularised the term in 1976, with a variant name being the Durgan Dragon.

Monstrous Measurements: Estimated to measure between 15 and 20 feet in length, Morgawr is characterized by its grey skin, long neck, and several large humps along its body, resembling a water-dwelling dinosaur from 1960s films. It is often described as having a humped body, a long tail, and a small head with a black-brown hue, akin to a sea lion.

Terrifying Tracks: Morgawr has been observed moving in shallow waters and is thought to be amphibious. Its four flipper-like limbs resemble those of a plesiosaur.

Beastly Behaviours: Adding to its mystique, Morgawr is said to be attracted to naked women, especially young Wiccans, according to claims made by Tony Shiels.

Deadly Diet: Its diet primarily consists of conger eels, which thrive in the waters around Cornwall. This makes it a formidable predator in its aquatic habitat.

Watery Abode: Sightings of this legendary creature peaked in the mid-1970s, particularly along the 'Morgawr mile' coastline between Rosemullion Head and Toll Point in Cornwall, and especially in the area of Falmouth Bay.

Scary Sightings

1876: Sightings of the sea serpent known as 'Morgawr,' meaning Sea Giant in Cornish, date back to when two fishermen caught the creature in their nets in Gerrans Bay, Cornwall. Morgawr is regarded as one of the most famous sea serpents in the world.

1906: On August 3, officers Spicer and Cuming, aboard the American transatlantic liner *St. Andrew* reported seeing a sea monster with an 18-foot-long head and substantial jaws while rounding Land's End, Cornwall.

1975: Two witnesses claimed to see a humped figure with stumpy horns and bristles in its long neck, holding a conger eel in its mouth.

1976: Mary F. sent two photos of Morgawr to the *Falmouth Packet*, describing it as looking "like an elephant waving its trunk, but the trunk was a long neck with a small head at the end, resembling a snake's head." She noted the creature had humps on its back that moved unusually, stating, "the animal frightened me. I would not like to see it any closer. I do not like the way it moved when swimming." Neither Mary F. nor the negatives of the photographs have ever been traced. Noted mystery writers and photographers Janet and Colin Bord examined first-generation copy prints and "feel that these photographs could be genuine."

1976: Tony "Doc" Shiels claimed to have photographed the creature lying low on the water. He noted stumpy horns and described the animal's body as 15 feet long.

1985: A significant sighting occurred on July 10, when Sheila Bird and her brother Eric observed a 20-foot grey creature for several minutes off Porthscatho in Falmouth Bay before it sank vertically and vanished.

1985: A Mrs Waldon reported a sighting while watching her husband swim in the sea. She noticed a large silhouette with a long neck.

1987: A diver observed a long neck rising 1 meter from the sea.

1995: In early September, Gertrude Stevens spotted Morgawr off Rosemullion Head, describing it as having a small head on a long neck and a broad, flat tail.

1999: In August, John Holmes recorded footage of an animal in Gerrans Bay with a snakelike head and neck.

2000: One of the more recent sightings occurred on May 16 when a couple, Irene and Derek Brown, spotted a creature about 200 yards out to sea. They described it as having several humps and a flexible neck resembling a cobra poised to strike. Irene dashed to get her camera, but the creature submerged in a commotion just as she returned, with the couple estimating its length at 15 feet. They remarked, "it was like a water-based dinosaur, reminiscent of those creatures seen in 1960s films."

Beastly Evidence

Film and Photography:

An Anonymous Photo: The 1975 photograph submitted anonymously by Mary F. to the *Falmouth Packet* newspaper allegedly depicts Morgawr, a large creature with a humped body and long neck, spotted near Pendennis Point, Cornwall. However, the image's authenticity is contentious due to its association with hoaxes involving figures like Tony 'Doc' Shiels. This connection raises scepticism about the legitimacy of the sighting, leading to speculation about whether such encounters arise from actual unknown creatures or are merely products of imagination fuelled by storytelling.

The Holmes Film: In August of 1999, John Holmes recorded video footage of an animal in Gerrans Bay with a head and neck resembling Morgawr's classic snakelike head.

Beastly Theories

A Paranormal Plesiosaur? There is a local belief that the presence of these creatures signals a bad omen, often forecasting a scarcity of fish or inclement weather. While it is uncertain whether this folklore represents a traditional blend of myth and practical knowledge common to many ancient cultures, we can confidently assert that the 'paranormal status' of ethno-known animals worldwide typically reflects a socio-spiritual interpretation of unclassified biological specimens. These interpretations are shaped by the superstitions and cultural conventions of the communities that observe them.

It's a Kind of Magic! This section explores the possibility of hoaxes or embellished tales derived from local folklore, propagated by the self-proclaimed wizard and questionable family theatre performer Tony 'Doc' Shiels. Shiels is believed to be behind a series of cryptid hoaxes, including the Owlman of Mawnan and the discredited Loch Ness Muppet photos. His dubious photographs and elaborate stories circulated throughout the 1970s and 80s raise questions about the authenticity of such claims and their roots in community culture.

An Errant Elephant Seal: Morgawr could be a lost elephant seal that found its way into Cornish waters. Elephant seals, known for their large size and occasionally solitary behaviour, could be mistaken for mythical creatures by those unfamiliar with them. Given their extensive swimming capabilities, it's reasonable to hypothesize that an elephant seal could venture far from its typical habitat, driven by food scarcity, ocean currents, or even a migratory instinct. As these seals are not native to the region, sightings and interactions with locals may have led to the mythological framing of Morgawr, demonstrating how genuine encounters with local fauna can intertwine with folklore and the supernatural.

THE DSV ALVIN MONSTER

What's in a Name? The creature sighted by Marvin McCamis and Bill Rainnie during a dive with the submersible *DSV Alvin* in 1965 is often referred to as the "Alvin plesiosaur" due to its resemblance to the prehistoric marine reptile, the plesiosaur.

Monstrous Measurements: According to McCamis, the sea serpent was about 40 to 50 feet long, featuring a thick body and a long neck with a snakelike head.

Terrifying Tracks: Due to the creature's underwater habitat, no physical tracks are associated with the sighting. However, the absence of definitive proof, like photographs or physical evidence, has led to speculation about its existence.

Beastly Behaviours: The creature was described as having a powerful and graceful swimming motion. During the sighting, it was observed moving quickly away from the submersible, which suggests it was an agile swimmer comfortable in its environment. Its presence this deep below the ocean indicates, as many researchers have speculated about these creatures, that similar to some turtles, they may, in fact, possess the ability to breathe underwater through a process called Cloacal respiration.

Deadly Diet: While its diet remains unknown due to the lack of direct observation or evidence, as an enormous marine reptile, it may have fed on fish or other sea creatures.

Watery Abode: The sighting occurred in the Tongue of the Ocean, a deep channel between the islands of Andros and New Providence in the Bahamas, serving as a habitat for various marine life.

Scary Sightings

1965: During a deep-sea dive off the Bahamas, the *DSV Alvin* submersible, piloted by Marvin McCamis and Bill Rainnie, allegedly encountered a sea serpent described as a reptilian longneck. The sighting occurred in the Tongue of the Ocean, a deep-water area between Andros and New Providence islands.

McCamis reported spotting the creature at a depth of about 5,300 feet, initially mistakenly referring to it as a utility pole due to its thick shape. He then realized it was a large creature with flippers, a long neck, and a snakelike head, which swam away before they could capture it on camera. This sighting, recorded in the submersible's "wet log," was later removed from the final version, making McCamis reluctant to discuss it further.

The encounter gained notoriety through Fortean researcher Charles Berlitz, who published McCamis's account in his 1977 book *Without a Trace*. In 1999, McCamis confirmed the sighting to cryptozoologist Scott Mardis, correcting Berlitz's date, stating it occurred in July 1965, when Alvin was operational. J. Manson Valentine, a colleague of Berlitz, illustrated the creature based on McCamis's description, which he identified as resembling a plesiosaur.

Beastly Evidence

Log Jamming: Despite McCamis's firsthand account and the event recording in the submersible's log, the official documentation was allegedly altered, preventing concrete evidence from being acknowledged. Artists have illustrated McCamis's description, but no physical evidence or photographs exist.

Beastly Theories!

A Case for Living Plesiosaurs? The ongoing fascination with plesiosaurs often revolves around the idea that these prehistoric creatures might still inhabit our oceans today. While sceptics argue that plesiosaurs and other dinosaurs went extinct 66 million years ago, there are compelling reasons to consider the possibility that they have survived in isolated marine environments.

One argument favouring the existence of living plesiosaurs is the vastness of our oceans. Many species remain undiscovered in these deep waters, where sightings are rare. Cryptozoologists posit that these creatures could evade human detection in the most remote areas of the sea. Reports of sightings, such as those of Nessie, Champ, and Ogopogo, suggest that marine reptiles resembling plesiosaurs might still exist.

While sceptics highlight the frequency at which we observe modern marine animals like dolphins and whales, it's essential to consider the different ecological behaviours of potential plesiosaur descendants. Unlike these well-known species, which are frequently sighted, plesiosaurs may have developed unique habits contributing to their elusiveness. Their deep-sea habitats could mean longer intervals between surfacing for air, reducing encounters with humans. As apex predators, any surviving marine reptiles may also exhibit cautious behaviour towards boats and divers, leading to fewer observed interactions.

Critics also question why evidence of attacks by living plesiosaurs hasn't surfaced, arguing that such a large predator would leave a trail of evidence. However, it's plausible that their numbers are so limited that encounters leading to visible evidence are rare. Moreover, the lack of evidence does not necessarily invalidate the possibility of their existence; the ocean is still largely unexplored, and many marine species remain poorly understood.

The creature reported by two men in a submarine, located over a mile beneath the ocean's surface, remains an enigma. It could have been a long-extinct marine reptile, a misidentified species like a sperm whale, or an entirely new organism. The debate continues, with strong emotions on both sides. Until more definitive evidence is found, the idea of living plesiosaurs remains a tantalizing possibility, urging us to keep an open mind while observing the mysteries of the deep.

CRYPTOZOOLOGICAL KRAKENS & MASSIVE MEDUSAS

Def.

Cryptozoological krakens and massive medusas refer to large, often fantastical cephalopods, such as mythical squids and octopuses. These creatures, known for their elusive nature, are reported in diverse habitats, including freshwater and uninhabitable environments. Their presence sparks intrigue about the hidden depths of our oceans and inland waters.

AMIKUK

What's in a Name? The Amikuk, a creature from Yup'ik folklore, is known for its shapeshifting abilities and menacing traits. Its human form is called a Qamungelriit, signifying a being that has taken on a more human appearance.

Monstrous Measurements: This legendary creature is often described as exceptionally long and human. With spindly limbs, its arms can extend up to 8 feet, while its legs measure between 6 and 7 feet. At times, it may have four limbs, enhancing its terrifying presence. Encountered in the sea, the Amikuk is said to have hairless skin and a slick, leathery texture, making it a truly fearsome being.

Terrifying Tracks: Unknown.

Beastly Behaviours: The Amikuk is a legendary creature from Yup'ik folklore, known for its relentless hunting tactics in water and on land. It ambushes kayakers by lying beneath the ice and "swimming" through the soil, creating quicksand that saps the strength of those who resist. The Amikuk can invade a person's body, causing collapse and shapeshift into a human form called Qamungelriit, prompting elders to advise individuals to accept any gifts it offers. If shot, it multiplies into eight beings that emit a thumping sound, instilling fear and enabling surprise attacks. Renowned for dragging individuals and kayaks underwater, the Amikuk can also break through the ice and burrow underground to pursue those who try to escape.

Deadly Diet: The Amikuk is a formidable carnivorous predator known for its stealthy ambush tactics while hunting on the water. Once it captures its prey, it drags them underwater and attempts to drown them. Legends suggest that the Amikuk can multiply into eight distinct entities when shot, enhancing its elusive and fearsome reputation.

Watery Abode: The Amikuk primarily inhabits the murky depths of quicksand-like earth, swampy bogs, and the frigid waters along the Alaskan coast. It is equally adept at navigating the ocean's depths and burrowing through the world, allowing for seamless transitions between these environments as it hunts. The creature is said to construct nests on land from peculiar materials resembling leaves, which are believed to hold magical properties.

Scary Sightings: While modern encounters with the Amikuk are non-existent, they remain a source of fear among First Nations people. Eyewitness accounts from Yup'ik elders recount sightings of this elusive being while travelling across the ice. It has been observed pulling sledges in a straight line, showcasing its supernatural ability to traverse challenging terrains.

Beastly Evidence

A Monster Mask: The Portland Art Museum has a traditional Yup'ik mask symbolizing the Amikuk on permanent display. This artefact underscores the cultural importance of the Amikuk within Yup'ik lore, highlighting its role in regional mythology and contemporary beliefs.

Drink the River Dry! Naturalist Edward William Nelson observed that: "Several dry lake beds in that area were shown to me, believed to have been drained by these creatures when they swam out to sea, creating a channel with their passage through the earth. It is said that if the Amikuk returns, the water comes back from the sea and refills the lake."

Beastly Theories!

An Animus Octopus! In First Nations folklore, the Amikuk is portrayed as a misunderstood creature with origins linked to colossal octopuses swept inland by powerful storms trapped in lakes and swamps. Over time, these majestic beings adapted to their surroundings, leading to tales of their fearsome nature, characterized by long, spindly tentacles and dark, leathery skin. They became notorious predators, lurking in shallow waters and striking unexpectedly at kayakers and fishermen, their strong arms capable of dragging victims beneath the surface. Despite their monstrous reputation, there is a reverence for the Amikuk, with some legends depicting them as guardians of hidden treasures, their nests woven from enchanted furs rumoured to have the power to mend or bring prosperity. Thus, the Amikuk embodies nature's duality, serving as a reminder of the wild's power and mystery, blurring the lines between monster and protector and highlighting the need for respect towards the unknown forces in both land and water. As these legends evolved, it became clear that the Amikuk symbolized not just a predator of fear, but a creature rooted in nature's duality. It serves as a reminder of the power and mystery of the wild, blurring the lines between monster and guardian and urging respect for the unknown forces that inhabit both land and water.

KRAKEN

What's in a Name? The term "Kraken" originates from the Norwegian word "Krake," which means a creature similar to a giant squid. First noted by Francesco Negri in 1700, it may also relate to a term for "uprooted tree," reflecting the squid's tree-like appearance. Its scientific name, *Architeuthis dux*, was assigned by Danish naturalist Japetus Steenstrup in 1857. The creature has various names, including Aale tust (meaning "tuft of eels"), Anker-trold ("anchor-troll"), and Kolkrabbi.

Monstrous Measurements: The Giant Squid can reach about 55 feet, while the Kraken from Norwegian mythology is described as a super-giant squid with a body 1.5 miles in circumference. Sightings have suggested creatures over 100 feet long, including one reported in 1969 off Vieques Island, Puerto Rico. The Kraken appears as several small islands surrounded by seaweed, with a dark brown colour, light speckles, a high, broad forehead, large eyes, and a pointed tail. Its tentacles can be as large as medium-sized ships.

Terrifying Tracks: Giant sucker marks on sperm whales indicate the presence of massive squids, but verifying marks over 1-2 inches is difficult. A 46-foot giant squid found in Newfoundland had suckers measuring about 2.5 inches in diameter.

Beastly Behaviours: The Kraken is notorious for creating large eddies and attacking ships by wrapping its tentacles around their masts. In one account, sailors sought refuge with St. Thomas after fending off a massive squid, highlighting its fierce reputation. Fishermen who venture a few miles from shore on calm, hot days often find unexpectedly shallow depths of 20 to 30 fathoms instead of the expected 80 to 100 fathoms. These depths attract plentiful shoals of cod and ling, suggesting that the Kraken may lurk below, manipulating the seafloor to draw in fish. When fishermen notice the creature surfacing, they must quickly row away. As it emerges, the Kraken appears as a collection of skerries with seaweed-like growths, and its tentacles can rise as high as ship masts. Eventually, it sinks again, creating a dangerous suction vortex.

Deadly Diet: The Kraken is said to lure fish to the surface and prey on large marine animals like whales. Historical records note giant squids attacking ships and killing crew members.

Watery Abode: Present in both the Atlantic and Pacific Oceans.

Scary Sightings

1801: Pierre Denys de Montfort documented a votive picture in the chapel of St. Thomas, St.-Malo, France, depicting a massive squid or octopus attacking a ship by coiling its arms around the masts and rigging. This event occurred off the coast of Angola. The sailors vowed to make a pilgrimage to St. Thomas for safety, and they managed to free their ship by cutting off the creature's tentacles. Following their harrowing experience, they travelled to St.-Malo, where the picture illustrating their adventure was displayed.

Late 19th Century: During his investigations, Denys de Montfort spoke with various whalers in Dunkerque, France, who recounted tales of giant squids. One American whaler, Captain Reynolds, described an experience with a severed squid arm measuring 45 feet in length and 2 feet 6 inches in diameter. Retired Danish captain Jean-Magnus Dens recounted a terrifying encounter off the coast of Angola, where a gigantic squid attacked his ship, resulting in the deaths of three crew members. The crew managed to drive five harpoons into the creature before they overcame it, with Dens estimating the length of its arms to be over 35 feet.

1872: A 46-foot giant squid specimen washed ashore in Bonavista Bay, Newfoundland, providing physical evidence of its existence. The suckers on this specimen measured 2.5 inches in diameter, contributing to ongoing discussions about the size of these elusive creatures.

1875: Frank Bullen described a dramatic night battle between a sperm whale and a giant squid in the Strait of Malacca, Indian Ocean. While this account may be exaggerated, it highlights the interaction between these two formidable sea creatures. The size of sucker marks found on sperm whales has been suggested as evidence of large giant squids but marks greater than 1-2 inches in diameter are challenging to verify.

1969: Dennis Braun and two other marines from the *USS Francis Marion* observed a colossal squid estimated to be 100 feet long near Vieques Island, Puerto Rico. They watched this incredible sighting for more than ten minutes, marking one of the few known instances of a living specimen being seen at the surface.

Beastly Evidence

Carta Marina Monster: The earliest known representation of the Kraken is in Olaus Magnus' 1539 map, the *Carta Marina*, which depicts various sea monsters. Magnus describes a Norwegian sea creature resembling a fish with tentacles and another with tusks. He called them "two enormous sea monsters, one with ferocious teeth, the other with horns and a horrendous flaming gaze." The eye circumference measures approximately 16 or 20 feet. The exact measurement is unclear, but applying an average of 12 inches per foot suggests an eye diameter of about 4.9 to 6.2 feet. In 1555, Magnus expanded on this in *Historia de Gentibus Septentrionalibus*, describing a black creature similar to both whales and squids, with a body measuring 46 to 52 feet and features like long root-like horns and large, flaming red eyes. These descriptions may have resulted from observations at night, and the "flaming eyes" might indicate bioluminescence.

First Impressions Last: The first recorded use of the term "Kraken," referenced as "sciu-crak," was by Italian writer Negri in his 1700 travelogue, *Viaggio settentrionale*, describing it as a large fish with many horns or arms, distinct from sea serpents. 1741 Egede described the Kraken as a many-headed, clawed creature comparable to the Icelandic hafgufa. Erik Pontoppidan further popularized the Kraken in 1753, categorizing it as multi-armed and hypothesizing it as a giant sea crab or octopus, influencing interest in the creature in the English-speaking world. Although Pontoppidan is often credited with being the first to name the Kraken, a German source suggests his description was the first available in German.

Montfort's Monster: Denys-Montfort published in 1801 about two giants: a "colossal octopus" attacking ships and the "Kraken octopod," considered the largest organism in zoology. This ties into Pliny's accounts of giant cephalopods.

Beastly Theories!

A 'Giant', Giant Squid! The Kraken, a giant cephalopod of the Atlantic and Pacific Oceans, was scientifically recognized after remains washed ashore near Ålbæk, Denmark, in 1853. Danish naturalist Japetus Steenstrup described the giant squid (*Architeuthis*) in 1857, with known specimens reaching about 55 feet. Evidence, including massive squid arms found in whale stomachs, suggests even larger creatures exist. Historian Otto Latva points out that the association between giant squids and the Kraken myth emerged in the late 19th century, influenced by Enlightenment ideas and the classification of marine animals.

The Colossal Squid: The Kraken legend may have originated from sightings of the colossal squid, which can grow to 43-100+ feet and has attacked ships. Pliny the Elder referred to a "monstrous polypus," which aligns with descriptions of the colossal squid.

A Giant Octopus: In 1802, French malacologist Pierre Denys de Montfort recognized two "species" of giant octopuses. His engraving of an octopus attacking a ship accompanied his accounts of encounters, including one off Angola. Montfort suggested colossal octopuses might have caused the loss of ten British warships in 1782.

Whirlpools and Waterspouts: Sailors faced perils from many whirlpools, like Norway's famous Moskstraumen, the Maelstrom. Could these have led to folktales about the Kraken, who was strong enough to pull a ship below the waves?

COLOSSAL OCTOPUS

What's in a Name? The colossal octopus is a fascinating creature closely related to squid, both of which belong to the cephalopod family. These remarkable invertebrates are defined by their soft bodies, eight long arms lined with suckers, and impressive intelligence. The term "colossal" aptly describes their exceptional size, making these octopuses some of the most captivating marine enigmas. Scientific names include *Octopus giganteus*, assigned by Addison E. Verrill in 1897. They are also known by variant names such as Bermuda Blob and Lusca.

Monstrous Measurements: Known varieties of octopi's range in size from a few inches in circumference to an astonishing 23 feet in length. Some speculate that an elusive species might exist in the ocean's depths, potentially measuring over 100 feet across and weighing up to 10 tons. The only reported carcass of a colossal octopus was found at 18 feet long and 10 feet wide, with arm fragments extending up to 36 feet. Their colouration typically appears greyish-brown, and their arms range from 8 to 75 feet long.

Terrifying Tracks: Unknown, although it must be assumed that if they were ever to come on shore, traces of their enormous bulk and eight long sucker-adorned tentacles would be evidenced in the sand.

Beastly Behaviours: Colossal octopuses are shy and reserved compared to their more aggressive relatives, the squid. However, they can exhibit dangerous behaviours when provoked. Their impressive intelligence allows them to solve problems and demonstrate strong defensive tactics in their natural habitat.

Deadly Diet: As carnivorous predators, colossal octopuses feed on crustaceans, fish, and other marine creatures. They utilize their suction-cup-lined arms to capture prey, showcasing their exceptional hunting skills.

Watery Abode: Colossal octopuses inhabit the dark depths of the ocean, primarily residing on the seafloor. This lifestyle complicates the discovery of their remains, as their bodies decay without leaving noticeable traces on the surface. Their range includes the Hawaiian Islands and the Philippines and extends through the North Atlantic Ocean, from the east coast of Florida to Bermuda, Belize, and south Texas.

Scary Sightings

1896: Two boys discovered a massive octopus carcass washed ashore near St. Augustine, Florida. Despite the significance of this find, no scientists, including leading experts, travelled to observe it.

1912: An octopus with arms measuring 13 feet long was sighted off Toulon, France.

1950: Madison Rigdon encountered an octopus the size of a car surrounded by sharks off Lahilahi Point, near Makaha, Oahu, Hawaii. This creature defended itself with a remarkable 30-foot tentacle equipped with suckers the size of dinner plates.

1950: Off the Kona Coast in Hawaii, fisherman Val Ako spotted a monster octopus with tentacles 75 feet long and suckers as large as auto tyres. His family adviser revealed that this octopus would visit the island annually for a month with a female companion.

1952: Constable John Morrison found a cephalopod half out of the water near Broadford on the Isle of Skye, Scotland. After kicking it, the creature gripped his ankle with a 6-foot tentacle. Morrison escaped from his boot and killed the octopus with rocks and garden shears. It was later identified as a red flying squid (*Ommastrephes bartrami*), an occasional visitor to British waters.

1936: While stationed at Pearl Harbor, Robert Todd Aiken discovered a group of six large octopuses, measuring 40 feet from tip to tip, off the shore of Oahu. He attempted to bring film director Robert Hale to the location to document the sighting, although it's unclear if any footage was successfully captured.

1989: Fourteen people in an 18-foot motorized canoe off Iligan Bay in the Philippines witnessed a huge octopus with 8-foot tentacles seize their boat and rock it violently. After ten minutes of struggle, the canoe capsized, and the passengers were either rescued by fishermen or managed to swim to shore.

Beastly Evidence

A Cryptid Carcass: In November 1896, two boys cycling along the beach south of St. Augustine, Florida, discovered the remains of an enormous creature washed ashore. Local amateur naturalist Dr. DeWitt Webb examined the mutilated body, measuring eighteen feet long and ten feet wide, with unattached arms reaching up to 36 feet in length and a diameter of 10 inches. Initially, Webb believed it to be the carcass of a colossal octopus and reached out to Yale Professor Addison Verrill, a leading cephalopod expert, who, based on photographs, agreed that the creature might have had a living diameter of up to 150 feet. However, Verrill abruptly changed his mind after examining a tissue sample preserved in formalin, declaring the creature to be a whale. The controversy lingered until Forrest Wood, director of Marine Studios, discovered that Webb's sample was still stored at the Smithsonian Institution. He persuaded the museum to allow Dr. Joseph Gennaro of the University of Florida to analyse the samples. Gennaro's examination revealed the tissue was consistent with octopus rather than blubber or whale, a conclusion later supported by biologist Roy P. Mackal. In 1995, four scientists re-evaluated the samples, proposing instead that the remains belonged to whale skin—finding support in the amino acids analysed. However, this claim has faced scepticism, as critics argue that removing whale skin intact would have been highly challenging to solidify it into the three-foot-thick mass observed on the beach. This ongoing debate leaves the true identity of the creature shrouded in mystery.

Beastly Theories!

A Colossal Octopus: The rarity of colossal octopus discoveries can be attributed to their bottom-dwelling behaviour; carcasses remain on the ocean floor to decompose, leaving minimal evidence for scientists to uncover. As ocean exploration continues to expand, the possibility of encountering a colossal octopus becomes increasingly enticing, hinting at the vast mysteries of marine life yet to be discovered. The North Atlantic's variety of octopus is particularly noteworthy. The largest known species is the Giant Pacific octopus (*Enteroctopus dofleini*), which can exceed a radial spread of 20 feet and weigh over 100 pounds. A smaller relative, *E. megalocyathus*, inhabits the warmer eastern waters of the South Pacific and South Atlantic, particularly off the coasts of Chile and Argentina. Marine biologist Michel Raynal has suggested that a larger form of cirrate Octopus, like *Cirroteuthis*, may also play a role in the narratives surrounding colossal octopuses.

A Hidden Hydra: The legendary Hydra from Greek mythology, depicted as a serpentine creature with multiple heads, may have been influenced by sightings of large octopuses. One notable species, the presence of octopuses with arms longer than 10 feet, could have inspired tales of the fearsome six-necked, twelve-footed sea monster

Scylla, which plagued Odysseus and his crew in the Strait of Messina, Italy. Similarly, the feared nine-headed Hydra that Heracles faced in the marsh of Lerna near Árgos in Greece reflects the fascination and fear towards these formidable cephalopods.

An Outsized Octopus: The Common Octopus (*Octopus vulgaris*) typically has an average radial size of 1 to 2 feet, but reports exist of outsize specimens measuring between 8 to 9 feet. Although records of octopuses exceeding these dimensions are scarce and often vague, individual specimens have been observed in British waters with radial spreads of just over 6 feet. The Giant Pacific octopus holds the record for the largest known Octopus, surpassing 20 feet in radial spread and often exceeding 100 pounds. An exceptional specimen captured near Victoria, British Columbia, in 1967 weighed 156 pounds and stretched 23 feet from arm tip to arm tip. Unofficial reports suggest there may be individuals weighing over 300 pounds, with claims of one reaching an astonishing 400 pounds. This species can be found in habitats ranging from southern California to Alaska and extends across the Pacific as far as Japan, while *E. megalocyathus* is localized in the eastern South Pacific and South Atlantic off Chile and Argentina.

GIANT JELLYFISH

What's in a Name? The term "giant jellyfish" describes several enormous cryptid jellyfish encountered in oceans around the globe. It is sometimes also known as Nomura's jellyfish.

Monstrous Measurements: Among these colossal creatures, the lion's mane jellyfish stands out, boasting a bell diameter of up to 7.5 feet and tentacles that can extend an astonishing 120 feet or more. Reports of giant jellyfish have included specimens measuring 50 to 100 feet in diameter, exceeding previously established records and suggesting the possibility of even larger beings lurking in the ocean's depths.

Terrifying Tracks: With their huge bulbous bodies and vast, flowing tentacles, giant jellyfish are unlikely to survive on land. However, some encounters have involved sightings of enormous jellyfish wrapping around fishing vessels, even impeding navigation and fouling up the ship's rudder with their long tentacles.

Beastly Behaviours: Giant jellyfish are often characterised as slow-moving, gracefully drifting through ocean currents. However, they also exhibit predatory behaviours that can be alarming; some reports indicate they are capable of preying on sharks, a strikingly unusual behaviour for invertebrates.

Deadly Diet: These gigantic creatures are believed to have a diverse diet, consuming a range of marine life, including smaller fish, sharks and potentially even humans. Their tentacles are equipped with specialised cells known as nematocysts, which deliver potent stings to capture prey, drawing it towards their mouths in the centre of their bell.

Watery Abode: Giant jellyfish inhabit various marine environments, in the North Atlantic and South Pacific Oceans. Typically found in temperate and tropical waters, they thrive in deeper, cooler regions, far from coastal areas, where conditions are conducive to their growth.

Scary Sightings

1953: Australian diver Christopher Loeb reported a chilling encounter while exploring a deep underwater chasm. As he descended, a shark measuring around 15 feet followed him curiously but did not attack. When Loeb reached a ledge above a dark abyss, he felt a sudden drop in water temperature. Moments later, a large, pulsating brown mass emerged from the depths. It was enormous, an acre, with dull brown colouration and ragged edges. As it floated past him, the cold intensified, and the shark became paralysed in its presence. The massive entity reached out to the shark, and Loeb watched in horror as the creature engulfed it, sinking back into the chasm as the water warmed again.

1969: Divers Richard Winer and Pat Boatwright encountered a large jellyfish 50 to 100 feet in diameter while diving 14 miles southwest of Bermuda. It displayed deep purple colouration with a pinkish outer rim. Winer, engaged in oceanographic work for General Electric, noted the jellyfish's slow movement and lack of water disturbance around it as it ascended from the depths. Although the conditions were challenging for visibility, Winer estimated the jellyfish's size and watched it float away before sinking back into the dark waters.

1973: The crew of the Australian ship *Kuranda* collided with a colossal jellyfish while travelling in the South Pacific between Australia and Fiji. Captain Langley Smith described the jellyfish as having tentacles that exceeded 200 feet in length and observed a slimy mass 2 feet deep coating the deck. Tragically, one crew member died after being stung by a tentacle. An SOS call brought the salvage tugboat *Hercules* to assist in dislodging the jellyfish, which was tentatively identified as a lion's mane jelly after samples were analysed in Sydney.

2005: A young man from Japan contacted the authorities, claiming that a jellyfish as large as a car had devoured his family while they were swimming in shallow waters. The police believed he was fabricating the story to cover up a potential crime, leading to his arrest on murder charges. After serving time, he took a polygraph test, which suggested that he was not lying. While some think he may have manipulated the results, others believe he could have encountered a massive, previously unknown species of jellyfish capable of consuming humans.

Beastly Evidence

Kuranda Carcass: Physical evidence of giant jellyfish has been documented through various encounters. One notable incident occurred in 1973 when the Australian ship *Kuranda* collided with an enormous jellyfish draped over the forecastle. This jellyfish was measured to have tentacles extending up to 200 feet. Subsequent analyses of the substance left on the ship's deck revealed characteristics consistent with those of a lion's mane jellyfish.

Beastly Theories!

Lion's Mane Jellyfish: This is the largest known jellyfish, primarily residing in the cold northern seas. However, reports of even larger specimens have emerged from temperate and tropical waters. This jellyfish is found in the North Atlantic and North Pacific Oceans, particularly in shallow coastal areas. Larger individuals display deep red or purple hues, while their smaller counterparts are yellow or brown. Although the nematocysts can deliver painful stings, they are typically not lethal. A remarkable specimen studied by Alexander Agassiz in 1865 in Massachusetts Bay boasted a bell that measured 7 feet 6 inches in diameter and tentacles that stretched an astonishing 120 feet.

Cryptid Jelly: The sightings of giant jellyfish have given rise to various theories among sceptics and enthusiasts alike. Some propose these sightings could be misidentified known species, while others entertain the notion of undiscovered marine creatures. Reports suggest that environmental conditions play a role in the emergence and growth of these giant jellyfish, prompting speculation about unexplored marine ecosystems. Alongside these jellyfish, another group of unidentified cryptid marine invertebrates has been reported in the Pacific Ocean. These shapeless creatures, which are sometimes thought to prey on sharks, are often mistaken for giant jellyfish. However, not all possess the long tentacles associated with the species, leading to alternative theories regarding their existence.

THE LUSCA

What's in a Name? "Lusca" originates from Caribbean mythology and is derived from a Bahamas Creole word. It is also known as the Giant Scuttle, 'Him of the Hairy Hands', Lucsa, and Luska. The name reflects its mollusc characteristics, particularly its tentacles, as a shortened form of Mollusca, which includes octopuses and squids.

Monstrous Measurements: The Lusca is often depicted as a hybrid between a shark, an octopus, an eel, and a squid, with reported widths of up to 50 feet. It features phosphorescent eyes and tentacles with sucker tips, with some accounts claiming lengths of 75 to 200 feet.

Beastly Behaviours: This creature is believed to be nocturnal, surfacing at night, especially during full moons. Witnesses have reported it dragging boats and people into the depths. The Lusca can alter its colouration and has been known to attack humans who venture too close, leading to the disappearances of vessels.

Deadly Diet: The Lusca primarily feeds on fish, crustaceans, and small sharks, utilizing effective hunting strategies that include lurking and aggressive strikes to capture prey.

Watery Abode: Lusca's inhabit underwater caves and deep-sea trenches in the Caribbean, particularly around the Bahamas and Latin America. They prefer environments that provide concealment, such as the complex cave systems of blue holes in the Bahamas, which can reach depths of 200 feet and support abundant crustacean life.

Scary Sightings

1896: The St. Augustine Monster was discovered on the coast near St. Augustine, Florida. Initially speculated to be a Lusca, it was later identified as decomposing tissue from a sperm whale.

2005: An underwater photographer claimed he was attacked by a 50-foot-long octopus, which took his camera and retreated into a cave.

Date Unspecified: At dusk, a swimmer near a blue hole was suddenly pulled underwater. He escaped but later found significant sucker marks on his thigh from the encounter.

Beastly Evidence

A Deep Dive: A crew of divers set out to capture the Lusca and soon encountered something massive, tugging at their traps, breaking lines easily. One trap was pulled with such force that it dragged their boat at a speed of one knot. Sonar revealed a large, pyramid-shaped creature below. After a while, the line went slack, and when they retrieved the trap, it was twisted and damaged.

A Legless Beast: On January 18, 2011, a giant octopus-like creature washed ashore on Grand Bahama Island. Only the head and mouth were found, leading local fishermen to estimate the whole body could be 20 to 30 feet long. This incident sparked speculation that it might have been a Lusca.

A Television Terror: In an episode of *Destination Truth*, a team explored blue holes in search of Lusca evidence. While diving to 150 feet, they detected unusual sonar activity and noticed movement from a large creature. Team leader Josh Gates thought he was merely seeing part of the wall but was pulled out for safety due to increasing concern. Later, at a depth of 175 feet, sonar again indicated something substantial nearby, and Gates saw movement once more, but visibility was poor. Movement picked up by FLIR cameras hinted at a large entity, prompting the team to turn off their boat lights to avoid drawing attention. Upon reviewing the footage, they noted what resembled a large tentacle from a massive octopus or squid.

Beastly Theories!

A Cryptid Chimaera: The Lusca, steeped in local urban folklore, emerges as a chimaera of superstition and maritime tales. Often perceived as a hybrid of a shark and an octopus, it embodies the fears and fascination of coastal communities. Descriptions vary widely, with some attributing dragon-like features or multiple heads, while others see it as a sinister spirit. This blending of legend transforms Lusca into a powerful symbol of mystery, representing the cultural landscape shaped by stories that thrive in the depths of the sea.

A Change of Direction: Tidal surges and vortices have fascinated sailors and oceanographers for centuries, leading to fantastical tales of sea monsters. Historical examples, such as the notorious Maelstrom at the Lofoten Islands in Norway, showcase how violent ocean currents have often been misconstrued as the actions of mythical creatures lurking below. Sailors experiencing intense turbulence would describe their encounters in ways that evoked images of leviathans stirring in the depths. Similarly, the Bermuda Triangle's mysterious vessel disappearances have been attributed to powerful underwater currents and methane hydrate eruptions, which mimic the effects of monstrous forces dragging ships under.

Notable incidents, such as the "Great Storm" of 1703, further illustrate how tidal forces can distort perceptions at sea, as survivors recounted harrowing tales of ships vanishing into swirling waters, reinforcing legends of sea monsters. In modern times, whirlpools like the Corryvreckan off Scotland continue to spark stories of shadowy shapes beneath the surface. These examples highlight how natural oceanic phenomena create illusions that captivate the imagination, ensuring that tales of monstrous beings endure, reflecting humanity's timeless affinity for storytelling and the mysteries beneath the ocean's surface.

CUERO

What's in a Name? Cuero is the Spanish word for "cowhide" and has various names, such as Cuero unudo and Trelquehuecuve. "Cuero" means "hide." The Mapuche called it Trelque huecuve, meaning "evil spirit hide," where "Trelque" is "hide" and "huecuve" means "evil spirit."

Monstrous Measurements: El Cuero has dark, rough skin and a flattened, wide, and thin body, resembling a tanned cowhide. It ranges from 2 to 5 feet across and weighs approximately 65 pounds. Its body is circular and flat, featuring wide pectoral fins and a long, whip-like tail without a barb. The edges are ringed with sharp claws, nails, or hooks. It possesses eyes on stalks, with four larger eyes on the dorsal surface. The mouth is extendable, akin to a sturgeon.

Terrifying Tracks: Although this creature is believed to come on land occasionally, no tracks or sign of it have been reported.

Beastly Behaviours: Most active in the evening, this creature can move across land and creates large wakes in the lake. It enjoys basking in the sun on the bank. According to South American natives, El Cuero is a voracious predator. The monster is said to surge out of the lake like a crocodile, overwhelming its prey. It then uses its proboscis to puncture the skin and suck out the internal organs and blood. Although it lives in deep water at the bottom of lakes and inlets, it is also believed to be amphibious, coming out onto the shore to bask in the sun. Some researchers think the creature might be partially marine. It is powerful enough to drag animals as big as a horse into the water. However, it can be dispatched by throwing Thorny Branches into its hide-like centre, which instinctively contracts and causes the creature to die, being punctured upon the sharp thornlike branches of the Quisco.

Deadly Diet: Any medium-sized animals or humans unlucky enough to wander too close to the water's edge, where it waits in ambush to drag them into the depths. Some stories report that it prefers to decapitate its prey.

Watery Abode: Lago Lacar and Lago Nahuel Huapí, located in Neuquén Province, Argentina, along with other lakes in the region, including some in Chile, are rumoured to host El Cuero, a lake monster believed to inhabit both lakes and live in caves. Folklore also mentions a smaller and more aggressive variant called the "cuertio" that is said to exist in Lake Lacar.

Scary Sightings

1810: Father Juan Ignacio Molina, the first European naturalist to describe Chilean fauna in his book *Essay on the Natural History of Chile*, mentioned a monstrous fish or dragon known as Ghyryvilu (or Vulpangue, the fox-snake). Locals warned that this man-eating creature lurked in certain Chilean lakes, deterring them from swimming. Descriptions of the creature varied, with some depicting it as a long serpent with a fox's head, while others described it as circular, resembling an extended bovine hide.

1965: Ambrosio Meilivio recounted a cuero attack he learned about in his youth, where a man named Ramil was killed at Lake Carrilaufquen. After being thrown from his horse near the water's edge, Ramil fell atop something that was a hide. It quickly wrapped around him and dragged him into the lake.

Date Unknown: Numerous controversial human encounters have been reported. One tale tells of a woman washing clothes by the lakeside while her baby slept nearby. Suddenly, the creature erupted from the water like a crocodile and swallowed the infant before vanishing as quickly as it appeared.

1974: Fisherman René Zuker reported seeing a small ray in Lake Nahuel Huapi, just a few yards from the Limay River, around 40 years before January 2014. He described it as hand-sized, appearing half-rotten and being consumed by insects.

1976: Allegations emerged of giant freshwater rays spotted in Lago Gutiérrez and Lago Moreno in Argentina's Río Negro Province, both of which flow into Lake Nahuel Huapi. Legend states that a dive team seeking a tourist bus that had fallen into the lake encountered large rays at the lake's bottom. The story gained credibility when confirmed by Walter Hormastorfer, Chief of the Prefectura Naval.

1996: Several witnesses observed a moving object resembling a stone in Lago Lolog, located in Argentina's Neuquén Province, where local lore claims a cuero resides.

2014: René Zuker reported witnessing and photographing a small freshwater stingray at a depth of around 20 feet while standing on a pier in Lake Nahuel Huapi.

Beastly Evidence

Film & Photography: An alleged photograph of a creature in Lake Nahuel Huapi was taken in January 2014 by fisherman René Zuker. Some cryptozoologists suggest it may show a velvet catfish (family *Diplomystidae*), a little-known freshwater fish endemic to the

Southern Cone, which appears larger due to light refraction at the lake's surface.

Literary License: In his 1914 book *Chiloé y los Chilotes*, Francisco J. Cavada describes the creature as La Manta or Cuero on page 104, stating: "Rays resemble this being but lack claws, as do squids. Could the tentacles be mistaken for claws? If it is a freshwater ray, how did it reach Patagonia?"

Beastly Theories!

'Bordering' on Myth! Notice how the Cuero myth is specifically restricted to what was once the land of the Mapuche people. The absence of similar legends further south, in the territory inhabited by various Tehuelche groups, underscores this specificity. It is crucial to note that the Myth exists exclusively in the regions historically part of the Mapuche territory or in areas where Araucanized Tehuelche groups absorbed elements of the Mapuche culture, including language and some of their myths. In contrast, the Southern Tehuelche groups, particularly those south of the Senguer, Chico, and Mayo Rivers in Chubut province—Southern Patagonia—do not possess similar folklore surrounding the Cuero. Instead, while there are legendary creatures in this region's lakes, none correspond to the Cuero mythos. One plausible reason is the geographical and climatic barriers posed by the colder weather of the southern areas, which may have hindered the dissemination of these myths. Furthermore, the Tehuelche residing in areas devoid of stingrays were unlikely to develop myths that involved them. Thus, it raises an interesting question: Could the Cuero be a cautionary tale rooted in Mapuche tradition, aimed at keeping curious children away from the potentially dangerous waters?

A Ribauld Ray! The debate around the Cuero often extends to discussions about its identity, with theories proposing it might represent a giant freshwater ray or even a freshwater cephalopod. The esteemed Argentine writer Jorge Luis Borges famously categorized the Cuero as a freshwater octopus, highlighting the creature's mysterious and multifaceted nature. Notably, there are obvious differences between South America's freshwater stingrays and the Cuero, suggesting a complex evolution of myths surrounding aquatic creatures. The discovery of giant dead stingrays washed ashore likely left a significant impression on any Mapuche individual who encountered such a sight. This startling spectacle could easily inspire a myth.

Nahuelito: The Cuero is oftentimes referenced in discussions about Nahuelito, a cryptid typically described as resembling a plesiosaur, which is said to inhabit Lago Nahuel Huapi. Some proponents of these myths suggest that the presence of the Cuero is evidence of the ancient origins of lake monster tales in this region, with roots extending back to pre-Hispanic times. However, using one cryptid to explain another can verge on circular reasoning. To illustrate this point, one certainly does not explain the phenomena of alien encounters merely by labelling them as visitations from the fairies, meaning simply that the relationships between such myths often demand a more minute exploration.

OKLAHOMA OCTOPUS

What's in a Name? Freshwater Octopus: A medium-sized cephalopod named after the state where it is found.

Monstrous Measurements: Rumoured to be the size of a horse, this freshwater cephalopod resembles an octopus with long tentacles and leathery, reddish-brown skin. Legend suggests it grows between 2 and 3 feet long and inhabits North American rivers.

Beastly Behaviours: The creature is said to attack and kill unsuspecting swimmers. The Octopus of Oklahoma has allegedly terrorized local waters for over 200 years, with some attributing several unexplained drownings to its attacks. Despite sightings, the drowning victims showed no lacerations from tentacles. Contributing factors may include high alcohol consumption among recreationists, leading to miscalculations and accidents.

Deadly Diet: This species shares a diet similar to marine octopuses, consuming freshwater species akin to its marine counterparts. Its large tentacles enable it to drag humans underwater.

Watery Abode: The Oklahoma octopus is a cryptid believed to inhabit several artificial freshwater lakes, including Lake Thunderbird, Oologah Lake, and Lake Tenkiller. Sightings have also been reported in Lake Norman. All these lakes, created by damming rivers for flood control, provide recreational opportunities and the backdrop for tales of the Octopus of Oklahoma. Lake Tenkiller offers visibility from 8 to 28 feet deep, allowing clear water views for those who have claimed to spot this elusive creature. Other notable locations include the Licking River in Kentucky and the Kanawha and Blackwater Rivers in West Virginia.

Scary Sightings

1933: Robert Trice and R. M. Saunders were fishing on the Kanawha River near Charleston, West Virginia, when they caught a 3-foot octopus. However, recent research by Mark Hall has confirmed this incident to be a hoax.

1959: A grey octopus was spotted surfacing and moving onto the bank of the Licking River near Covington, Kentucky.

1999: A dead octopus resting on fossil beds was discovered on the bank of the Ohio River at the Falls of the Ohio State Park in Jeffersonville, Indiana. It was identified as either a Caribbean arm stripe octopus (*Octopus burryi*) or a bumblebee two-stripe octopus (*O. filosus*), an Atlantic species that showed no signs of decomposition.

Beastly Evidence

A Freshwater Frytopi? In July 2003, a fisherman discovered a small red octopus in Lake Conway, Arkansas. Authorities believe it may have been a discarded pet that outgrew its aquarium. This incident sparked rumours of larger octopuses in the area, but officials explained that the octopus survived in the freshwater for a time before being found.

Beastly Theories!

A Freshwater Octopus? The Oklahoma Octopus may represent the possibility of a freshwater octopus species. As a cephalopod, it would be the only known freshwater-dwelling octopus, highlighting a remarkable adaptation to low-saline environments. While this concept may seem unique, it's important to note that numerous marine species, such as certain requiem sharks, thrive in freshwater ecosystems, like the Ganges River shark. This raises the intriguing possibility that undiscovered octopus species could be adapted to similar habitats and are waiting to be identified.

An Abandoned Pet: Some sceptics doubt the existence of freshwater octopi, yet there is evidence of them surviving in such environments. A notable case involved a common octopus found in Lake Conway, Arkansas, released as a pet. These individuals may cling to structures like dam gates. Additionally, elderly octopi may wander searching for habitat, although they typically avoid toxic waters like the Ohio River.

Catfished: The legend of a lake-dwelling octopus may stem from the misidentification of large catfish, which can grow several feet long and weigh hundreds of pounds, particularly in Oklahoma lakes. These formidable fish could easily be mistaken for octopuses, especially in murky waters. Environmental factors such as floods or storms might also transport marine animals like jellyfish or squid into freshwater lakes, further complicating sightings. As a result, these instances of unfamiliar aquatic life could lead to confusion among observers, suggesting that local legends may be based more on misinterpretation than on actual octopus encounters.

An Urban Legend: The legend of the Oklahoma octopus is rooted in Native American folklore, which tells of a mysterious freshwater octopus residing in several artificial lakes in the state, including Lake Thunderbird and Lake Tenkiller. This creature is described as being the size of a horse, with reddish-brown skin and long tentacles. It is said to prey on unsuspecting swimmers. The legend's origins are unclear, but some attribute it to ancient tales of aquatic beasts, inspired by the numerous drownings in Oklahoma lakes. While some consider the octopus a cryptid, others regard it as a myth, reflecting the deep curiosity and fear surrounding the unknown in these waters and among Indigenous peoples.

THE OIL PIT SQUID

What's in a Name? The term "Oil Pit Squid" originated in automotive workshops after a squid-like creature was discovered in a motor oil change pit. This name has become synonymous with eerie legends about these beings.

Monstrous Measurements: Oil Pit Squids measure 6 to 8 inches long and about 1 inch in diameter. Their greyish-red bodies and multiple tentacles give them a unique and unsettling appearance.

Beastly Behaviours: The specific behaviours of the Oil Pit Squid are undocumented. Anecdotal evidence suggests they may resist conventional extermination methods, indicating their adaptability to harsh environments.

Deadly Diet: The diet of the Oil Pit Squid remains unknown.

Watery Abode: These squids thrive in oil-emulsion pits filled with harmful substances like antifreeze, chemicals, and motor oil, creating a toxic habitat.

Scary Sightings

1996: Workers at the GMC Delphi Interior and Lighting plant in Anderson, Indiana, reported sightings of Oil Pit Squids while cleaning a sludge pit. Descriptions included creatures up to 10 inches long swimming in toxic liquid. One worker noted finding a squid-like creature with an eye.

Beastly Evidence

A Captured Specimen: One worker captured a squid-like creature in a jar, but it mysteriously disappeared before any research could be conducted. Shortly after the public discovery, the pit was drained, and no further evidence of the squids was found.

Beastly Theories

A Mixed Bag! Various theories surround the potential origins of certain mysterious organisms, including the idea that they may have evolved from mutated earthworms or bacterial growth. In contrast, others suggest similarities to a "Water Bear." Some consider the possibility that sightings could be hoaxes, while alien spores have also been proposed as a potential source. Additionally, enthusiasts entertain that these beings might represent a previously unknown species adapted to extreme environments, similar to extremophiles found in deep-sea vents.

JELLY SQUID OF LONDON BRIDGE

What's in a Name? The "Jelly Squid of London Bridge" is named for its curious mix of Jellyfish and squid-like features and the location it was encountered.

Monstrous Measurements: Witnesses described the creature as about 5 feet long and as thick as a human body. It had a grey, elongated square head with numerous green tentacles or tassels, enhancing its otherworldly appearance.

Beastly Behaviours: The Jelly Squid surfaced and submerged rhythmically for about a minute. Witnesses noted a strange metallic or mechanical feel, yet it appeared biological. Its slow swimming against the current hints at unique propulsion abilities.

Deadly Diet: The creature's diet remains a mystery, but its jellyfish-like traits suggest it may consume small fish, plankton, or other aquatic organisms, ensnaring prey with its long jellyfish-like tentacles.

Watery Abode: This creature was only observed on one occasion in the River Thames, a historic and busy commercial waterway. The river meets the North Sea via the Thames Estuary in the southeast of

Great Britain where this creature undoubtedly gained entry to this inland water. However, whether it originates from this body of water or further afield is anyone's guess.

Scary Sightings

2014: Since Roman times, the River Thames has hosted various mysterious visitors. Notably, in April 2014, two brothers spotted the Jelly Squid while crossing London Bridge. They described it as having a greyish square head and green tentacles, swimming slowly against the current. Despite attempts to photograph it, their images were too poor to capture the creature. Other witnesses were present, fuelling discussion about its identity.

2015: A year later, one brother's normally calm son panicked during a mudlarking trip under London Bridge, insisting they leave the area, claiming he sensed something unusual.

Beastly Evidence

A Camera Phone Conundrum! While both brothers who witnessed the jelly squid attempted to photograph the creature with their camera phones, poor quality and distance hindered adequate documentation. Nevertheless, vivid descriptions from witnesses, who claimed to have been among a crowd observing the creature from the bridge, provide a convincing chronology of what they encountered that day.

Beastly Theories

Bell Jellyfish: This sighting is unusual and unique, simultaneously resembling both a squid and jellyfish. It certainly does not match any cephalopod or medusa species known to science. After a brief rummage through the archives, I found photographic evidence of a giant bell jellyfish, 4ft across, which was sighted in a Cornish river in May of 2014, and I know that many of these types of jellyfish, although not typically sighted in rivers, are frequently sighted along the coasts of Britain. But the bell jellyfish has an orange-pink hue and does not match the description of the London Bridge creature.

Box Jellyfish: This jellyfish grows to about 10 feet long and 10 inches wide, featuring a pale blue, transparent body with a cube-like bell and tentacles containing 5,000 stinging cells that react to the presence of prey. It's one of the deadliest creatures on Earth, with many victims succumbing to heart attacks or drowning before reaching safety. Witnesses described a creature that resembles the box jellyfish, confused and covered in the brown silt of the Thames. While these jellyfish primarily inhabit northern Australia and the Indo-Pacific, they can swim at speeds up to four knots. Although they have adaptations allowing for more mobility, their presence in British waters remains unlikely.

Giant Squid or Robot Kraken? Could a large squid be behind the sighting? In 1925, a giant squid washed ashore at Withernsea Beach, but no squid species matched the London Bridge creature's description. There was an intriguing sighting of a squid-like creature in Bristol Harbour, captured on film exhibiting bioluminescence—a trait common to squids. However, this was later revealed to be a hoax by university students. The creature's identity remains a mystery: an unknown squid, a rare jellyfish, or something else entirely. Despite the lack of corroboration, the River Thames has seen many unusual visitors throughout its history.

TERRIFYING TURTLES

Def.

Terrifying Turtles are mythical turtle species that have been reported for centuries but are rarely scientifically verified. They include enormous marine turtles from mariners' tales and unusual forms inspired by cultural legends and ancient fossils, which are not formally recognised by science.

BEAST OF BUSCO

What's in a Name? The Beast of Busco is a legendary creature that takes its name from Churubusco, Indiana, where it is said to reside. It is often affectionately called "Oscar," named after the first person who reported seeing it. Other names for this creature include the "Phantom Churubusco Turtle."

Monstrous Measurements: An enormous snapping turtle measures around six feet across and weighs between 500 to 1,000 pounds. Descriptions often compare its shell size to that of a dining room table or the roof of a car, highlighting its massive presence.

Terrifying Tracks: Large tracks in the mud resemble those of an enormous snapping turtle.

Beastly Behaviours: Local legends provide various theories about the creature's behaviour. Some believe it may hibernate for years, waiting for unsuspecting prey. Witnesses have reported seeing the creature lurching out from the water in an attempt to catch fish; however, traditional baits and lures have failed to attract it.

Deadly Diet: While details about its diet remain speculative, the

Beast of Busco is believed to prey on fish and small waterfowl, considering its aquatic environment and presumed size.

Watery Abode: The creature is believed to reside in Fulks Lake, a small seven-acre body of water near Churubusco, Indiana. This lake is the focal point of numerous expeditions and legends. Another rumoured habitat for the creature is the Black Oak Swamp, located near to Hammond, Indiana. Fulks Lake, near Churubusco, Indiana, and Black Oak Swamp, near Hammond, Indiana, are associated with this mysterious being.

Scary Sightings

1898: The first recorded sighting of the Beast dates back to 1898, when farmer Oscar Fulk claimed to have seen a giant turtle in Fulks Lake. The legend of a turtle with a shell bigger than a dining room table originated about three miles outside downtown Churubusco, along a quiet dirt road leading to a small seven-acre lake known today as Fulk Lake. Oscar Fulk owned this land and allegedly was the first to see the large turtle swimming in the lake. Few details exist beyond this initial sighting, and Fulk's account garnered little interest among others in the community.

1948: In July, local fishermen Ora Blue and Charley Wilson also reported spotting the creature. They described seeing a massive alligator snapping turtle, estimated to weigh around 500 pounds while fishing on Fulk Lake. At that time, the land was owned by farmer Gale Harris who, along with others, also reported seeing the creature. Word of the sighting spread, leading to various expeditions to capture the Beast, including attempts to drain the lake and use motorboats. Despite a month-long hunt that briefly gained national attention, the Beast of Busco was never found, becoming a legendary creature that has fascinated and puzzled people for decades.

1949: Approximately 200 people witnessed the creature leap from the water, further fuelling the legends. The most intense search occurred in March 1949, when farmer Gale Harris mobilized a team to capture the Beast, which by then had gained substantial media attention.

Beastly Evidence

The Hunt for Oscar: In March 1949, Gail Harris, whose farm was where a mysterious turtle was spotted, initiated a significant effort to catch the creature. She employed scuba divers, deep-sea equipment, a female sea turtle as bait, a sump pump, and a dredging crane to drain the lake. Local newspapers in Fort Wayne highlighted the story, attracting thousands of people who flocked to the farm hoping to spot the turtle. On October 13, around 200 onlookers got their chance when the turtle leapt from the water to catch a duck used as bait. However, by December, the draining efforts were failing, and Harris fell ill with appendicitis, deciding to call off the search.

After many began to doubt the turtle's existence, Harris made several attempts to capture it, including draining the lake by pumping water into a sealed-off area with the assistance of Orville Bright and Kenneth Leitch. Unfortunately, the dam broke just as the lake was drained. Despite these numerous efforts, "Oscar" (named after the farm's original owner) was never captured.

A Media Frenzy! In early 1949, a UPI reporter from Fort Wayne sent the story to wire services, catapulting the turtle to national fame. Curious mobs of sightseers began to invade Harris' land, leading to the intervention of state police for traffic control. A photographer for *Life Magazine*, Mike Shea, took 299 photos at the site, but they were deemed unusable. In 1994, a documentary film titled *The Hunt for Oscar*, directed by Terry Doran, was released. Additionally, in July 1950, a massive turtle with a head as large as a human's was spotted swimming near a drain leading into the Little Calumet River after a swamp was drained near Black Oak, Indiana.

Turtle Town: One notable place is the unassuming town of Churubusco, where a recurring turtle theme is evident in the town's businesses, parks, and signage. The townspeople fondly remember the tales of an enormous snapping turtle that put their town on the map. A turtle shell labelled "Beast of Busco" hangs in the Two Brothers Restaurant in Decatur, Indiana. Additionally, a small concrete turtle statue is on the sidewalk at the main intersection in Churubusco. The Beast of Busco has become a part of Indiana folklore and culture, inspiring books, songs, movies, and festivals. Every June, Churubusco celebrates Turtle Days, a carnival honouring the town's famous residents. Various statues, signs, and souvenirs feature the turtle's image. Some residents still believe the Beast of Busco is alive and well in Fulk Lake, awaiting another opportunity to reveal itself to the world.

Beastly Theories!

Make it Snappy! The theories about the Beast of Busco differ significantly. Some residents believe this creature is a genuine and enormous snapping turtle that has successfully evaded capture for many years. Conversely, sceptics contend that it is simply a product of imagination or creation by the locals to enhance the charm of their quiet town. Whether a genuine relic from ancient times or just a myth, the Beast of Busco continues to be an intriguing mystery that sparks curiosity and fascination.

Is it feasible for such a large and ancient creature to thrive in a small, contemporary lake? What is the origin and essence of this Beast? How has it endured and evaded capture for such an extended period? And where could it be now? These questions linger in the minds of those captivated by the Beast of Busco.

The alligator snapping turtle (*Macroclemys temminckii*), frequently associated with these legends, is said to reach a maximum weight of 400 pounds. It features a large head with hooked upper and lower jaws, noticeable dorsal ridges, and an additional row of scutes along the sides of its shell. This species resides in the Mississippi River drainage areas of Mississippi, Louisiana, Arkansas, and Missouri, but it may occasionally venture farther away.

HOAN KIEM TURTLE

What's in a Name? The name "Hoàn Kiếm" translates from Vietnamese to "returned sword," referencing the legendary tale that inspired the lake's name. The Hoàn Kiếm turtle is scientifically named *Rafetus hoankiemensis*, given by researcher Ha Dinh Duc.

Monstrous Measurements: The Hoàn Kiếm turtle is considered one of the largest freshwater turtles in the world, measuring between 5 to 6.5 feet in length and about 3 feet in width. These remarkable creatures can weigh up to 440 pounds. Their distinctive appearance features a grey, mottled upper shell and a pinkish belly. Their skin is olive green, adorned with yellow-speckled faces and hog-like snouts.

Terrifying Tracks: While specific tracks are rarely documented due to the turtle's elusive nature, locals and visitors often note that the tracks resemble those of a large softshell turtle.

Beastly Behaviours: The Hoàn Kiếm turtles are usually shy and elusive, rarely surfacing in the densely populated area of Hanoi. Their secretive nature has allowed them to survive unnoticed in Hoàn Kiếm Lake for centuries until recent years.

Deadly Diet: Details regarding the diet of the Hoàn Kiếm turtle are not extensively documented. However, like other freshwater turtles, it is presumed to have a varied diet, including aquatic vegetation, small fish, and other organic materials from the lake. Remarkably, it has even been observed eating a cat!

Watery Abode: The Hoàn Kiếm turtle is found only in Hoàn Kiếm Lake, situated in the heart of Hanoi, Vietnam. This small, algae-covered lake, surrounded by the city's vibrant life, represents a unique aspect of the past that has persevered into modern times.

Scary Sightings

1428: The first recorded sighting of the Hoàn Kiếm turtle occurred when King Lê Thái Tổ celebrated his victories over the Chinese. While boating on the lake, a giant turtle surfaced and retrieved the king's sword. In honour of this legendary moment, the king renamed the lake Hoàn Kiem, which means "returned sword," believing the blade had been restored to his dragon protector.

1967: A 550-pound, seven-foot-long male turtle climbed ashore and died. It was preserved and placed in a glass case at Ngọc Sơn Temple, with a plaque indicating it was over 500 years old.

1998: The Hoàn Kiếm turtle was captured on camera for the first time —fuzzy footage aired on television, generating excitement across the capital. In March of the same year, an amateur filmmaker recorded three turtles surfacing for air.

2016: The last known Hoàn Kiếm turtle was found dead, marking the sad end of an era for this legendary creature whose existence we had only recently come to acknowledge as fact.

Beastly Evidence

The Golden Turtle God: The legend has been linked to tales of giant turtles in Vietnam for centuries. The story began in the 15th century with Lê Lợi, who became emperor and founded the Lê dynasty. He received a sword called Heaven's Will from the Golden Turtle God, Kim Quy. After driving out the Ming army, Lê Lợi went boating on a lake, where the Golden Turtle surfaced to reclaim the sword, prompting him to rename the lake Hoàn Kiếm Lake, meaning "The Lake of the Returned Sword." This tale of Lê Lợi and the giant turtle remains a cherished part of Vietnamese folklore.

Film & Photography: Still images documented the presence of giant turtles in November 1993 and March 2000. After a 1998 video aired, a biologist suggested they might represent a new species, although some experts expressed scepticism regarding this classification. On March 24, 1998, an amateur cameraman filmed three turtles surfacing for air, confirming their existence in the lake, which had previously been thought to be a legend.

Get Stuffed! A stuffed specimen of the world's largest freshwater tortoise, R. leloii, is displayed at Ngoc Son Temple on an island in Hoàn Kiem Lake. This specimen, preserved after its death on June 2, 1967, weighed 200 kg (440 lbs) and measured 1.9 meters (6 ft 3 in) long. It died from injuries inflicted by a fisherman who abused it. The turtle has a greenish-brown carapace, a pink belly, and a large head. Before this, there was uncertainty about the species' existence.

Egg'cellent News! On April 7, 2000, an egg measuring 1 inch by 2 inches, believed to be from one of the turtles, was discovered. An attempt to incubate it was unsuccessful. Current status: The number of remaining individuals in the lake is unknown.

A National Icon! The turtle serves as a national icon in Vietnam, symbolizing independence and protection of the capital. It is celebrated in Hanoi's art and architecture, particularly at Tháp Rùa (Tortoise Tower), a 19th-century structure on Hoàn Kiếm Lake. Nearby, Ngọc Sơn Temple features an entrance with a relief of the turtle swimming away, sword on its back. The Hoàn Kiếm turtle is also likened to a Vietnamese Loch Ness monster, a centuries-old cryptid that has sparked fascination and excitement in the city.

Beastly Theories!

A New Species? After studying large turtles since 1991, Professor Ha Dinh Duc believes they may be a new species, potentially named *Rafetus hoankiemensis*. While some attribute them to *Pelochelys bibroni*, Dr. Peter C.H. Pritchard suggests they could be part of *Trionyx swinhoei* or a distinct species. Duc and others propose genetic differences, indicating they could be *Rafetus vietnamensis*. However, this is debated among biologists. Duc also theorizes that these turtles were brought to Hoàn Kiếm Lake by Emperor Thái Tổ.

Swinhoe's Softshell Turtle: This species can weigh over 300 pounds and is the only known captive specimen in the Shanghai Zoo. Some biologists once speculated that Hanoi's Hoàn Kiem Lake turtles might represent a new species, *Rafetus leloii*, but further research revealed they were Yangtze giant softshell turtles. Although not linked to a legend, *Rafetus swinhoei* is recognized as the world's rarest freshwater turtle. Field surveys in northern Vietnam are ongoing to locate additional specimens. At the same time, two surviving individuals have been identified in Đồng Mỏ Lake and Xuan Khanh Lake, with efforts underway to protect these habitats from commercial fishing and floods.

A Witness to Extinction! In 2011, concerns over the Hoàn Kiếm turtle's health prompted city authorities to capture it for treatment. After several failed attempts, the turtle was finally captured in April and placed in an enclosure. Despite efforts to clean its polluted habitat, the turtle was released in July but died in January 2016 at over 100 years old. Its death was a significant cultural loss for Vietnam. The preserved body is now housed in Hanoi's Museum of Nature, leading to discussions about introducing a similar species to keep the legend alive despite ongoing environmental challenges.

NDENDECKI

What's in a Name? The name "ndendecki," which can also be spelled "ndendeki," is believed to originate from a Lingala (Bantu) word. This name is often called the "dinosaur turtle" because of its enormous size. It is also known by the variant name "Ndendecki."

Monstrous Measurements: The ndendecki is characterized by a rounded shell measuring 12 to 15 feet in diameter. This remarkable size surpasses that of any known species of aquatic turtle currently alive, including the largest fossil freshwater turtle, *Stupendemys*.

Terrifying Tracks: Reports indicate that the ndendecki leaves behind large tracks in the soft, muddy banks of the Likouala aux Herbes River. These tracks' exact size and shape remain unclear, as sightings are rare.

Beastly Behaviours: The ndendecki is an aquatic creature that is submerged in rivers and lakes. It is considered non-aggressive, feeding slowly on organic matter at the bottom of its watery habitat.

Deadly Diet: This giant turtle primarily feeds on organic detritus found in its aquatic environment, making it a benign presence in the rivers and lakes of the Likouala.

Watery Abode: The ndendecki is reported in the Likouala aux Herbes River in the Republic of Congo. This vast and unexplored area is characterized by swamps, which serve as a haven for diverse wildlife.

Scary Sightings

An Elusive Animal! Sightings of the ndendecki have primarily come from local villagers near Boha, who describe encounters with this giant turtle. Eyewitness accounts suggest that it is a dinosaurian creature of legend, in a land of legends, living among other cryptid creatures such as the Mokele Mbembe, Emele Ntouka, Mbielu, Mbielu, Mbielu and J'ba F'fofi fuelled by the mysterious folklore and ancient beliefs of the people who inhabit these dense swamplands.

Beastly Evidence

Cryptid Quest! In the 1980s, Prof. Roy P. Mackal led expeditions to the Likouala region in search of the mokele-mbembe, a water creature resembling a small sauropod dinosaur. Although his team did not encounter this creature, they learned of other cryptids, including the ndendecki, or "dinosaur turtle," reported by locals. Eyewitness accounts compiled by Gilbert Bonguenele Manengue, a security agent from Boha, described the ndendecki as a massive freshwater turtle with a shell 12-15 ft in diameter, surpassing known species like the *Stupendemys*. Fortunately, the ndendecki is harmless, feeding on detritus along the river and lake bottoms.

Beastly Theories!

An Extraordinary Softshell: The ndendecki may be a large, undiscovered variant of the African softshell turtle (*Trionyx triunguis*), which usually grows to about 3 feet. Congolese zoologist Dr Marcellin Agnagna suggests that local reports of 12 to 15-foot specimens might be based on oversized older turtles rather than exaggeration. This cryptid turtle, reported from the Likouala aux Herbes River in Congo, may be linked to enormous individuals of T. triunguis in the area.

SOAY GIANT TURTLE

What's in a Name? It is named after the island of Soay, located on the west coast of Scotland, where it was first encountered. It is also known as The Sea Monster of Soay.

Monstrous Measurements: The creature resembles a 3-meter-long turtle with a saw-edged dorsal crest and large scales. Its gullet is red, and its wide, split-mouth is filled with pointed structures. The beast also has large, prominent eyes. A leatherback turtle can grow up to 2.2 meters in length.

Terrifying Tracks: Flippers resembling those of a turtle.

Beastly Behaviours: Heavy breathing, moves similarly to a large turtle. Breathes through its mouth, creating a whistling noise.

Deadly Diet: Unknown but judging by the similar oral structure observed in leatherback turtles, it feeds exclusively on jellyfish.

Watery Abode: The beast of Soay owes its name to a tiny island near Great Britain, one of the observation sites. It is located on the west coast of Scotland.

Scary Sightings

_1959:_ Off the coast of Soay Island in Scotland, author Tex Geddes and engineer James Gavin encountered a monster while shark fishing. They first heard the creature breathing, and upon turning toward the sound, they found themselves face to face with a fearsome reptile. The men described the creature as having a dark, rounded head, a red slash for a mouth, and spiked structures inside. Sharp, serrated ridges ran along the length of its humped back. Based on their observations above the water's surface, they estimated the creature measured between 6 to 10 feet in length. Their account of the monster spread through Britain like wildfire, accompanied by a highly embellished, dragon-like illustration of the beast.

_1971:_ Nessie-hunter Tim Dinsdale discovered a giant dead turtle in a storage shed in Mallaig, near Soay. He estimated its weight at around 1,500 pounds.

Beastly Evidence

A Media Monstrosity: The sighting and accompanying story quickly gained traction, being featured in national news media outlets such as the *Illustrated London News*. Tex served as the primary catalyst for this coverage, writing about the encounter with the prominent zoologist and writer Maurice Burton.

Beastly Theories!

Touche' Turtle! The legend of the Soay Island Sea Monster began in September 1959 when Tex Geddes and James Gavin reported a strange sighting. Initially, Geddes thought the creature was a turtle. However, as it drew closer, he described it as a large, hump-backed animal with a spiked mouth and a serrated back. The accounts of the two men varied slightly: James estimated the monster to be around 6 to 8 feet long, while Tex claimed it was between 8 and 10 feet. They may have encountered a Leatherback Sea Turtle, which can reach lengths of 7 to 8 feet and has spiky features, leading to a case of mistaken identity.

Big Daddy! Another interesting turtle-related fact is that the *Archelon ischyros*, known as the Father of All Turtles, is the largest known turtle species. These ancient marine creatures could measure up to 16 feet long and 12 feet wide, and may have weighed as much as 11,000 pounds during the Late Cretaceous period. Fossils have been discovered in South Dakota, Kansas, and Colorado. Interestingly, there have been alleged modern-day sightings of the Archelon in various locations, including the Grand Banks in the North Atlantic Ocean, the Gulf of Urabá in Colombia, and off the west coast of Scotland.

FATHER-OF-ALL-THE-TURTLES

What's in a Name? The "Father of All Turtles" is a giant sea turtle identified as a sea monster by Belgian cryptozoologist Dr Bernard Heuvelmans in his 1968 work, *In the Wake of the Sea Serpents*. The name originates from native Sumatran fishermen who believed in a legendary sea deity that could transform into a colossal marine turtle, embodying myth and mystery.

Monstrous Measurements: The "Father of All Turtles" resembles a tortoise, featuring a tortoise-like head, large prominent eyes, and a wide toothless mouth. Its slender neck supports a rounded carapace with a unique saw-toothed ridge covered in large scales. This marine giant possesses two pairs of powerful flippers and can reach lengths estimated between 14 and 45 feet.

Terrifying Tracks: The creature leaves huge, distinctive flipper tracks in the sand.

Beastly Behaviours: It breathes through its mouth, producing a whistling noise that sends shivers down the spine of anyone who encounters it.

Deadly Diet: Unknown.

Watery Abode: It is said to inhabit the depths of the North Atlantic Ocean and the Caribbean Sea, where this magnificent creature roams in search of sustenance.

Scary Sightings

1494: Christopher Columbus reports seeing a whale-sized turtle near the Dominican Republic. The turtle was described as having a long tail with fins.

1883: March 30: The schooner *Annie L. Hall's* crew mistakes a colossal turtle for a capsized ship near the Grand Banks. The turtle measures approximately 40 feet long and 30 feet wide, with flippers around 20 feet long.

1883: November: Capt. W. L. Green and fishermen report a separate sea monster sighting off Long Branch, New Jersey.

1955: March 8: L. Alejandro Velasco, stranded on a raft in the Gulf of Urabá, Colombia, sees a yellow turtle approximately 14 feet long.

1956: June: The cargo steamer *Rhapsody* spots a 45-foot turtle near Nova Scotia, with flippers measuring about 15 feet long and able to raise its head 8 feet out of the water.

1959: September 13: Tex Geddes and James Gavin observe a large animal in the Inner Hebrides, Scotland, 4-8 feet wide at the waterline.

1971: In August, Tim Dinsdale discovered a dead giant turtle weighing around 1,500 pounds in a storage shed in Mallaig, Scotland.

Beastly Evidence

The Shell House: The earliest report of colossal turtles dates back to the 3rd century AD, when Roman scholar Claudius Aelianus mentioned their enormous shells, up to 23.5 ft in circumference, used as roofing material in the Indian Ocean. Sceptics argue these shells might have been fossils, particularly from the prehistoric giant tortoise *Megalochelys atlas* found in Nepal's Siwalik Hills. However, fossil shells are too heavy and brittle for that purpose.

A Cryptid Cartographer: In 1154 AD, Moroccan scholar Muhammad al-Idrisi referred to similarly large turtles, up to 33 ft long, in the Sea of Herkend near Sri Lanka, claiming females could lay up to a thousand eggs. Though he had never visited Asia, he had gathered extensive details from Islamic explorers. However, turtles typically lay around a hundred eggs, suggesting that some of these reports may have been exaggerated.

Beastly Theories!

An Anomalous Giant: The Atlantic leatherback turtle (*Dermochelys coriacea coriacea*) can reach 7-8 feet long and weigh 800 pounds. Some theory reports of giant turtles in the Atlantic may be misidentifications of these turtles, which can grow over 9 feet and have the most enormous flippers of any sea turtle. The white/yellow colour seen in sightings might be due to colour mutations or albinism. Leatherbacks thrive in cold waters and are often spotted near Quebec and Newfoundland, supporting their identification in historical sightings.

Archelon Ischyros: This extinct turtle, measuring up to 16 feet long and weighing 11,000 pounds, lived about 70 million years ago. Fossils have been discovered in regions like South Dakota and Kansas. Some researchers speculate that modern sightings of giant turtles could be linked to surviving specimens of Archelon, citing its massive size and unique features.

The World Turtle: Mythological accounts of giant turtles appear in diverse cultures worldwide, including Hindu and Native American stories. Such legends may have originated from encounters with creatures like *Archelon ischyros*, although this remains speculative. Eyewitness reports of large turtles surged in the 1950s, leading cryptozoologist Bernard Heuvelmans to categorize them as the "Father of All Turtles." While science has yet to confirm the existence of a gigantic turtle, the name is already established for future discoveries.

LEELANAU LAKE MONSTER

What's in a Name? The creature is known as "Leelanau," named after Lake Leelanau, which is believed to be its home. The name translates from the local Ojibwa language to "delight of life."

Monstrous Measurements: This creature features a long, stump-like neck, a lengthy tail, and two large eyes. Unlike typical lake monster reports, Leelanau doesn't resemble plesiosaur-like beings, indicating it could represent a unique species.

Terrifying Tracks: Unknown.

Beastly Behaviours: The creature remains motionless to avoid detection, only diving away if it senses a threat to its concealment. It possesses a form of epidermal camouflage that makes its long, turtle-like neck resemble an old, gnarled tree trunk. This camouflage allows the creature to evade notice by remaining completely still until any potential human observers pass by. However, if its camouflage is compromised, the beast will suddenly dive and flee.

Deadly Diet: Unknown.

Watery Abode: Lake Leelanau, or "Carp Lake," consists of two connected lakes in Leelanau County, Michigan. The northern lake exceeds 120 feet in depth, while the southern lake is about 62 feet deep. Both are said to be home to this mysterious lake monster.

Scary Sightings

1910: A teenager named William Gauthier had a frightening encounter with an elusive creature. While perch fishing in a rowboat near Carp Lake, Gauthier ventured into uncharted waters and moored his boat next to a dead cedar stump. Suddenly, he was startled by two enormous eyes that opened at his eye level. Frozen in terror, he watched as the creature dove beneath his rowboat, revealing its impressive length as its head surfaced on one side while its tail remained above water.

Gauthier, hailing from a prominent local family, had decided to fish in a new lake section that summer. After passing several dead cedar trees, he was about to experience the shock of his life. The moment his rope touched the branch, the creature revealed itself. It abruptly submerged after staring into its enormous eyes for what felt like an eternity. Gauthier claimed he could see the creature's head on one side of the boat while its tail remained visible on the other.

Beastly Evidence

A Cryptid Aquarium: Local legend states that the beast first appeared after the Lake Leelanau dam was built in the late 1800s to power the Leland Sawmill. According to various sources, the dam sealed off the lake's largest outlet and trapped the creature inside. After its construction, the water level rose by 10 to 12 feet, flooding the surrounding land and creating a marshy environment where the beast is said to have thrived.

Beastly Theories!

Epidermal Camouflage: The juvenile witness only recognized the stump when its eyes opened, suggesting the creature had remarkable camouflage, similar to stick bugs. This raises the question of how often people staring at half-submerged trees are seeing a cryptid. William Gauthier's failure to identify the creature until its eyes opened indicates that Leelanau possesses extraordinary disguising abilities, allowing it to blend into the marshy environment of Lake Leelanau and prompting further inquiries into its evolutionary traits and behaviour.

The Last of Its Kind? Gauthier's great-grandson recalls that his great-grandfather was terrified by an unusual encounter on Lake Leelanau, which caused him to avoid fishing there for years. Around the turn of the century, others reported similar disturbing experiences but hesitated to come forward due to fear of ridicule. Many years have passed since the last sighting, leading investigators to believe any creature from that time has expired. However, unwary boaters may have unknowingly passed by a living creature, mistaking it for a rotting stump.

A Peculiar Plesiosaur or Primitive Turtle? The fossil record is incomplete, and many extinct and living species may still be waiting to be discovered. Leelanau may represent an unknown form of archaic turtle, or a unique, undiscovered type of prehistoric plesiosaur adapted to North America's swampy environments. Intriguingly, it hasn't been linked to familiar lake monsters or known extinct species, suggesting it may belong to an unclassified genus.

PERNICIOUS PINNIPEDS

Def.

Pernicious pinnipeds refer to particular pinniped species, such as seals, sea lions, and walruses, which are often regarded as cryptids. This classification includes unclassified species within the suborder *Pinnipedia* and known species exhibiting unusual physiological traits, such as gigantism or dwarfism. Additionally, these pinnipeds may be found in atypical environments, such as freshwater habitats or isolated regions.

CARIBBEAN MONK SEAL

What's in a Name? The Caribbean monk seal, named for its locational appellation, *Monachus tropicalis*, is also known as the West Indian seal or sea wolf.

Monstrous Measurements: Caribbean monk seals measured 7 to 8 feet long and weighed 375 to 600 pounds. They had a robust body, with males slightly larger than females. Their colouration ranged from brown to grey on the back, with a lighter underside, and adults were darker than the younger seals, which had a yellowish hue. They had short foreflippers with small claws and slender hind flippers. Their rounded heads featured broad muzzles, wide-spaced eyes, upward-opening nostrils, and pronounced whisker pads with long, light-coloured whiskers. Algae sometimes grew on their fur, giving them a greenish appearance.

Terrifying Tracks: Historically, Caribbean monk seals left their tracks scattered across low sandy beaches where they would haul out to rest. Although detailed tracking data is scarce due to their extinction, it is known that they favoured secluded atolls and islands for resting.

Beastly Behaviours: Approachable and unaggressive, often socializing in groups of 20 to 40 and sometimes up to 100. They primarily fed on fish and crustaceans. They were slow and curious on land, making them easy targets for hunters. Their lengthy pupping season peaked in early December, with mothers nursing their pups using four retractable nipples. Newborns measured about 3 feet long and weighed 35 to 40 pounds, typically born with a sleek black coat.

Deadly Diet: Primarily feeds on fish and crustaceans, thriving in the abundant marine life found in its habitat.

Watery Abode: Caribbean monk seals inhabit the warm waters of the Caribbean Sea, particularly off the coasts of Haiti and Jamaica. They extend throughout the northern and western Caribbean and the Gulf of Mexico. They prefer secluded sandy beaches above high tide but occasionally venture to mainland coasts and deeper offshore waters, feeding in shallow lagoons and reefs.

Scary Sightings

1952: The last confirmed sighting of a Caribbean monk seal occurred in 1952 at Serranilla Bank, located in the waters west of Jamaica and off the eastern coast of Nicaragua.

2008: The species was officially declared extinct by the United States after an extensive five-year search. This analysis was conducted by the National Marine Fisheries Service of the National Oceanic and Atmospheric Administration (NOAA). The Caribbean monk seal is closely related to the endangered Hawaiian monk seal, which is found exclusively in the central Pacific Ocean surrounding the Hawaiian Islands, and the Mediterranean monk seal, a vulnerable species primarily located in the waters of Greece.

Beastly Evidence

Fishermen's Tales: An assessment in 1997 involving interviews with 93 fishermen in northern Haiti and Jamaica found that over 22% recognized monk seals from pictures, indicating some knowledge of the species. This percentage was significantly higher ($P < 0.001$) than those who identified control species unlikely to have been observed. However, it was similar to the number of manatees known to occur in the region. Additionally, more than 95% of respondents identified common local species. Further questioning revealed that 16 of the 21 fishermen who selected monk seals had seen them in the past 1-2 years, with descriptions aligning with monk seals, suggesting that the Caribbean monk seal may not be extinct.

The Quest for a Gentle Giant! On April 22, 2009, *The History Channel* aired an episode of *Monster Quest* speculating that an unidentified sea creature in Florida's Intracoastal Waterway could be the extinct Caribbean monk seal. However, no conclusive evidence supports this, and alternative views suggest it might be a misidentified West Indian manatee.

Beastly Theories!

A Fatal Disposition: The Caribbean monk seal (*Neomonachus tropicalis*), also known as the West Indian seal, went extinct primarily due to extensive overhunting of oil and meat, and overfishing their natural prey. These seals were particularly vulnerable to humans, as their unaggressive and curious nature made them easy targets. While large sharks served as their natural predators, human actions were the most significant threat.

Historically, Caribbean monk seals congregated in groups of 20-100 and primarily fed on fish and crustaceans. Sluggish on land, seals had a long pupping season, with newborns measuring about 1 meter long and weighing 16-18 kg. The Caribbean monk seal nasal mite, which lived in the seal's nasal cavity, also went extinct with its host.

The first half of the twentieth century saw a sharp decline in sightings of these seals. The last confirmed sighting was in 1952 at Serranilla Bank. Although unconfirmed sightings by local fishermen persist, many biologists believe these reports are of wandering hooded seals rather than the extinct monk seal.

LAKE TITICACA SEAL

What's in a Name? Affectionately called "Teetee" by the local people or referred to as the Lake Titicaca Monster. Lake Titicaca itself derives its name from an Aymara term that means "puma" ("titi") and "grey" or "white hairs" ("caca"). This name might refer to the sacred rock known as "thakhsi cala," found on Isla del Sol. The lake is also referred to as Lago Huiñaymarca or Lago Chucuito.

Monstrous Measurements: The Lake Titicaca Monster is a legendary aquatic creature said to inhabit Lake Titicaca, which spans Peru and Bolivia. It's often described as a 12-foot-long monster with a bear-like head and smooth coffee-brown skin, resembling a seal or manatee. Other accounts depict it as a gigantic, serpent-like being with glowing eyes and sharp teeth, capable of capsizing boats or blending into the dark waters. Its appearance varies across folklore, with some versions showing multiple tentacles or crocodilian features.

Terrifying Tracks: While the specifics remain unknown, locals have reported seeing large furrows and signs resembling a seal-like creature, albeit one of enormous dimensions!

Beastly Behaviours: The Lake Titicaca Monster is a territorial creature instinctively driven to protect its domain. Typically seen sunning on beaches near sheltered coves, it emerges primarily in response to threats to its territory. While not inherently malicious, it disregards human life when defending its sacred waters and will react aggressively to disturbances from boats or human activities. This creature embodies nature's raw power, operating under a code of survival and protection rather than malice. Over the years, locals and visitors have reported mysterious disappearances and boat accidents attributed to the monster, with some claiming to have heard its terrifying roar echo across the lake.

Deadly Diet: Lake Titicaca is a biodiversity hotspot featuring over 530 aquatic species, including the endangered Titicaca grebe and large Titicaca water frog. It is home to native fish like Orestias, catfish and water birds such as the white-tufted grebe and Chilean flamingo. This ecosystem also includes freshwater snails, amphipods, and rich vegetation like totora. These species may contribute to the diet of the elusive "Lake Titicaca monster," with the large water frog and Orestias fish being essential for its survival in this unique environment.

Watery Abode: Lago Titicaca, particularly around the Copacabana Peninsula and Strait of Tiquina, features sheltered coves near Tiquina, Copacabana, and Santiago Huata. The Isla del Sol (Island of the Sun) is the creature's home, holding deep spiritual significance and numerous myths connecting the monster to the island's sacred energy.

Scary Sightings

1910: Native Americans and European settlers had reported encounters with particular creatures multiple times.

1914: Geographer Millicent Todd Bingham noted that manatees, also known as sea cows, inhabited Lake Titicaca. She described how they frequented grottoes along the shore and were occasionally seen resting on remote beaches.

Beastly Evidence

SEAL the Deal! A local man, Miguel Garcés, possessed a tooth retrieved from the carcass of the Lake Titicaca Monster discovered on the beach near Copacabana.

Beastly Theories!

An Unknown Freshwater Seal: The only seals that live exclusively in freshwater are the Baikal seal (*Phoca sibirica*) from Lake Baikal in Siberia and the Caspian seal (*Phoca caspica*) found in the Caspian Sea. There are also cryptids similar to Teetee that some researchers believe represent unknown populations of freshwater seals, like the Ambize.

A Long-Necked Seal: Longnecks are often classified as sea serpents and lake monsters, making them some of the most commonly reported cryptids. Although different classification systems exist, they are considered large, long-necked pinnipeds. Historically, many people believed that longnecks were surviving plesiosaurs or related creatures, a theory that still persists today. Since the late 19th century, some cryptozoologists have suggested that sightings of longnecks in oceans closely relate to reports of freshwater lake monsters in temperate regions.

A Common Nature Spirit: The Lake Titicaca Monster has been part of local folklore for centuries, and is viewed as a guardian spirit of the lake by indigenous tribes. Beliefs suggest it might be an ancient creature hiding in the lake's depths, appearing when nature is out of balance or human activities disrespect the area. Some stories link the monster to Incan mythology, depicting it as a protector of the Inca Gold hidden in the lake. It is said to create whirlpools and waves to capsize boats or trap prey, highlighting its dangerous nature. While often seen as malevolent, it can also be viewed as a guardian, punishing those who trespass on sacred traditions.

STELLARS SEA APE

What's in a Name? The creature is named after George Steller, who noted its resemblance to 'Simia Marina Danica' in a 1558 book. It has had various scientific names, including 'Siren cynodephala' (coined in 1792) and 'Trichechus hydropithecus' (coined in 1800). It's also known as Steller's sea monkey.

Monstrous Measurements: This creature measures 5 to 6 feet in length, boasting a long, tapered, and robust body covered in reddish fur underneath and grey on its back. Its head resembles a dog's, featuring pointed ears, large eyes, and long drooping whiskers while lacking front flippers or pectoral fins. The tail is bilobate, with the upper lobe significantly larger than the lower one. When submerged, its red belly takes on a cow-like appearance.

Beastly Behaviours: Very playful by nature, it can lift itself out of the water by one-third of its length and maintain that position for several minutes.

Deadly Diet: It primarily feeds on species of bull kelp (*Nereocystis luetkeana*), which are common in the Gulf of Alaska.

Watery Abode: The creature has been observed near the Shumagin Islands, located at the southern tip of Alaska and part of the Aleutian Islands.

Scary Sightings

1741: German naturalist George Steller, the physician aboard the *St. Peter*, encountered a peculiar creature near the Shumagin Islands in the Gulf of Alaska. He described it as approximately five feet long, with a dog-like head, pointed ears, long whiskers, and a shark-like tail. Its body was covered in thick greyish hair and lacked forelimbs. Steller and his crew observed this enigmatic animal for two hours as it playfully interacted with a piece of seaweed, lifting a third of its body out from the water in a human-like manner. Despite Steller's attempts to capture it, after multiple missed shots the creature vanished beneath the waves. During the demanding Great Northern Expedition, Steller faced one of the ocean's most mysterious creatures. Or did he?

1965: Writer and navigator Miles Smeeton reported a similar sighting off the north coast of Atka Island in the Aleutian Islands. He described the creature as roughly the size of a sheep, noting its long, reddish-yellow fur and features reminiscent of a Tibetan terrier, including a droopy moustache. Accompanied by his daughter Clio and friend Henry Combe on his ketch, the *Tzu Hang*, Smeeton observed the animal's graceful diving movements about four miles from shore. In his book *Misty Island*, he recounted this fleeting encounter, emphasizing the similarities to Steller's earlier observations, with only two sightings recorded over two centuries.

Beastly Evidence

Cryptid Classification: Initially classified as 'Simia marina' and other names, the creature was misidentified as a northern fur seal based on diary descriptions and sightings on Shumagin Island. A sketch labelled it a "sea ape," though this account was imperfect. In 1936, it was suggested the creature could have been a playful bachelor fur seal, explaining its perceived lack of forelimbs in low light.

Beastly Theories!

A Northern Fur Seal: It was suggested that a young northern fur seal (*Callorhinus ursinus*) might have been present in Steller's accounts despite the crew's familiarity with various seal species. The first sighting of this unique animal occurred during Steller's time on the rookeries of Ostrov Bering in the Commander Islands. Steller may have mistakenly identified the seal's hind flippers as a tail, contributing to the confusion surrounding this species. Northern fur seals are known for their thick fur and distinctive features, including a prominent mane in males. They possess remarkable abilities to dive deep for food, primarily consuming fish and squid.

An Arctic Leopard Seal: Another intriguing marine creature noted by Steller could be a young specimen of the Arctic leopard seal (*Hydrurga leptonyx*). This seal's lack of external ears is a characteristic shared by many authentic seals. Leopard seals are formidable hunters renowned for their powerful jaws and hunting skills. They are unique in their family for preying on warm-blooded animals, such as penguins, and displaying agile swimming capabilities in icy Antarctic waters.

A Hawaiian Monk Seal: Steller also noted the presence of a solo Hawaiian monk seal (*Monachus schauinslandi*), which displayed behaviours and size that matched his description of the elusive creature. Nonetheless, this seal typically does not venture far from the Hawaiian Islands, making it an unlikely candidate for Steller's Sea Ape. Hawaiian monk seals are among the few tropical seal species recognized for their rounded bodies, smooth fur, and notably playful behaviour. They are critically endangered, due to habitat destruction and human interactions, highlighting the urgent need for their conservation.

A Long-Necked Seal: Longnecks are often classified as sea serpents and lake monsters, making them some of the most commonly reported cryptids. Although different classification systems exist, they are considered large, long-necked pinnipeds.

BUNYIP

What's in a Name? The Bunyip, known among some Aboriginal Australians as the Kianpraty, is a mythical creature from Australian folklore often depicted as a malevolent spirit inhabiting swamps, billabongs, and waterholes.

Monstrous Measurements: Descriptions of the Bunyip vary widely, featuring characteristics reminiscent of birds and alligators. Many accounts tell of an emu-like head with a long bill and serrated edges, a thick, muscular body, and powerful limbs equipped with long claws. The creature is reported to range from 4 to 4.5 feet in length, but when standing on its hind legs with its head upright, it may reach a terrifying height of 12 to 13 feet.

Terrifying Tracks: Its tracks resemble those of alligators, ducks, or creatures with flipper-like appendages, adding to the mystery of its aquatic nature and habitat.

Beastly Behaviours: Revered in Aboriginal lore, this creature is known as a fearsome ambush predator that swims effortlessly and can reach speeds up to 31 mph. Primarily hunting at night, it is an opportunistic predator that preys on livestock and any humans who venture too close to the water's edge. Its bellow is described as blood-curdling, serving as a territorial marker.

Deadly Diet: The creature's diet is primarily determined by the food sources that wander into its territory. Local Aboriginal communities have reviled it for targeting livestock, as well as women and children.

Watery Abode: Reported to inhabit river basins and wetlands across Australia and Tasmania.

Scary Sightings

1818: One of the earliest documented sightings involved James Meehan and explorer Hamilton Hume, who discovered enormous bones at Lake Bathurst in New South Wales that they likened to a manatee or hippopotamus.

1845: The *Geelong Advertiser* published a detailed description of the Bunyip, marking the first recorded use of the name and igniting public fascination.

1847: Aboriginal people in the Grampians described eerie sounds from the water and later claimed to have seen a large creature with shaggy fur and bright eyes, believed to be a Bunyip.

1850s: Numerous reports from settlers and Indigenous Australians detailed sightings of an enormous aquatic creature with a long neck and a fearsome roar.

1870: Miners near McIvor Creek in Victoria reported witnessing a large creature emerge from the water. They described it as having thick fur and emitting a horrifying bellow.

1890: A farmer named Thomas D. Andrew claimed to have glimpsed a Bunyip while fishing at the Murray River, describing its massive tail and limbs after it splashed dramatically from the water.

1910: Naturalist Sir Thomas Mitchell recorded observations of a mysterious dark shape in the Gippsland swamps. The shape vanished into the water, leaving disturbed mud behind.

1970s: Renewed sightings came from locals in the Dandenong Ranges, who reported unsettling calls at night and glimpses of a shadowy figure near the water's edge.

1978: A group of teenagers swimming near Adelaide believed they spotted a Bunyip, describing a dark, shadowy figure that glided just beneath the surface before disappearing.

Beastly Evidence

A Fossil Fiend: In the 1830s, George Rankin discovered fossilized bones in the Wellington Caves of New South Wales. This significant find was later examined by Thomas Mitchell and identified by British anatomist Sir Richard Owen as belonging to the extinct prehistoric marsupial Diprotodon.

A Scary Skull: Reports from 1846 described a peculiar skull attributed to that of a Yowie, which resembled a deformed calf or foal. This discovery further heightened the intrigue surrounding the region's prehistoric remains.

A Pop Culture Cryptid: The Bunyip is a legendary creature in Australian culture. It is featured in various media, including *Scribblenauts*, *The Secret Saturdays*, horror films like *Bunyip* and *Red Billabong*, and children's literature like *The Bunyip of Berkley's Creek*. Bunyipas has a statue in Melbourne and appears in video games like *Ty the Tasmanian Tiger* and inspired Dingodile from *Crash Bandicoot*.

Beastly Theories!

A Rogue Pinniped: The legends of the Bunyip may have been inspired by known species such as leopard and elephant seals. Leopard seals are infamous for their aggression and size, while elephant seals can grow up to 16 feet long and weigh over 5,000 pounds. Both species inhabit the coastal regions of Australia and New Zealand, and their elusive behaviour could have contributed to Aboriginal folklore. One of these ocean giants could have ventured deep into Australia's inland waters, becoming hopelessly lost while aggressively hunting anything they encountered. This scenario provided the basis for the legendary phenomenon of the Bunyip.

Mythological Megafauna: One theory suggests that the Bunyip is a modern representation of the Diprotodon, a prehistoric marsupial that thrived during the Pleistocene era. This massive creature could have inspired descriptions found in Bunyip lore, accentuating modern fascination with "living fossils" and the concept that some creatures could have evaded extinction.

A Dreamtime Demon: In Aboriginal mythology, the Bunyip is associated with significant spiritual narratives, particularly as a Dreamtime demon. One tale describes how the Bunyip becomes a malevolent spirit after breaking the law of the Rainbow Serpent.

HAWKESBURY RIVER MONSTER

What's in a Name? Reports of a mysterious water monster date back to the ancient art of the Dharuk tribal Aborigines of New South Wales. This legend refers to the creature as Mirreeulla, which means "giant water serpent." Locally, it is known as the Hawkesbury River Monster.

Monstrous Measurements: Cave art depicts a creature with a snake-like head, long neck, large body, two pairs of flippers, and an eel-like tail. Reports of unusual slide marks resembling those of a crocodile have been found along the riverbanks. This description aligns closely with that of a plesiosaur, often identified as The Loch Ness Monster or Nessie.

Terrifying Tracks: Reports describe unusual slide marks resembling a crocodile along the riverbank.

Beastly Behaviours: This creature is a potential ambush predator and shows little concern for people and boats when not actively hunting.

Deadly Diet: Fish, livestock, and, if the legends are to be believed, the occasional fisherman.

Watery Abode: Sightings of these creatures have been reported from Wisemans Ferry at the western end of the river, extending eastward to the Broken Bay-Brisbane Waters expanse at the river's mouth.

Scary Sightings

1912: A report from the *Evening News* in Sydney described an alligator-like creature seen in South Creek, a tributary of the Hawkesbury River. Witnesses reported observing a strange swimming object approximately four feet in length.

1924: A report published in the *Windsor and Richmond Gazette* detailed eyewitness accounts of a "titanic seahorse." W.J. Riley and his brother described seeing a large creature about 5 to 6 feet long with a square-looking fishtail.

1980s: Fishermen reported a frightening encounter with a sea creature that surfaced beneath their aluminium boat, launching it out of the water by more than 9.8 feet. During this time, other reports emerged of boats found adrift with their occupants missing and other vessels that had capsized.

1997: A resident reported seeing a large, serpentine creature while fishing in the Hawkesbury River. An anonymous fisherman claimed to have seen a dark shape swimming just under the river's surface, estimating its length to be about 10 feet.

2011: A tourist spotted an eel-like creature while taking a boat tour on the Hawkesbury River. The witness described the creature as dark green and 8 to 10 feet long.

2014: A local family reported seeing a large, submerged creature while swimming in the river. They described it as having a long body and a large fin, similar to prehistoric depictions of marine reptiles.

2017: An incident involved kayakers who claimed to have been followed by a large, sinuous shape while navigating a narrow section of the river.

2020: A fisherman claimed to have spotted a large creature resembling a crocodile while trolling in the deeper waters of the Hawkesbury River, stating it was about 12 feet long.

Beastly Theories!

It's a 'Plesiosaur' to Meet You! The Hawkesbury River monster has often been compared to the plesiosaur, a prehistoric marine reptile known for its long neck and broad body. Reports of large, mysterious shapes surfacing from the river's depths mimic similar accounts from various bodies of water worldwide, where comparable creatures have been sighted. Some cryptozoologists suggest these sightings could result from misidentifications of known aquatic animals, such as large fish or turtles. Additionally, the river's size and depth may provide an environment that supports large, undiscovered species, fuelling the myths surrounding the existence of a surviving plesiosaur or closely related creature in the area.

A Marsupial Seal? One theory about the monster's identity is the existence of a marsupial seal, a concept based on Australia's unique evolutionary landscape. While no known marsupial seals exist today, it suggests that an extinct lineage may have adapted to a semi-aquatic lifestyle. Sightings in the Hawkesbury River could be attributed to large marine mammals resembling seals, leading to speculation about an undiscovered species. This idea challenges traditional views on mammalian evolution and broadens our understanding of ecological possibilities.

An Antarctic Adventurer! The idea of a lost leopard seal in the Hawkesbury River adds an interesting twist to the river monster's identity. While leopard seals are usually solitary and live in the ocean, a seal might wander into the river, explaining reported sightings. Aquatic animals can travel long distances, so these events are possible. People may misinterpret these encounters based on local stories, contributing to the legend of the mysterious river monster.

SECRET SIRENIANS

Def.

Secret sirenians denote specific species of sirenians, like manatees and dugongs, that are frequently considered cryptids. This category encompasses unclassified species within the sirenian order, other species believed to be extinct, and recognised species that display uncommon physical characteristics or inhabit unusual environments, including freshwater ecosystems or areas outside of their normal habitat.

ST HELENA MANATEE

What's in a Name? The creature is named after the island where it was first observed.

Monstrous Measurements: Length, 10 feet. Yellowish colour. Large, green eyes.

Wide jaws with large teeth. Bristly moustache.

Beastly Behaviours: This creature often rests or sleeps on the rocks along the shore.

Watery Abode: The island of St. Helena is located in the South Atlantic Ocean. It is home to the St. Helena Manatee, although its classification remains uncertain—whether as a sirenian or a seal.

Scary Sightings

1655: A Cornish traveller Peter Mundy journeyed to India on the *Aleppo Merchant* and briefly visited St. Helena on his way back in 1656. While walking near Chappell Valley, he encountered a large, injured creature on the beach. He described it as having a lion-like appearance with four prominent teeth. Despite differing opinions on its identity, Mundy called it a "sea lioness" and estimated its length to be ten feet. He documented the encounter in his journal, which included a sketch of the animal.

Beastly Evidence

You're History! Historical records from St. Helena indicate various sightings and captures of creatures called "sea cows" or manatees. Mentions of these creatures date back to the late 17th century. Notably, in 1691, a sea cow was reported in Windward just before a traveller's visit, with descriptions suggesting they resembled sea lions rather than true manatees, primarily due to their rocky shore habitat with no freshwater sources available. The last confirmed sighting occurred in 1810 when a creature was shot at Stone Top Valley beach, leading to debates among observers about its true identity. Some identified it as a sea lion, while others claimed it was a manatee.

A Supposed Sirenian? Scientific interest in these alleged manatees culminated in a study analysing conflicting reports. The conclusion was that the St. Helena "manatee" was a sea lion, specifically the Cape fur seal. This conclusion reflects a general scepticism surrounding the presence of manatees in the region, primarily based on descriptions provided by early observers. Researchers suggested that the enigmatic sea cows of St. Helena were misidentified marine mammals rather than true sirenians, shaping the narrative surrounding these mysterious creatures in the island's history.

Beastly Theories!

A Monster Imposter: Sirenian creatures, such as manatees and dugongs, have long been linked to mermaid sightings in cryptozoological lore. Notable claims involve the survival of the extinct Steller's sea cow, sightings of dugongs in New Guinea, and the possibility of undiscovered species in West Africa. Historical accounts of the three known manatee species—Amazon, Caribbean, and African—indicate that manatees were present around St. Helena, particularly in Manatee Bay. This leads to intriguing speculation that sightings of a "St. Helena Manatee" might have involved known species observed in distress, leading to misidentification or exaggerated accounts of their existence.

The South African Fur Seal: This easily recognizable seal is known for its distinctive appearance. With a robust body and a thick layer of fur, it is well-adapted to the cold waters of the Atlantic and Indian Oceans. These seals are nonmigratory, primarily staying close to the coasts of South Africa and Namibia, where they can often be seen basking on rocks and beaches. Due to their agile swimming abilities and playful nature, they may sometimes be mistaken for other marine mammals, such as the St. Helena Manatee, especially during casual observations. The manatee, being a large, slow-moving herbivore, has a more rounded body shape. However, both species share the same habitat in coastal regions, which can confuse casual observers, particularly since they coexist in the same waters around St. Helena.

A Southern Stowaway: The elephant seal species is the largest of its kind and is occasionally spotted around the remote island of St. Helena. Known for their impressive size and distinctive features, including large snouts and thick, wrinkled skin, these seals are more migratory than their South African counterparts, travelling thousands of miles for breeding and feeding. While primarily found in the Southern Hemisphere, their sporadic presence in St. Helena adds an element of intrigue, especially when viewed alongside the St. Helena Manatee. The significant size difference can mislead people into thinking they are seeing the manatee, particularly since both species might be observed swimming in the same coastal waters. The adaptations of elephant seals for diving may also lead them to interact with manatees, resulting in a blend of marine life that could confuse untrained observers. Their occasional presence could further contribute to misconceptions among locals and tourists unfamiliar with the diverse marine wildlife of the region.

STELLER'S SEA COW

What's in a Name? Steller's sea cow, or '*Hydrodamalis gigas*', is named after the naturalist Georg Wilhelm Steller, who found the species in 1741 near the Commander Islands in the North Pacific Ocean. In Russian, it is called "Kapustnik," which means "cabbage-eater," because it eats plants.

Monstrous Measurements: This Sirenian was a large marine animal that measured 20 to 26 feet long and weighed up to 22,000 pounds. It had a strong, round body covered in tough, dark brown skin. Its small head and unique tail shape helped it adapt to life in the water.

Beastly Behaviours: Steller's sea cow was a large, gentle animal that lived in the sea. It spent about four to five minutes underwater searching for food. This creature only ate plants, mostly seaweed like kelp and sea kale. It sometimes floated on its back while sleeping on the water's surface. Sadly, its easily accessible meat made it a target for hunters, which led to its quick decline and eventual extinction.

Deadly Diet: Its diet included different types of seaweed, making it a calm herbivore.

Watery Abode: It lived around the Gulf of Anadyr in Siberia, the Commander Islands in the Bering Sea, and Attu in Alaska. During the Pleistocene era, it had a larger range that stretched from Japan to Baja California, showing how well it could adapt to different marine environments.

Scary Sightings

1741: German naturalist Georg Wilhelm Steller discovered Steller's sea cow when he was shipwrecked on Ostrov Bering in the Commander Islands off Siberia.

1743-1763: Fur hunters regularly visited the Commander Islands, hunting Steller's sea cows for their meat, which was noted to be tasty.

1768: Steller's sea cow was declared extinct.

1770s: A. E. Nordenskiöld interviewed residents of Bering Island who claimed that sea cows were still being killed and consumed.

1830: Polish naturalist Benedykt Dybowski agreed that sea cows survived off Bering Island until at least this year.

1854: Two natives, Merchenin and Stepnoff, saw a sea cow spouting water from its mouth in the ocean.

1850s: Lucien Turner interviewed an Aleut woman whose father had seen sea cows off Attu in the Aleutian Islands, Alaska.

1890: A sea cow was allegedly stranded on the shore of the Gulf of Anadyr, Siberia.

Early 1950s: A harpooner named Ivan Skripkin described observing finless, 32-foot-long animals appearing each July near Bering Island.

1962: The crew of the Russian whaler *Buran* observed six dark-skinned marine animals, measuring 20-26 feet long, feeding in a lagoon near Cape Navarin, Chukot Autonomous Province, Siberia.

1976: Russian fisherman Ivan Nikiforovich Chechulin claimed to have approached and touched a live sea cow at south of Cape Navarin. The animal had a whale-like length and a long snout.

Beastly Evidence

Remains of the Day: Preserved remains of Steller's sea cows can be found in various museums worldwide. These include complete, partial, or composite skeletons, skulls, and isolated bones such as limb bones, vertebrae, and ribs. Some museums also claim to have scraps of preserved skin from this species. However, some experts argue these scraps may come from seals or whales.

One piece is at the Überseemuseum in Bremen, Germany. A Zoological Museum held a second piece, which may have been destroyed during World War II and is believed to have been misidentified as whale skin. A third piece is at the Zoological Institute of the Academy of Sciences in St. Petersburg, Russia, and is also thought to be a whale skin fragment found by A. Brandt. It is important to note that no museum or scientific institution claims to have a complete torso skin from a Steller's sea cow.

A 'Huge' Stamp of Approval! Steller's sea cow is depicted on a postage stamp from Russia's Commander Islands, a group in the Bering Sea, where this massive sea mammal once thrived.

Beastly Theories!

A Late Extinction? Evidence of Steller's sea cow comes from explorers, hunters, and locals who reported encounters. Officially extinct in 1768, it was discovered by naturalist Georg Wilhelm Steller in 1741. As a member of the Sirenia family, it grazed on kelp and sea kale but faced extinction due to hunting for its meat and skin. While most believe it was extinct by 1768, A. E. Nordenskiöld suggested it may have survived for an additional ninety years in the Commander Islands. The species was the largest known sirenian and was quickly hunted to extinction. Although there have been unconfirmed reports of large sea creatures that could be surviving sea cows, these may instead be misidentified narwhals or elephant seals.

An Oversized Elephant? In 1976, someone might have seen a wandering northern elephant seal that had strayed from its migration to the Gulf of Alaska. The elephant seal species is the largest of its kind and is known for its impressive size and distinctive features, including large snouts and thick, wrinkled skin. It would not be outside the realms of possibility for a large elephant seal to be mistaken for a Sirenian. Although, it hardly makes sense that any local hunters or fisherman would make this leap considering the common occurrence of large pinnipeds throughout this region.

THE RI

What's in a Name? The creature known as the Ri, or Ilkai, is an unidentified marine mammal recognised by various names in local dialects. The Barok people call it "ah ree," while the Susurunga community uses "Ilkai." Additionally, it is known as Pishmeri in Pidgin, meaning "fish-woman." These names reflect the cultural significance and awareness of the creature among the indigenous people of New Ireland, Papua New Guinea.

Monstrous Measurements: This marine mammal is characterised by a horizontal bilobate tail measuring 15 to 20 feet long and lacking a dorsal fin. It has a dark or light-brown body, measuring 5-7 feet, featuring a human-like head with long hair, frontal eyes, a protruding mouth, and fused arms at the sides. Females possess breasts, and their palms are ridged with long, sharp fingernails. The lower trunk ends with flippers, and its internal fat is yellow.

Terrifying Tracks: Unknown.

Beastly Behaviours: Often recognised by its large vertical swimming movements, which distinguish it from dugongs. It exhibits a social structure, with males, females, and juveniles often swimming together. Local fishermen report observing the ri mating in the surf and entering freshwater streams at night. It swims horizontally and can hold its breath for approximately ten minutes. The ri communicates through whistles and a cry resembling a human's expression of fear. It often rests on sandbars, where Barok fishermen may catch and consume it. This species primarily inhabits the water, leaving only occasionally to sunbathe on sandbars.

Deadly Diet: This creature can be seen hunting fish in shallow waters.

Watery Abode: Commonly found in the Bismarck Sea and the Solomon Sea, especially along the central and southern shores of New Ireland and between Buka and Bougainville islands. Sightings have also been reported near Manus Island and the northern coast of New Guinea and in shallow coastal waters around New Ireland, Lihir Island, and the Solomon Islands.

Scary Sightings

1973-1974: Gary Opit lived among Indigenous communities in New Guinea while studying the local flora and fauna. During his travels on the *Papuan Explorer*, a vessel transporting cargo along the northern coast, he observed a brown, round head resembling a human's on the water's surface on October 3. As the ship approached, the creature submerged gracefully. Opit noted that its elongated body was slim, unlike the bulky form of a dugong, which he had observed before. He was intrigued by its descent, as it dove tail-first, leaving him uncertain about its true identity.

1979: Anthropologist Roy Wagner observed a long, dark-bodied creature swimming along the surface of Ramat Bay, New Ireland. The animal quickly disappeared when a sawfish leapt from the water nearby.

1983: Wagner, alongside Gale Raymond and Richard Greenwell, spotted a ri from a distance in Elizabeth Bay, New Ireland. The animal surfaced briefly at ten-minute intervals but attempts to capture it with a net were unsuccessful. Members from the expedition noted glimpses of the creature on multiple occasions.

1985: Members of an expedition led by Thomas Williams and sponsored by the Ecosophical Research Association observed a ri from their diving ship, *Reef Explorer*—a local identified the creature as an ilkai. Captain Kerry Piesch entered the water with scuba gear and photographed a greenish-grey animal that measured around five feet and displayed graceful underwater movements. Subsequent observations led the team to conclude they were viewing dugongs. However, on February 15, they witnessed villagers removing a large dugong from the water, further confirming its presence in the area.

Beastly Evidence

The Wagner Expedition: Roy Wagner, an anthropologist, documented cultural awareness of the ri between 1979 and 1980. He collected testimonies that described its unique characteristics, including a long, dark body and front-facing eyes. Fishermen reported sightings of the ri near the Bismarck Sea and the Solomon Sea, where it was observed hunting fish in shallow waters. In 1983, Wagner and his research team conducted further investigations, confirming the animal was historically well-known and culturally significant to local communities. They noted its peculiar morphology, including a lack of a "dorsal "and unique swimming behaviour, leading to the confusion that the ri is a biologically distinct species.

Beastly Theories!

A Dodgy Dugong!? The ri, as reported by the Indigenous population of New Ireland, may represent an undiscovered species related to the dugong rather than a mere misidentification. Local narratives and consistent sightings suggest a significant cultural understanding of this marine creature, which lacks the dorsal fin typical of cetaceans, aligning more closely with Sirenian characteristics. While dugongs (*Dugong dugongs*) are known to inhabit the region, the physical distinctions noted by the indigenous people—such as a neck separating the head from the body and a narrower snout—warrant further investigation. Unlike dugongs exhibiting a streamlined body, the ri shows features suggesting it may not be a recognised species. Additionally, historical data indicates the dugong population's decline due to hunting and environmental stress, prompting potential migratory behaviour that could have led to unique local adaptations. Therefore, ongoing research could reveal that the ri is not just a variant of the dugong but a previously unidentified species that deserves attention in marine biology and cryptozoology.

What is a Fish? The concept of coverall names in ancient cultures suggests that "ri" could be a coverall term used by locals to describe various unusual animals. Just as Native Americans and people in the Tibetan plateau employ specific terms like "yeti" to categorise diverse wildlife, island residents may use "ri" to refer to different creatures with certain characteristics. This approach simplifies communication about unfamiliar animals, much like the English word "fish" encompasses everything from minnows to megamouth sharks. The text mentions specific animals like the finless porpoise and the southern rightwhale dolphin, which locals might classify under the term "ri" when encountering unique wildlife that lacks distinct names in their language.

MYSTIFYING MUSTELIDS

Def.

Cryptid mustelids are often described as large, otter-like mammals with four limbs. They inhabit both inland and marine waters and may represent undiscovered populations of species believed to be extinct or cryptids that have not yet been discovered.

IEMISCH

What's in a Name? The Iemisch, also known as the Iemisch Listai, is a creature from Patagonian folklore referred to as the "water tiger" in the Tehuelche language, a term also used for the marine otter. Its scientific name, *Neomylodon listai*, was established in 1898 based on fossils found in the Cueva del Milodón. In his work *The Mysterious Mammal of Patagonia*, Santiago Roth named it Iemisch Listai in 1899 after discovering a jaguar femur in the same cave. This creature is also known by several other names, such as: Chimchimen, Guarifilu, and Zorro-víbora.

Monstrous Measurements: The size of a puma, with a robust body, short legs, and a long, supple tail similar to an otter. It has a short, round head covered in coarse bay or dark brown fur, with a lighter ring around its eyes and no external ears. Its strong jaws feature large canine teeth, and its feet are plantigrade, with three webbed toes on the forefeet and four on the hind feet. It is described as larger than a puma, nocturnal, and amphibious, feared for its ability to drag horses into water with its claws.

Terrifying Tracks: Iemisch tracks resemble those of the jaguar.

Beastly Behaviours: Known for its burrowing habits and alarming tendency to seize and drown horses and humans from riverbanks, this carnivorous animal uses adept aquatic skills to hunt prey. Its capacity to seize and drown larger creatures indicates its predatory prowess, leading to local fears about its hunting abilities.

Deadly Diet: An opportunistic carnivore, it will take any prey, including humans, which ventures too close to its territory.

Watery Abode: The creature is believed to inhabit areas around Lago Colhué Huapi, Río Senguer, and Estancia Valle Huemeles in Chubut Province, Argentina, and extends into Santa Cruz Province and Aisén del General Carlos Ibáñez del Campo in Chile. Historically, its range included Río Negro Province to the eastern slopes of the Andes and the Straits of Magellan, living in caves and sheltered spots along lakes and river shores.

Scary Sightings

1848: An Iemisch was reported swimming down the Santa Cruz River, observed by the Tehuelche near Isla Pavón. Terrified, they fled inland, and the area was later called Iemisch-Aiken.

1870s: Ramón Lista encountered a large animal resembling a giant pangolin with hair instead of scales in Argentina's Santa Cruz Province. Bullets were ineffective against its tough skin.

1897: Florentino Ameghino claimed to have obtained a *Neomylodon* hide from an animal known as an Iemisch. His brother Carlos documented an encounter with a Tehuelche named Hompen, who allegedly killed an Iemisch with his bolas.

1900: French palaeontologist André Tournouër described an animal resembling a large puma spotted during his second Patagonian expedition. His guide referred to it as hymché.

1921: Martin Sheffield's family in Epuyén reported encounters with an Iemisch-like creature, which they described as a plesiosaur.

Sheffield's daughter Juana observed tracks and a large animal lying in the sun beside a lake.

1980s-1990s: Eloy Hutnik, a fisherman from Sarmiento, claimed to have seen a strange animal in Lake Colhué Huapí.

Beastly Evidence

A Scholarly Sabretooth? The Iemisch was first documented by Florentino Ameghino in 1897 and explored further in the 1955 book *On the Track of Unknown Animals*. It is a creature shrouded in myth and intrigue. According to follow-up research by Bernard Heuvelmans, local populations described the Iemisch as a blend of a jaguar and an otter, with reports indicating it could grow as large as an ox. Known as a "tigre d'acqua," the Iemisch was said to be equally agile in water and on land, accompanied by a "soul-wrenching scream." Additional studies by Robert Lehmann-Nitsche mentioned that he received a sample of the creature's skin from a rancher, which contained small bone plates believed to protect it from arrowheads. The sample was discovered near human remains, implying the creature may have been hunted.

Beastly Theories!

A Missing Mylodon: An undetermined species of giant ground sloth was identified from bones and tough, red-haired skin found in Cueva del Milodón in Chile, with some researchers suggesting it was the Iemisch. However, its amphibious and carnivorous characteristics do not match those of a terrestrial, herbivorous sloth. Mylodon remains date back to 13,000–8,600 years ago, indicating that sloths may have survived until around 3000 B.C. Criticism arose around the theory that Iemisch was a living ground sloth named *Neomylodon*, with some scientists proposing it might be a giant rodent instead. Many researchers questioned the existence of the Iemisch, viewing it as a myth, and argued that its traits contradicted those of a herbivorous ground sloth. Additionally, isotopic evidence from 2021 indicated that Mylodon may have scavenged meat, suggesting it was not strictly herbivorous.

An Otterly Ridiculous Hypothesis! An unidentified species of large otter or a surviving population of the Giant Otter (*Pteronura brasiliensis*) may explain accounts of the Iemisch. Some researchers suggest it was a giant otter, while others identify it as the marine otter (*Lontra felina*) or propose it as a unique species in southern Patagonia. Iemisch traits —like its amphibious lifestyle and long flat tail—are consistent with otters. Despite this, some believe it could be an unknown species related to the giant river otter, questioning its ferocity based on its nature. Investigations revealed scepticism about its existence due to a lack of native knowledge, and the term "Iemisch" does not align with recognised local languages.

A Forgotten Folktale: The tales of the Iemisch in Patagonia may stem from folk memories of jaguars that are now extinct in the region and from older big cat species whose bones were discovered by locals. The Pleistocene Magellanic jaguar, which once roamed southern Patagonia, and other prehistoric felids may have contributed to the Iemisch sightings. These sightings could reflect a blending of local lore and the uncovering of ancient fossils, leading to exaggerated stories of large, carnivorous animals in the area.

WAITOREKE

What's in a Name? The name "waitoreke" has unclear origins; Rev. Richard Taylor referred to it in the 1840s as "Waitoreke, otter" but noted it might be linked to seals. It's absent from Tregear's 1891 Māori dictionary and was deemed "ungrammatical" by Sir Peter Buck. Since European settlement, it has been called various names like "New Zealand otter" and "Māori otter." The Waitoreke (or variants like Waitoreki) is an otter/beaver-like cryptid believed to inhabit New Zealand.

Monstrous Measurements: Described as resembling a small otter or seal and is the size of a small badger, typically weighing between 15 to 25 pounds. Its pawprints are similar to those of a European otter, though smaller in size. This creature has brown fur, and some reports suggest it to be about the size of a cat, with short legs and a brownish coat.

Terrifying Tracks: Its tracks resemble those of a small otter.

Beastly Behaviours: Amphibious but primarily observed close to or in the water and said to shy away from humans.

Deadly Diet: Unknown; however, researchers suspect that, similar to the otter, it may feed on fish, small crustaceans, and other aquatic creatures.

Watery Abode: It is believed that this cryptid inhabits freshwater environments in the mountainous regions of New Zealand's South Island, particularly in its lakes and rivers.

Scary Sightings

1772: During his expedition in Dusky Sound, Captain Cook reported several crew members observed a "four-footed animal." The descriptions varied, but it was noted to be the size of a house cat, with short legs and a mouse like coloration. One sailor described it as having a bushy tail and resembling a jackal.

1840s: In interviews with Māori chief Tarawhatta, Walter Mantell documented further descriptions of the creature. According to these accounts, the animal measured about 2 feet from the nose to the base of the tail, featuring grisly brown fur, thick short legs, a bushy tail, and a head resembling a mix between that of a dog and a cat.

1855: Reverend Richard Taylor, in his book *New Zealand and Its Inhabitants*, mentioned the creature known as the Waitoreke, contributing to the ongoing discourse about its existence.

1864: Captain Frederick Hutton speculated that the creature observed in Dusky Bay might have been a type of dog. He noted that the crew had not encountered dogs in New Zealand at that time and referenced footprints attributed to an otter-like animal.

20th Century: Sightings of the Waitoreke persisted into the 20th century among settlers, farmers, trampers, hunters, and tourists, reinforcing the creature's mystery. Philip Houghton described a sighting near Martins Bay: "I saw it for three or four seconds, enough to get a good glimpse. It was a medium brown furred animal, about the size of a hare, but with different proportions and movement. Its body was solid with a small head that blended into the body. The hind part was larger than the front, and the legs seemed small compared to the body. The tail was long and tapered."

Beastly Evidence

Evidence That Can Be 'Pelt': Physical evidence for the existence of the waitoreke remains elusive. Julius von Haast obtained a pelt in 1868, which was notable for its brown fur with white spots and the absence of webbing between the toes. This inconclusive evidence resembles the fur of a quoll, raising questions about its true identity. The lack of more definitive specimens or remains has made it challenging to confirm the waitoreke's existence. Although introduced marsupials like the common brushtail possum have thrived in New Zealand since their introduction in 1858, efforts to introduce quolls and similar species have failed, suggesting that additional research into the possible relatives of the waitoreke might be required.

A Mini Monster Expedition? Despite the scant physical evidence, numerous sightings of the Waitoreke have fuelled interest in its existence. Reports dating back to the 1970s, particularly in papers by G. A. Pollock from 1970 and 1974, examined various sightings and led to a search of the area surrounding lakes Waihola and Waipori in Otago during the 1980s. These sightings often described the waitoreke residing in inland lakes and rivers, though definitive proof remains absent.

Beastly Theories!

A Colonial Cryptid! Since European settlement in the late 18th century, the animal has been mistakenly called the "New Zealand otter," "Māori otter," and others based on various theories. It is said to resemble a small badger and has pawprints similar to the European otter, though smaller. New Zealand's only endemic land mammals are bats. The land mammals introduced by early Polynesian and

European settlers include the kurī (dog) and kiore (rat). Importantly, otters are mammals and belong to the *Mustelidae* family, not marsupials.

Let's Get to Know an 'Otter! Could this creature be an introduced mustelid, a small population that never fully established itself but still endures, suffering from dwarfism due to a lack of genetic variability that has forced it into a bottleneck? Are modern sightings merely remnants of stragglers, left behind and slowly dwindling in number before reaching their inevitable extinction?

DOBHAR CHU

What's in a Name? The name "Dobharchú" is derived from the Irish word for "otter" and is linked to a mythical "king otter" in County Leitrim. The Eurasian otter is commonly referred to as "madra usice," meaning "water hound." Other names for this creature include Anchu, Dhuraghoo, Dorraghow, Doyarchu, King Otter, and Master Otter.

Monstrous Measurements: It looks like an otter but is much larger, about 10 to 15 feet long. It has a unique white coat with black tips on its ears and a black cross on its back, which makes it look quite fearsome.

Terrifying Tracks: The Dobharchú leaves behind large, clawed tracks, indicative of its massive size.

Beastly Behaviours: This creature is dangerous and aggressive. You can hear it coming by a unique whistling sound. It has a strong snout that can break rocks easily.

Deadly Diet: Believed to prey on fish and other smaller animals in its habitat, it may occasionally attempt to prey on humans.

Watery Abode: The Dobhar-chú is primarily reported in County Leitrim, Ireland, especially near freshwater lakes and rivers.

Scary Sightings

1722: A notable sighting reported the death of Grace (or Grainne) Connolly, who was allegedly killed by the Dobharchú while washing clothes at Glenade Lough in County Leitrim. Her grave featured an engraving of an unknown otter-like creature commonly believed to be the Dobhar Chu.

1968: Two local men were driving past Glenade Lough when they witnessed a creature that was dark-brown or black, estimated to be around 2.5 ft tall and 8-10 ft long, with a lengthy neck and tail.

1968: A similar creature was observed by a 15-year-old cyclist, who described it as larger than a horse, black in color, with a sheep-like head, long neck, tail, and four legs.

1999-2000: Near Portumna in County Galway, an unfamiliar animal resembling a larger, darker otter was spotted crossing the road.

2001: An otter-like creature was claimed to have been recently encountered during a debate on *Radio na Gaeltachta*.

2003: On Omey Island in Connemara, a sighting involved an animal that was larger than a Labrador, dark in colour, with orange-red flipper-like feet, which was seen swimming across Fahy Lough.

2009: Details were provided about a sighting on Omey Island, which included observations of strange yelping from the sand dunes near Fahy Lough.

Beastly Evidence

Otterly Incomprehensible: In April 1999, cryptozoologist and author, Gary Cunningham, noticed a large taxidermied otter at Hynes Pub in Cross Molina, County Mayo, which measured about 4.5 feet long and featured an unusually elongated form with a lengthy neck, longer hind limbs, and a bushy tail, diverging from typical otter characteristics. Its dark, almost black fur caught his attention, raising comparisons to the Dobhar-chú depicted on Grace Connolly's gravestone. Despite being aware that taxidermy can distort features, Gary felt the distinctiveness of this specimen could not be easily dismissed.

Beastly Theories!

The Seal Serpent Theory: There are several theories about the Dobharchú, one of which is the "Seal Serpent Theory" by Gary Cunningham and Rob Cornes. This theory suggests that many lake monsters in Ireland could actually be sea lions that have entered freshwater lakes through connected waterways. These large, otter-like creatures, when spotted by locals, can spark fear and contribute to the lasting monster myths in the region. Each sighting tends to exaggerate over time, creating more fantastical tales.

A Super Otter? The "super-otter" is a theorized creature that resembles a large, elongated seal and can reach lengths of 20 to 30 feet. This hypothetical animal is believed to undulate vertically and is primarily seen in the glacial Arctic regions during the summer, especially around Norway and Greenland. It is characterized by a tail as long as its body, a flattened head, and four webbed paws, with a brownish-gray coloration reminiscent of a walrus. The super-otter is known to make a puffing sound through nostrils located at the end of its snout. It is well-adapted to cold waters, surfacing only at temperatures between -5°C and +5°C, although it may reproduce in warmer conditions, as younger individuals have a lower tolerance for cold. With the last confirmed sighting recorded in 1848, its current existence remains uncertain.

Monster Morale: One well-known folklore monster that serves as a warning for staying away from deep water is the "Selkie." In Irish and Scottish legends, Selkies are shapeshifting creatures that look like seals in the water but can become human on land. Tales often tell of Selkies luring people into the sea with their enchanting songs.

These stories aim to keep kids safe by warning them about the dangers of deep water. Parents might tell their children that if they venture too close to the ocean or a deep lake, a Selkie could pull them in, never to return. This way, the myth acts as both a cautionary tale and an explanation for tragic water-related deaths, suggesting that mysterious creatures are behind the dangers that can lurk beneath the surface.

AHUIZOTL

What's in a Name? The term "Ahuitzotl" comes from Nahuatl, a Uto-Aztecan language, meaning "spiny aquatic thing" or "water dog." This naming refers to the way its fur tends to spike up when wet. Additionally, the name is associated with a mythological Aztec water monster known for luring people to their deaths. The name Ahuitzotl also serves as the mascot and namesake of a famous Aztec ruler, who was a renowned military leader and the uncle of Moctezuma II. This ruler would later face the Spanish Conquistador Hernan Cortés when he entered the kingdom.

Monstrous Measurements: The Ahuitzotl is an animal that resembles a small dog. It has a smooth black coat, small, pointed ears, and paws similar to those of a raccoon. A bony spur protrudes from underneath its tail, which ends in a tip that resembles a human hand. Overall, the Ahuitzotl has an otter-like appearance, combined with various unique features that contribute to its classification as a cryptid.

Terrifying Tracks: Resembling a raccoon or otter in appearance.

Beastly Behaviours: This amphibious animal mimics the sound of a baby crying to lure people to the water's edge, wherein it uses the hand-like appendage on the end of its tail to drag them beneath the surface and feast on their eyes, nails, and teeth. The Ahuizotl is known to cause fish and frogs in the river to jump frantically to the surface, drawing curious fishermen to the water's edge. Some rarer local tales suggest that this creature can even sink boats, a legend that continues to inspire local fishermen to appease the creature with offerings of fish to this day.

Deadly Diet: Fish, frogs, and any hapless humans that it can lure to the riverbank using its baby-like cry.

Watery Abode: Thought to have previously lived in the deep pools and caves near the location of the old Lake Texcoco in Mexico.

Scary Sightings

A Cryptid Conquistador! There haven't been any recent sightings of the Ahuizotl, but historical accounts mention that the conquistador Hernán Cortés informed the King of Castile about an incident involving one of his men being killed by this creature.

Beastly Evidence

A Monster Manuscript: The Ahuizotl is described in Book II of the *Florentine Codex*, a 16th-century ethnographic work on Mesoamerica by the Spanish Franciscan friar Bernardino de Sahagún. According to Sahagún, the Ahuizotl is "very similar to the teui, a small teui dog; it is diminutive and smooth, with glossy black fur that resembles rubber. The creature has small, pointed ears like those of a small dog, is slippery and sleek, and possesses a long tail. At the tip of its tail is a hand that resembles a human hand, while its actual hands are similar to those of a raccoon or a monkey."

Beastly Theories

Otterly Ridiculous! The Neotropical otter, while widely distributed, is now quite rare. Could sightings of this elusive animal have inspired the legends of the Ahuizotl? Despite some physical resemblances, it's unlikely that this otter is the basis for such tales, as it is not aggressive and lacks a prehensile tail. Furthermore, since the Aztecs called this species Aitzcuintli, it's highly improbable that they would confuse it with the mythical Ahuizotl.

A Cultural Cryptid? Many countries have legends about mysterious, otter-like creatures, such as Ireland's Dobhar Chu and New Zealand's Waitoreke. These stories might originate from real, undiscovered animals, but they also play significant cultural roles. For instance, the Aztecs viewed the Ahuizotl as a guardian of lakes and fish, believed to be sent by the gods to assist drowning victims in finding peace. There were strict burial rules for these victims, with only priests allowed to handle their remains. They were typically buried in a house situated on an island surrounded by water. The Ahuizotl is thought to be related to a water opossum, which may have experienced some form of religious deification or zoolatry.

LAKE TANGINYIKA MONSTER

What's in a Name? Named after Lake Tanganyika in which it is said to reside.

Monstrous Measurements: This creature measures about 164 to 197 feet long and has six loops, each around 15 feet long and 10 feet wide, totalling about 35 meters. It has a stiff, bright brown fleece and a pointed muzzle. Near its head, there are two small fins, but it doesn't have paws or true fins. Its large body tapers toward the tail but mostly stays the same thickness along most of its length.

Terrifying Tracks: It leaves tracks the size of an elephant, featuring two gigantic claws similar to those of a large bird, along the sandy banks of the lake.

Beastly Behaviours: The creature exhibits unusual vertical swimming patterns, particular to an aquatic mammal, swiftly undulating through the water. Local lore suggests it appears once every five years, terrifying nearby residents, who believe that it has a taste for human flesh, particularly that of fishermen.

Deadly Diet: Although there are many fish species in the lake, and local superstition suggests this creature is a man-eater, it has never been observed preying on anything.

Watery Abode: The creature has been reported in Lake Tanganyika, which borders Burundi, the Democratic Republic of the Congo, Zambia, and especially along the western frontier of Tanzania

Scary Sightings

_1893:_ The first documented sighting of a lake monster in Lake Tanganyika occurred when Joseph Augustus Moloney of the Stairs Expedition reported that an Mpala missionary claimed to have seen a 30-foot "sea serpent" on two occasions—once in the lake and once resting on the shore.

_1907:_ Naturalist Lord Walter Rothschild shared accounts from an English officer of the South African police who reported seeing an amphibious creature with tusks in the southern part of Lake Tanganyika. This creature, often described with tusks or fangs, has been linked to the legendary water lions or unknown proboscideans.

_1914:_ Reports continued as a German doctor, M. V. Thierfelder, working during a sleeping sickness epidemic, encountered the lake monster while hunting. Along with a local teacher named and an African boy, Thierfelder trekked near a bay of Lake Tanganyika. He described seeing a creature resembling a monstrous serpent, moving with a unique vertical undulating motion instead of the typical horizontal swimming pattern of snakes. Thierfelder observed six loops of the creature rising from the water, estimating its length to be around fifty meters (111-168 feet), with each loop measuring approximately four and a half meters (13 feet) long and three meters (9 feet) in diameter. The creature was covered in a thick brown fleece and had fin-like structures near its head.

_1928:_ German reports indicated that ships had spotted a "saurian" on Lake Tanganyika, initially mistaken for an island until it dived. The report included findings of mysterious tracks on the lakeshore resembling those of a gigantic bird, much larger than elephant tracks, alongside a dragging trail indicating a thick tail.

Beastly Evidence

A Big Bird? Reports from 1928 described mysterious tracks left by a "saurian" creature. Witnesses noted seeing tracks with two gigantic claws reminiscent of those of a large bird, dwarfing even elephant footprints, alongside drag marks of a hefty tail. Nevertheless, it's essential to consider that these accounts could be influenced by colonial tall tales, which were often used to entertain and captivate audiences back home.

A 5-Year Critter: Over the years, witnesses have reported rare sightings of a monster, believed to appear every five years. During the colonial era, the German government even offered a reward for a "freshwater shark" said to inhabit the lake. Legends of "great fish" that devour canoes have further enhanced their mythological character.

Beastly Theories!

A Super Otter: The "super-otter" is a theorised creature that resembles a large, elongated seal and can reach lengths of 20 to 30 feet. This hypothetical animal is believed to undulate vertically and is primarily seen in the glacial Arctic regions during the summer, especially around Norway and Greenland. It is characterised by a tail as long as its body, a flattened head, and four webbed paws, with a brownish-grey colouration reminiscent of a walrus. The super-otter is known to make a puffing sound through nostrils located at the end of its snout. It is well-adapted to cold waters, surfacing only at temperatures between -5 °C and +5°C, although it may reproduce in warmer conditions, as younger individuals have a lower tolerance for cold. With the last confirmed sighting recorded in 1848, its current existence remains uncertain. However, if such a creature does exist, it is outside of its normal hypothetical habitat in Lake Tanganyika.

A Throwback Cetacean: The Lake Tanganyika monster, often described through anecdotal reports and local legends, could represent a surviving form of an ancient elongate whale species that adapted to freshwater environments. This hypothesis suggests that a population of these elongated marine mammals might have found refuge in Lake Tanganyika, evolving unique traits suited for its specific ecosystem. Over millennia, these creatures could have developed distinct characteristics to navigate the lake's deep waters and diverse habitats, while still retaining some of the ancestral features of their marine relatives.

A Giant Otter: The creature is a large otter or a group of otters. Its flexible body and undulating tail resemble those of known otters, which could explain reports of humps in the water. Although described as much larger, giant river otters can grow up to 6 feet in length. Additionally, the woolly fur observed in Lake Tanganyika's monster, similar to that of sea otters, suggests it may be a large otter species misidentified as an unknown creature. Observations of giant river otters display group behaviour, which could also account for sightings of a larger creature.

THE BEAST OF BODALOG

What's in a Name? The beast was named after the Bodalog farm where it was seen: the Bodalog Family Farm, near Rhayader, in mid-Wales. Due to its peculiar method of leaving its victims' bodies intact, save for two puncture wounds in their necks or sternum, some local media outlets also gave it the monstrous moniker of "The Welsh Water Vampire."

Monstrous Measurements: The Beast of Bodalog is a semi-mythical Welsh water vampire described as limbless, serpentine, or wormlike. It has two prominent fangs, which it uses to drain blood.

Terrifying Tracks: Leaves long flattened furrows or corridors in the grass that appear like a large serpent has left them.

Beastly Behaviours: This mysterious monster is wholly nocturnal and amphibious, preferring to lie hidden in the river by day, only slithering onto shore after dark to prey upon cattle grazing in the fields (preferably sheep), which it kills by sinking its fangs into their neck or sternum and draining them of their lifeblood. Evidence of the animal's nightly depredations can usually be seen in the corridors of the flattened ground it leaves, showing its passage from the river and a litter of intact cattle cadavers strewn about its path back from the fields.

Deadly Diet: Prefers to drink the blood of sheep, which it drains via making puncture wounds in the neck or sternum.

Hairy Habitat: Reputed to stalk the River Wye, especially those areas close to the Bodalog Family Farm, near Rhayader, the oldest town in Mid-Wales.

Scary Sightings

1988: The beast's presence was first felt between September and December 1988, when several farms in the area reported mysterious sheep deaths. The animals, initially appearing intact, were later found to all share a common fang-like puncture wound in either their throats or sternums, where their blood had been drained, vampire-like, by a stealthy unknown predator. By mid-October 1988, many more sheep had been lost, with the Bodalog Farm, owned by the Pugh family, losing forty sheep to the beast. These inexplicable events understandably led to local conspiracy theories, including a police cover-up and the rumour that a vampire had taken up residence in the area. Finally, they culminated in an organised hunt for the beast, led by armed villagers and a pack of experienced fox hounds, who tracked the scent of this sanguinivorous serpent back to the river's edge.

Beastly Evidence

Waste Not Want Not! Numerous sheep carcasses were discovered on the Bodalog Family Farm, exhibiting puncture wounds in both the sternum and throat regions. Additionally, large, elongated furrows were observed between the farm and the River Wye. As of mid-October, an unidentified animal was reported to have killed at least 35 sheep. Foxhounds tracked its scent back to the river; however, the animal was not observed, and no identifiable pawprints were found.

The *Daily Mail* reported on 10 October 1988 that various hypotheses were proposed regarding the creature's identity, including potential involvement from species such as otters, dogs, minks, and snakes. University scientists who examined the sheep carcasses stated they could not determine which animal could have caused the puncture marks.

Beastly Theories!

Big Cat Bonanza: Since The Dangerous Wild Animals Act of 1976, sightings of large predatory cats, like melanistic leopards, have become common in Britain. Initial attacks were believed to be from a juvenile cat honing its skills, but this theory changed when long furrows were found leading from the river to the sheep kills. The frantic behaviour of foxhounds, which followed the scent to the banks of the River Wye, further confirmed the presence of a larger predator.

An Ancient Beast Beavering About! Wales has its water monster mythology, with the Afanc or Addanc being one of the most notable. This creature, which can appear as a crocodile, beaver, serpent, dwarf, or demon, plays a part in Welsh legends, including those of King Arthur and Merlin. The term Afanc broadly refers to any unidentified monstrous or malevolent being. Some speculate that the Afanc may have been a real creature, a rare remnant population that survived into the Middle Ages. The River Wye, stretching 155 miles and offering ample food and shelter, might occasionally host such an ocean-going visitor. Legends suggest that people near the River Wye once made annual human sacrifices to appease a giant worm in the river. Could this long-lived creature have reappeared in 1988, angered by the lack of tribute, and affected local livestock?

Secret Snakes: Britain has two native snake species: the venomous adder and the grass snake, neither of which can prey on sheep. The Aesculapian snake, a non-native species, also doesn't pose a threat. This suggests that large constrictors like boas, pythons, and anacondas could be responsible for the flattened furrows near the sheep corpses. However, since none of the sheep were consumed, these large snakes are not the culprits. There is also the draining of the animal blood, something that a large constrictor would not do, as these snakes consume their prey whole.

STRANGE CETACEANS

Def.

Strange Cetaceans refer to whales and dolphins that science has not formally recognised. Reports of these creatures emerge from all the world's oceans, particularly in the Antarctic and Pacific regions. Their existence is often supported by anecdotal evidence, with many encounters describing creatures that seem to be unfamiliar varieties of well-known species.

ALULA WHALE

What's in a Name? The name Alula is an alternate designation for Caluula, a village located on the Gulf of Aden in Somalia. Donald S. Heintzelman assigned the species the scientific name *Orcinus mörzer-bruynsus* in his 1981 publication, *A World Guide to Whales, Dolphins and Porpoises.*

Monstrous Measurements: The Alula resembles a sepia-brown killer whale, measuring 20 to 24 feet long and weighing an estimated 1.8 to 2 tons. Its high, rounded forehead characterizes it, and its body features white, star-shaped scars, which are often attributed to interactions with giant cephalopods. The dorsal fin reaches about 2 feet in height, comparable to that of a female killer whale, and no significant sexual dimorphism is observed. The head shape resembles that of a pilot whale, featuring a small snout.

Beastly Behaviours: They are reported to reach a cruising speed of 4 knots and travel in groups of 4 to 6 individuals.

Deadly Diet: This species is believed to prey on large squid, as evidenced by the presence of star-shaped scars on its body. Additionally, similar to its killer whale relatives, smaller cetaceans, such as dolphins, may also be part of its diet.

Watery Abode: Reports indicate their presence in the deep coastal waters from the eastern Gulf of Aden to Socotra, with sightings most frequently recorded in April, May, June, and September.

Scary Sightings

Before 1971: The Alula whale was initially documented by W. F. J. Mörzer Bruyns, a naval officer and historian. Throughout his voyages, he claimed to have encountered several unidentified cetaceans. Without a field guide during his tenure as a captain, he published his own *Field Guide of Whales and Dolphins* in 1971, which featured accounts of the cryptic cetaceans he had observed. Mörzer Bruyns witnessed pods of the Alula whale on several occasions in the deep coastal waters of the eastern Gulf of Aden, north of Caluula in Somalia. He recounted that a group of four swam directly toward the vessel during their first encounter. Observing the dorsal fins, he initially assumed they were *Orcinus orca*. However, once they passed the ship at less than 50 yards beneath the surface in the tranquil, clear waters, it became clear they belonged to a different species. He remarked that the dolphins exhibited indifference toward the vessel, neither altering their path nor diving. He sighted them during crossings in April, May, June, and September, typically swimming just beneath the surface with their dorsal fins visible above the water. One duty officer noted witnessing them pursue a group of smaller dolphins trying to flee, but he indicated that both species might have been aiming for the same prey.

8 May 1987: The *SS ACT 1*, commanded by Captain J. F. Rowe, documented a sighting of what they believed to be the Alula whale in the 1988 edition of the *Marine Observer* publication. 2nd Officer A. Tibbott made an observation while the vessel was navigating the Indian Ocean during its passage from Fremantle to Suez. He reported that at 0645 GMT, a dark-brown whale exhibiting a prominent dorsal fin was spotted from the front, swimming just beneath the surface, approximately 100 meters ahead of the ship. When it came within 40 meters, it evaded by diving, keeping its flukes submerged the entire time. No spout was visible, and while a definitive identification could not be made, he indicated that the distinctive dorsal fin and dark-brown colouration pointed towards this being an Alula whale.

Beastly Evidence

Fisherman's Tails: No physical or photographic evidence of the Alula Whale has been obtained; however, the accounts of a naval officer and sea captain provide substantial testimony. In recent years, several previously unknown cetacean species have been identified, highlighting the challenges of confirming species due to the vastness of the ocean, which serves as a refuge for these undiscovered, intelligent, sonar-equipped cetaceans.

Beastly Theories!

Algae Accumulation: One explanation for the sightings of the Alula Whale is that its distinct brown colouration results from an accumulation of diatoms on its skin. Diatoms are microscopic algae that cling to surfaces in marine environments, and their growth can lead to skin discolouration. This phenomenon has been observed in Antarctic Killer Whales, which live in cold waters where shedding skin occurs more slowly, allowing for a greater buildup of these organisms. In warmer waters, like those of the Arabian Sea where the Alula Whale is reported, the conditions would typically not support such an accumulation, raising questions about this rationale's relevance to the Alula Whale.

Variety is the Spice of Life! Another theory suggests that the Alula Whale might represent a unique colour variant of the Killer Whale (*Orcinus orca*). Variations in pigmentation are common in cetacean species, leading to distinct phenotypes within the same species. This explanation could also encompass the possibility that what has been classified as the Alula Whale may instead be misidentified as False Killer Whales (*Pseudorca crassidens*) or Pilot Whales (*Globicephala spp.*). These species are known for their social behaviour and can exhibit similar characteristics, making accurate identification challenging.

War Wounds! Some researchers propose that the star-like markings observed on the Alula Whale might not be a natural colouration pattern. Instead, they could be scarred due to interactions with their prey, such as squid or other cetaceans. These markings may resemble distinct patterns but could indicate past encounters or attacks, suggesting a more complex ecological interaction. Such scars are common in species that prey upon aggressive marine life.

DIMORPHIC BEAKED WHALE

What's in a Name? It refers to its two distinct colour forms. The scientific name is Mesoplodon species A. The common name is Unidentified beaked whale.

Monstrous Measurements: This beaked whale ranges from 16-18 feet in length, featuring a long beak, flat head, and low triangular dorsal fin. Males have a white swath, reddish-brown heads, and dark flanks, while females are grey-brown. Two colour morphs exist: uniform grey-brown and black-and-white, with the latter being larger and scarred. Their appearance includes white markings that develop with age. This species belongs to the family *Ziphiidae*, noted for its distinctive features and is documented in photographs.

Beastly Behaviours: Typically observed moving in tight groups at a moderate pace.

Deadly Diet: Feeds on squid and other cephalopods.

Watery Abode: Found in the Eastern Pacific Ocean from central Mexico to Peru, favouring deep water. Observed off Mexico, Panama, and Peru, as well as in the open ocean.

Scary Sightings

Various Dates: In approximately sixty-five instances, the dimorphic beaked whale has been spotted at sea.

Beastly Evidence

Film & Photography: A set of aerial photographs was captured by a helicopter in November 1999. Shortly afterwards, during a marine mammal identification course led by Aguayo and Urbán in Bahia de Banderas, Jalisco, participants P. Hernández and J. L. López managed to capture two photographs of the whales, including one featuring an adult male showcasing its distinctive "racing stripes."

Due Diligence: Marine biologists Robert L. Pitman, Anelio Aguayo, and Jorge Urbán published the most comprehensive information about this species in *Marine Mammal Science* in 1987. These researchers reported 24 confirmed and eight tentative sightings of the dimorphic beaked whale, observed individually or in small to medium pods in the tropical latitudes of the eastern Pacific Ocean, specifically off the coasts of Mexico, Panama, and Peru. These sightings occurred during marine mammal survey cruises conducted by the Southwest Fisheries Center.

Amateur Audacity: It's pretty audacious that non-scientists like Loren Coleman and Patrick Huyghe felt entitled to bestow the alternative name "shovel-headed whale" upon this species without the rigorous validation that is essential in the scientific community. Such presumptions in naming can undermine the thorough work and dedication of scientific researchers in the field.

Beastly Theories!

False ID: The Dimorphic Beaked Whale's uncertain classification has led researchers to consider several candidates that could represent this species. The Lesser Beaked Whale, described in 1991 and measuring 11 to 12 feet, overlaps geographically with the Dimorphic Beaked Whale, and its previously overestimated size may align with unidentified sightings. The Pygmy Beaked Whale, recognized shortly after initial sightings of the Dimorphic Beaked Whale, exhibits similar size and morphological traits, making it a match. Longman's Beaked Whale, known only from two skulls and lacking live observations, adds to this cryptic species' intrigue due to its tentative classification and limited range. Lastly, Bahamonde's Beaked Whale, represented by a single skull and synonymized with the spade-toothed whale, may provide insights into closely related species.

GREEK DOLPHIN

What's in a Name? The name "Greek dolphin" is derived from the area where it has been commonly observed in the Mediterranean Sea, primarily off the coast of Greece, where it gained its name due to the frequency of sightings.

Monstrous Measurements: The Greek dolphin closely resembles the striped dolphin which is common in the Mediterranean but lacks the distinctive black stripes of that species. It has a dirty white colouration with smoky brownish and grey smudges behind its dorsal fin, a white underside, and a brown dorsal area, along with a white streak on its side. Additionally, the Greek dolphin is smaller and stockier, characterized by a short and stout snout. It does not have the diagnostic dark stripe that runs from the underside of the tail to the eye or the pale grey, finger-shaped marking below the dorsal fin found in striped dolphins.

Beastly Behaviours: These dolphins are social, often seen in pods of up to fifty individuals. Though they usually travel in smaller groups of two to ten, they may also display solitary behaviour at times. They can reach speeds of 15 knots in open water.

Deadly Diet: The dietary habits of the Greek dolphin are not well-documented because its status is unverified. However, as other related species in the Mediterranean usually eat fish and squid, the Greek dolphin has a similar diet.

Watery Abode: Primarily observed in deep waters of the eastern Mediterranean Sea, along the coastline of Greece and around the island of Sardinia.

Scary Sightings

1971: The first reported sighting of the so-called "Greek dolphin" occurred in 1971, raising intriguing questions about the marine fauna of the well-mapped Mediterranean region. Notable marine biologist W. F. J. Mörzer Bruyns documented multiple sightings, including calves near Stromboli and potential newborns. Some of these sightings may have involved the striped dolphin species. The Greek dolphin, a cryptid known for its elusive nature, has been seen frequently off the coast of Greece, prompting discussion about Bruyns's role in marine discovery. He has also reported other species, such as the Alula whale and the Iligan dolphin, leading some to wonder if his numerous discoveries might be too fortunate to be entirely credible.

Beastly Evidence

Missing in Action: To this day, no physical specimen of the Greek dolphin has been found, nor has photographic evidence been captured. This absence suggests either a pre-discovery extinction or misidentification of an existing species.

Beastly Theories!

Can a Dolphin Change Its Stripes? The debate over the Greek dolphin's identity raises questions about whether it could be a variation of the striped dolphin or a cryptid, similar to the Corfu Island Creature. This has intrigued cryptozoologists, who consider potential genetic mutations and environmental factors. Additionally, the field includes the elusive "Senegalese dolphin" and an unidentified small-toothed cetacean in the Philippines, pointing to the existence of unknown dolphin species.

The Corfu Island Creature: The Corfu Island Creature, also known as the Grecian Dolphin, is a dolphin-like animal that sparked controversy among cryptozoologists following a viral photo taken by Scottish tourist Harvey Robertson during a boat cruise near Parga, off the coast of Greece. Theories about its identity ranged from a hoax or a mutated dolphin caused by nuclear waste to an alien life form, with some speculating it resembled a pike fish or a long-snouted manatee. However, it was eventually identified as a plastic freeboard fender. Explanations for the creature varied widely, with some comparing it to a beaked whale while others humorously described it as the “love child of a hippo and a crocodile.” Interestingly, it did bear a passing resemblance to Ambulocetus, an extinct early cetacean known as the "walking whale," which could swim and walk, hunt like a crocodile, and possessed unique adaptations for underwater living.

HIGH-FINNED SPERM WHALE

What's in a Name? The high-finned sperm whale, also known as the high-finned cachalot, is a variant of the sperm whale distinguished by its notably tall dorsal fin. It was first described by Sir Robert Sibbald in 1687 when he reported encountering a stranded female in Orkney. Later, Carl Linnaeus classified the species under the scientific name *Physeter tursio* in the 10th edition of *Systema Naturae* in 1758.

Monstrous Measurements: Measuring between 30 and 100 feet in length, with an average size of 60 feet. Distinguished by a large dorsal fin resembling a ship's mast, it differs from other sperm whales, such as *Physeter macrocephalus* and *Kogia* species, which lack this feature. This species has robust jaws and functional teeth in both the upper and lower jaws, aiding in capturing large cephalopods and sharks, particularly in males. These adaptations also help them in combat against predators like orcas and rival whales.

Beastly Behaviours: Behavioural patterns remain speculative, with reports primarily highlighting its impressive size and distinctive dorsal fins. These creatures are believed to exhibit deep-diving abilities and a strong social structure and also to engage in confrontations with orcas when threatened. Additionally, individuals possess a specialized sac in their intestines filled with dark red liquid, which can be expelled to create a large cloud of ink in the water. This ink serves as a defence mechanism for younger individuals or during retreats from hostile encounters.

Deadly Diet: This species primarily feeds on squid and various fish, although its diet is not well documented due to its unclear classification. It typically targets smaller squid but is capable of subduing larger prey, such as the colossal squid. Its diet also includes giant squid, octopuses, sharks, rays, and other large fish, but it does not consume other whales or marine mammals.

Watery Abode: Believed to reside in the North Atlantic Ocean, especially near the Orkney and Shetland Islands, as well as in Nova Scotia.

Scary Sightings

1687: Sir Robert Sibbald reported a stranded female whale on Orkney, describing its dorsal fin as similar in size to a mizzen mast, estimating the fin height to be between 20 and 80 feet.

1758: Carl Linnaeus listed high-finned sperm whales in the 10th edition of *Systema Naturae*.

1946: A sighting near Annapolis Basin, Nova Scotia, where locals reported a large black whale trapped for two days, with dorsal fin length estimates ranging from 10 to 100 feet.

1902: A group of whales observed in the Antarctic with high sabre-shaped dorsal fins, estimated to be 20 to 30 feet long.

1910-1911: Additional expeditions in the Antarctic observed similarly sized cetaceans, approximately 30 feet long, with uniformly black backs and pointed dorsal fins.

1964: Off the coast of Chile, unidentified cetaceans with high dorsal fins were photographed, and their differing appearance from prior observations was noted.

Beastly Evidence

Sir Sibbald Sighting: In 1687, Sir Robert Sibbald reported a stranded female whale on Orkney, describing its dorsal fin as being similar in size to a mizzen mast, with an estimated height between 20 and 80 feet.

Black Beast of Annapolis: On September 27, 1946, there was a sighting near Annapolis Basin, Nova Scotia, where locals reported a large black whale that had been trapped for two days. Estimates of the dorsal fin's length varied, ranging from 10 to 100 feet. Apart from these sightings, no other evidence has been found to support the existence of this cryptid whale.

Beastly Theories!

An Orca Imposter? The idea of high-finned sperm whales may stem from sighting misidentifications of other cetaceans, such as orcas or pilot whales. Some hypotheses propose that stories of this creature began with exaggerated reports of stranded marine animals. While modern naturalists have dismissed the existence of the high-finned sperm whale, the intrigue surrounding these mythical sea creatures continues, inspiring speculation and wonder within marine folklore.

A Sub Sperm Whale: The high-finned sperm whale is distinguished from the common sperm whale by its tall, mizzen mast-like dorsal fin and long, narrow pectoral flippers, which make up 18 to 27% of its body length. Unlike the common sperm whale's uniform dark grey colour, high-finned sperm whales show pronounced countershading, featuring dark blue tops and white underbellies, along with varying white streaks around the eyes and jaw, giving them an orca-like appearance. They also have smooth, rubbery skin, unlike the wrinkled skin of typical sperm whales. Older individuals may have barnacles, particularly on their heads, flippers, and dorsal fins.

GIGLIOLI'S WHALE

What's in a Name? Giglioli's whale was scientifically named *Amphiptera pacifica* after the ship *Magenta* where the first reported sighting occurred. It honours Italian zoologist Enrico Hillyer Giglioli, who documented the species in the 19th century. It is also known as Mongitore's Monstrous Fish and the Rhinoceros whale.

Monstrous Measurements: This whale can reach lengths of up to 60 feet. It has a grey green back and a greyish-white underbelly. It has a large, blunt muzzle with a lower jaw longer than the upper and two dorsal fins spaced about 6 feet apart.

Beastly Behaviours: Giglioli's whale shares behaviours with other baleen whales. Its unique double dorsal fins distinguish it from current whale species. Observations of its swimming patterns emphasize its distinct role in the marine ecosystem.

Deadly Diet: Dietary habits remain unclear due to their unproven existence. It is speculated that, similar to other baleen whales, it feeds on small fish and plankton, although the absence of observable throat pleats suggests a different feeding mechanism.

Watery Abode: Believed to inhabit deep waters of the South Pacific and North Atlantic Oceans, with potential sightings in the Mediterranean Sea.

Scary Sightings

1867: The first recorded sighting occurred on September 4, when Enrico Hillyer Giglioli observed the creature about 1,200 miles off Chile aboard the *Magenta*.

1898: In October, a similar whale was spotted by Alexander Taylor and the crew of the fishing boat *Lily* off the coast of Stonehaven, Scotland.

1983: A sighting occurred on July 17, when French zoologist Jacques Maigret observed a similar creature in the Mediterranean Sea.

Beastly Evidence

A Modern Mystery! Despite detailed eyewitness accounts, evidence for Giglioli's whale remains elusive. Modern zoologists question the validity of these sightings, suggesting they may result from rare genetic mutations rather than the discovery of a new species, especially due to the decline in sightings with increased shipping.

Beastly Theories!

A Wonky Whale: Contemporary researchers theorize that reported anomalies may stem from genetic defects or environmental factors. If such a species existed, it would have been documented by commercial whalers, raising scepticism about its existence today.

Some FIN New? The presence of two dorsal fins in sharks serves a hydrodynamic purpose. This may have developed into a micro-adaptation, suggesting that a "doubled-finned" hydrodynamic structure can occur, indicating a potential adaptive trait rather than a distinct species.

RHINOCEROS DOLPHIN

What's in a Name? The rhinoceros dolphin, scientifically called *Delphinus rhinoceros* and later proposed as *Cetodipterus rhinoceros*, is a unique species recognized for its horn-like second dorsal fin near its head. It was first recorded in 1824 by naturalists Jean René Quoy and Joseph Gaimard during their voyage from Hawaii to Australia. In 1991, cryptozoologist Michel Raynal suggested *Cetodipterus rhinoceros*.

Monstrous Measurements: This dolphin species can reach lengths of about 10 feet and features a striking pattern of spotted black and white skin, similar to orcas. It has a smaller dorsal fin located near its neck, distinguishing it from other dolphins. The rhino dolphin resembles an orca but has a front half with spotted skin and an extra smaller dorsal fin on its head. Its size is double that of the common porpoise.

Beastly Behaviours: This species collaborates when hunting, often forming strong bonds with Giglioli's whales to create a mutually beneficial relationship. The dolphins utilize echolocation to locate schools of fish and guide the whales to these feeding areas. In exchange, the whales, due to their large size, protect the dolphins from potential threats.

Deadly Diet: Its diet primarily consists of fish.

Watery Abode: Primarily reported in the waters of the North Pacific Ocean. Sightings have been reported around areas such as Palmyra Atoll and Cornwall, England.

Scary Sightings

1741: A fish approximately 14 meters long washed up on the shores of Sicily. An illustration depicted the creature with two dorsal fins and a hole in its back, used for breathing, hinting at cetacean characteristics.

1819: A significant sighting occurred in the North Pacific of a pod of dolphins exhibiting two dorsal fins, with a second fin positioned just behind the head and small white markings on the front half of their bodies.

1856: A sighting in Lantivet Bay, Cornwall, included several dolphins with two dorsal fins swimming alongside common dolphins.

1857: In the southwest of England, one or two dolphins with two dorsal fins were observed among a group of normal dolphins. These dorsal fins appeared further back on the body compared to earlier sightings.

Beastly Evidence

On the Cusp? The rhinoceros dolphin is a cryptid with considerable anecdotal evidence and historical accounts suggesting its existence. However, it lacks any tangible proof, as no specimens have been found. This absence of physical evidence leaves its official classification uncertain, raising questions about its existence and taxonomy.

As a result, various theories have emerged regarding the identity of this mysterious creature.

Beastly Theories!

Deformed Dolphin, Weird Whale? There are numerous theories regarding the rhinoceros dolphin's peculiar appearance. Some researchers believe that the animals seen might be mistaken for beaked whales. In contrast, others propose the possibility of a rare genetic mutation that could lead to the presence of extra dorsal fins. Moreover, the dolphins' odd features might also be due to misinterpretations of their behaviour, such as a calf positioning itself against its mother. The discussion remains ongoing as scientists strive to unravel the mysteries surrounding this intriguing marine species.

A Giglioli's Whale: Rhinoceros dolphins are often seen associating with Giglioli's whale, which has two dorsal fins—one located near the head, where the neck would be on terrestrial animals, and another positioned farther back than the dorsal fins of other dolphins. These dolphins are large and feature a black colouration adorned with large white blotches. Researchers have speculated that sightings of these unique fin placements could be attributed to optical illusions or could simply involve dolphins with remoras attached to them. While supernumerary dorsal fins are recognized as a genuine mutation, none have been documented a significant distance from the standard dorsal fin location, let alone on the head.

FIENDISH FISH

Def.

Fiendish fish are creatures rumoured to inhabit secret waters. They are often described as enormous and possess unique physiological features and behavioural characteristics not typically observed in their known counterparts.

BATHYSTHERA INTACTA

What's in a Name? The *Bathysphaera intacta,* or "the untouchable bathysphere fish," was named by William Beebe (another one of several unique species' sightings) after an extraordinary sighting during his deep-sea explorations from the Bathysphere. The term "bathy" means "deep" in Greek, while "sphere" signifies the hollow steel vessel he used for his underwater observations. The name "intacta" has generated some debate, as it could imply notions of virginity or self-reproduction. Some have suggested it might be more fittingly named "*Bathysphaera intangibilis,*" which means "incapable of being touched" or "uncapturable by the mind."

Monstrous Measurements: The *Bathysphaera in*tacta can reach a formidable length of approximately 6 feet. Its large eyes enhance its predatory capabilities, and its body features a single line of pale blue bioluminescent photophores, distinguishing it from its relatives.

Beastly Behaviours: The *Bathysphaera intacta* is an ambush predator, equipped with short, undershot jaws filled with luminous fangs that are perpetually held open while swimming. Its unique tentacles, tipped with luminous red and blue barbels, serve both as feelers and lures in the dark depths of the ocean.

Deadly Diet: While specific dietary habits remain unconfirmed due to the fish's rarity, it is assumed that *Bathysphaera intacta* preys on other fish, utilizing its bioluminescence to attract prey in the abyssal darkness.

Watery Abode: The *Bathysphaera intacta* is believed to inhabit the deep waters around Nonsuch Island in Bermuda, at depths of over 2,200 feet. Its natural habitat consists of the dark, cold waters of the North Atlantic Ocean.

Scary Sightings

1932: The *Bathysphaera intacta* has only been recorded once in history. On September 22, 1932, William Beebe, after concluding a live radio broadcast, spotted it during a dive in his bathysphere. He described the moment as both thrilling and unforgettable, noting that he observed two individuals at a depth of 2,100 feet.

In his book *Half Mile Down*, published two years later, Beebe detailed this remarkable encounter. He elaborated on his encounter, writing:

> Several minutes later, at 2100 feet, I had the most exciting experience of the whole dive. Two fish went very slowly by, not more than six or eight feet away, each of which was at least six feet in length. They were of the general shape of large barracudas but with shorter jaws, which were kept wide open all the time I watched them. A single line of strong lights, pale bluish, was strung down the body. The usual second line was quite absent. The eyes were very large, even for the great length of the fish. The undershot jaw was armed with numerous fangs which were illumined either by mucus or indirect internal lights. Vertical fins well back were one of the characteristics which placed it among the sea dragons, Melanostomiatids and were clearly seen when the fish passed through the beam. There were two long tentacles hanging down from the body, each tipped

> with a pair of separate, luminous bodies, the upper reddish and the lower one blue. These twitched and jerked along beneath the fish, one undoubtedly arising from the chin, and the other far back near the tail. I could see neither the stem of the tentacles nor any paired fins, although both were certainly present. This is the fish I subsequently named *Bathysphaera intacta*, the Untouchable Bathysphere Fish.

Otis Barton, who operated the bathysphere and had a known rivalry with Beebe, regretted missing this extraordinary sighting of the Giant Dragonfish, as mentioned in his later publication, *The World Beneath the Sea* (1953).

Beastly Evidence

In the Eye of the Beholder: The primary evidence of the *Bathysphaera intacta's* existence comes from Beebe's account in his book *Half Mile Down*.

Beastly Theories!

Fisherman's Tails: During his four years of deep-sea research around Nonsuch Island, Bermuda, Beebe reported five unidentified cryptid fish, including the giant dragonfish (*Bathysphaera intacta*), pallid sailfin (*Bathyembryx istiophasma*), five-lined constellation fish (*Bathysidus pentagrammus*), three-starred anglerfish (*Bathyceratias trilynchus*), and the abyssal rainbow gar, which he tentatively placed in the needlefish family (*Belonidae*). His claims have drawn scepticism from the scientific community, akin to a gambler consistently rolling lucky sevens. Additionally, the need to secure funding and attract attention from eager journalists could have led Beebe to embellish his discoveries. While the excuse of "the one that got away" has often been used by explorers lacking concrete evidence, Beebe was regarded as a reliable zoologist. It's possible he may have misidentified these fish due to the cramped conditions of his deep-sea submersible, which operated over 2,100 feet below the surface.

A Giant Dragonfish: The largest known dragonfish, the obese dragonfish (*Opostomias micripnus*), reaches about 1.8 ft in length, while Beebe's giant dragonfish (*Bathysphaera intacta*) measures around 6 ft. Despite naming it a new genus and species, Beebe admitted that this classification was primarily an educated guess based on its resemblance to the scaleless black dragonfish (*Melanostomias bartonbeani*). A notable issue with Beebe's claims is that in the 91 years since his sighting, no verification of his abyssal fish has occurred. Nevertheless, *Bathysphaera intacta* remains listed in taxonomic records as a valid species.

CHALLENGER DEEP FLATFISH

What's in a Name? The Challenger Deep Flatfish is named after the Challenger Deep, the deepest known point in the Mariana Trench, located in the North Pacific Ocean. It shares its name with the British Royal Navy survey ship *HMS Challenger*, which conducted the first depth measurements of this abyssal region during its expedition from 1872 to 1876.

Monstrous Measurements: The Challenger Deep Flatfish is similar to a sole, characterized by a flattened body shape. It has two distinct eyes positioned on the top of its head.

Beastly Behaviours: The Challenger Deep Flatfish dwells in total darkness at extreme oceanic depths, where its behaviours are unknown.

Deadly Diet: Unknown

Watery Abode: These flatfish inhabit deep, dark recesses of the ocean floor in areas where no natural light penetrates.

Scary Sightings

1960: On January 23, 1960, during an expedition in the bathyscaphe *Trieste*, piloted by Jacques Piccard and Don Walsh, a flatfish was observed swimming away as they descended to the bottom of the Challenger Deep. It was described as about one foot long and six inches wide, possessing distinctive eyes that spotted the submersible entering its domain.

Later recalling their encounter, they said:

> As we were settling this final fathom, I saw a wonderful thing. Lying on the bottom just beneath us was some type of flatfish resembling a sole, about one foot long and six inches across. Even as I saw him, his two round eyes on top of his head spied us — a monster of steel — invading his silent realm. Eyes? Why should he have eyes? Merely to see phosphorescence? The floodlight that bathed him was the first real light ever to enter this hadal realm. Here, in an instant, was the answer to the question that biologists had asked for decades. Could life exist in the greatest depths of the ocean? It could! And not only that, here apparently, was a true, bony teleost fish, not a primitive ray or elasmobranch. Yes, a highly evolved vertebrate, in time's arrow very close to man himself. [...] Slowly, extremely slowly, this flatfish swam away. Moving along the bottom, partly in the ooze and partly in the water he disappeared into his night.

Beastly Evidence

A Deep Dive: Documented during the historic descent of the *Trieste*, which stayed at a depth of 35,797 feet for twenty minutes on January 23, 1960, and observed this hitherto unknown species of flatfish.

Beastly Theories!

Sea Cucumber: Torben Wolff proposed the creature might be a sea cucumber, the cushion-shaped *Galatheathauria aspera*, which has an oval form. At such depths, eyes would be ineffective. He suggested that if this "flatfish" is genuine, it could be an extremely rare or critically endangered abyssal fish, potentially extinct due to deep-sea fishing threatening abyssal biodiversity. However, since neither pilot was a marine biologist, a misidentification is possible.

An Unknown Flatfish: The presence of this flatfish raises fascinating questions about life in extreme conditions. Its adaptation to great depths indicates that complex vertebrate life can thrive in environments once deemed inhospitable. Further research may reveal insights into its behaviours, diet, and role in the abyssal ecosystem.

LAKE KANAS MONSTER

What's in a Name? Kanas, a name of Mongolian origin, means "gorgeous and mysterious." Local legends tell of a lake monster that has haunted Kanas Lake for generations, much like the Loch Ness Monster. Some ancient tales even connect the lake to Genghis Khan, suggesting his body was preserved underwater and protected by the elusive creature after his death.

Monstrous Measurements: The creature resembles a giant redfish akin to the taimen, growing up to 33 feet long. It has a 3-foot head, spiny dorsal rays, and powerful tail fins that generate significant waves when submerged. Local legends claim the lake is home to enormous fish or similar beings measuring 10 to 15 meters long.

Beastly Behaviours: The Kanas Lake Monster is rumoured to cause enormous waves, creating a chaotic scene on the tranquil surface of the lake. Local lore tells of the creature emerging from the depths to drag animals into the icy waters. It's claimed the beast, often likened to the Loch Ness Monster in Scotland, would occasionally emerge to drag horses into the water before eating them.

Deadly Diet: Local legends suggest that a monster preys on livestock, especially cattle and sheep, causing fear among farmers and herdsmen near the lake. Witnesses have reported strange hoof prints at the lake's edge, often leading to eerie, red-tinged waters. In a notorious 1970s incident, a herdsman discovered his horses missing, with only tracks indicating something dark had occurred.

Watery Abode: Kanas Lake is a beautiful alpine lake located in the Altai Mountains of Xinjiang, China. Created around 200,000 years ago by glacial movements, it reaches a depth of about 390 feet and has crystal-clear waters that change color with the seasons, enhancing its mystique.

Scary Sightings

1943: A Russian account noted a 6-foot fish weighing 243 pounds; current records show a max of 4.9 feet and 101 pounds, though larger fish sightings continue.

1970s: A herdsman discovered that his ten horses had vanished after a nap, with only hoof marks and red-tinged water left behind, despite extensive searching by the villagers.

1980: The first official sighting of the Kanas Lake Monster was reported by *Guangming Daily*, describing a giant red object over 15 meters long.

1988: Fishermen reported three 13-foot specimens in July.

2004: A sighting by Fang Wei, an employee of the Xinjiang Meteorological Service Centre, heightened local interest.

Beastly Evidence

1985: Biologist Xiang Lihao and his students reported capturing images of a school of around sixty large fish in July 1985, but the photos were never made public. Fishermen later claimed to have caught three 13-foot specimens, yet solid evidence of the creature remains limited.

1985: During a 1985 visit to Kanas Lake, researchers observed sudden waves, and a massive blood-red, rainbow-shaped fish estimated at over 10 meters long. After deploying a large fishing net to catch it, the net mysteriously vanished and was later found torn two kilometres upstream. Researcher Huang Renxin speculated the creature could be a *Hucho taimen*, typically known to grow up to two meters long.

2005: A scientific expedition costing $1.5 million aimed to find the giant trout but failed to produce any evidence.

2007: The CCTV documentary series *Approaches to Science* filmed one large *Hucho taimen* in the lake using underwater cameras and sonar. However, at just three meters long, it was much shorter than earlier sightings suggested.

2012: Wang Hongqiao, a worker at Kanas Lake, filmed what he asserted were three lake monsters creating water spray while swimming. The footage was taken from a high observation platform, but experts concluded it showed a school of large fish instead of monsters.

2022: In May, multiple tourists filmed large shadows moving across Kanas Lake, reigniting curiosity about the lake's mysteries. A journalist from *Cover News* inquired about the sighting but was told that the "lake monster" was merely *Hucho taimen*.

Beastly Theories!

Dragon God: The Kanas Lake Monster has captured imaginations for centuries. Theories range from a prehistoric fish to a vengeful lake guardian tied to Genghis Khan's mausoleum. The blend of folklore and beautiful surroundings attracts tourists and monster hunters eager to uncover the truth behind what is considered China's Loch Ness Monster. Legend has it that Genghis Khan named the lake during his travels west, and after his death, his body was buried in its depths, guarded by water monsters. In Mongolian, Kanas translates to gorgeous and mysterious. Local villagers believe a giant creature, known as the Kanas Lake Monster, inhabits the 390-foot-deep lake.

A Local Myth: A chilling theory suggests a monster lurks beneath the lake's clear waters. The narrative spread, leading to more legends of the beast dragging away livestock. Today, Kanas Lake, surrounded by breathtaking mountains, attracts tourists eager for its beauty and to catch a glimpse of China's Loch Ness Monster.

A Giant Taiman: One explanation is the enormous Siberian taimen, a large freshwater salmon that typically grows up to 6 feet long but can reach two meters. With increasing online sightings in the 21st century, researchers explored the truth behind these water monsters. While scientists speculate that *Hucho taimen* could explain some sightings, the mystery remains regarding the case of the ten vanished horses.

Giant Trout: The enigma persists, drawing more tourists hoping to see China's Nessie. Some speculate the area may be encouraging or even faking sightings to increase tourism. Environmental protection expert, Yuan Guoying, believes the so-called monster is actually a group of Siberian giant trout from the salmon family.

THE LAU

What's in a Name? The Lau is a freshwater monster from East Africa, named in the Nuer and Dinka languages, both of which belong to the Nilo-Saharan language family. It has several alternative names, including Jâk, Jâk-anywong (meaning "punishing spirit"), Nyal (Shilluk), and Nyama.

Monstrous Measurements: The Lau has a serpentine shape with legs and varies significantly in size, being estimated between 12 to 100 feet long, with some descriptions suggesting it could match the size of a donkey or horse. Its colour ranges from brown to dark yellow. The creature's head features a 3-inch crest similar to that of a crowned crane, with some accounts noting four membranous bones around its mouth, while others report catfish-like barbels.

Terrifying Tracks: Creates noticeable furrows indicative of a large animal moving between swampy areas of its terrain.

Beastly Behaviours: Produces a booming call at night and makes loud gurgling sounds from its stomach, especially during the rainy season.

Deadly Diet: The dietary habits of the Lau are not well-documented, but it is thought to hunt aquatic creatures in its environment.

Watery Abode: Inhabits riverbank holes in the Bahr al 'Arab, Bahr al Ghazal, Bahr al Zera¯f, Bahr al Jabal, and other tributaries of the White Nile. Its range spans from Malaka¯l to Rajja¯f and from Lake No to Shambe in Sudan.

Scary Sightings

Late 19th Century: A 40-foot Lau was spotted near Wa¯w, Sudan.

1914: A complete Lau skeleton was found in the Bahr al Zera¯f and given to the Nuer people as charms.

1916: A 12-foot Lau was observed in the Bahr al Zera¯f.

1918: Loud gurgling sounds attributed to the Lau were reported in the Bahr al 'Arab.

1937: William Hichens published a photograph of a wooden effigy resembling a Lau's head, carved by Mshengu she Gunda from Tanzania.

Beastly Evidence

An Ethno-Known Animal: There is no physical evidence supporting the existence of the Lau as a genuine cryptid species, despite reports of enigmatic skeletons and traditional effigies resembling it.

Beastly Theories!

A Colossal Catfish: Some speculate it might be an undiscovered species of large catfish known for producing growling sounds and having features like long barbels and a crest-like dorsal fin. Certain catfish can crawl on land at night, and while they lack vocal cords, they can still generate growling noises. Some possess venomous spines, while others can deliver electric shocks. The Nile electric catfish can grow to 5 feet, while the Wels catfish in Europe can nearly reach 10 feet and weigh over 500 pounds.

A Large Lungfish: The marbled lungfish is another option to consider. This species can grow over 6 feet long and is found in the lakes and swamps of East Africa.

A Cryptid Chimaera: This theory suggests that the Lau may be a composite creature, combining traits of various dangerous aquatic species. Composite creatures in folklore, like Sekhmet (Egyptian lioness) symbolizing nurturing and ferocity, or the Greek chimera (lion head, goat body, serpent tail) representing chaos, reflect cultural values and fears. Similarly, the Japanese kirin (deer, horse, dragon) embodies good fortune, while the Native American thunderbird signifies strength and guardianship.

Nonspecific Nomenclature: The term "Lau" may serve as a broad classification for elongated aquatic creatures, encompassing a range of fish species found in the Nile and other rivers across Africa. Descriptions of the Lau paint a picture of a captivating yet formidable creature, stirring curiosity and thoughtful consideration regarding its potential presence in the enigmatic waters of East Africa.

LAKE ILLIAMNA MONSTER

What's in a Name? The Lake Iliamna Monster is named after its home in the southwestern portion of the U.S. state of Alaska.

Monstrous Measurements: Descriptions of the Lake Iliamna Monster vary widely due to mixed cultural folklore and eyewitness reports. It is thought to be a serpent-like creature around 30 feet long, featuring visible fins, a large head—often described as either wolf-like or shark-like—and smooth, metallic-coloured skin.

Beastly Behaviours: The creature is described as being reclusive, with reports highlighting its remarkable skill in diving deep and remaining submerged in the cold lake waters for extended durations.

Deadly Diet: Although concrete evidence regarding the diet of the Lake Iliamna Monster is lacking, it is presumed that this large aquatic creature primarily preys on fish and smaller aquatic organisms within the lake.

Watery Abode: Iliamna Lake, located in southwestern Alaska, is a prominent natural body of water known as an inland sea. It measures 77 miles long and 22 miles wide, covering over 1,012 square miles, making it the largest lake in Alaska. The lake reaches depths of up to 988 feet and is situated about 50 feet above sea level. Access is primarily via floatplanes, as no roads connect to nearby communities, although small boats can traverse the Kvichak River in summer.

Scary Sightings

1942: Bush pilot Babe Alyesworth and passenger Bill Hammersley observed several large, dull aluminum-colored fish while flying over Iliamna Lake. They noted the creatures had broad, blunt heads, elongated bodies, and vertical tails that swayed side to side, indicating they were not whales. Upon closer inspection from lower altitudes, they surmised the fish were longer than 10 feet, resembling mini submarines rather than typical fish.

1945: Larry Rost, a pilot with the U.S. Coast and Geodetic Survey, reported sighting a giant fish over Lake Iliamna, estimating its length to be more than 20 feet and also describing it as coloured like dull aluminium.

1959: Cryptozoologist Tom Slick enlisted Alyesworth for an aerial survey of the lake; however, no significant sightings were recorded.

1963: An unnamed biologist observed a 25-30-foot fish from above that remained submerged for an extended duration of 10 minutes without surfacing for air.

1967: Chuck Crapuchettes, a missionary in Alaska, reported seeing a large creature while flying in a floatplane. He attempted to radio for assistance, but no confirmation was received before the creature vanished.

1977: Pilot Tim LaPorte, along with two passengers, spotted a 12-14-foot fish at the surface of Pedro Bay. As the aircraft approached, the fish dove, creating a large splash that revealed a vertical tail.

1987: Resident Verna Kolyaha reported observing a large black fish with a distinctive white stripe on its fin.

1988: Multiple locals reported similar sightings of a large black fish swimming near the surface of the lake.

2017: Kakhonak village residents observed a large creature approximately one mile offshore, estimating its length at 50-60 feet. They reported it exhaled like a whale, with smaller creatures following closely behind.

Beastly Evidence

A Beastly Biology: Despite numerous reported sightings, physical evidence of the Lake Iliamna Monster remains scarce. The area's pristine ecosystem contributes to the lack of traceable evidence. Eyewitness accounts constitute the primary basis for ongoing speculation about the creature's existence. Notably, in 1963, a biologist from the Alaska Department of Fish and Game observed an 8-10-meter-long creature swimming below the surface for over ten minutes without surfacing.

Taxicab Tales: In 1977, pilot Tim LaPorte, along with two passengers, spotted a dark, 4-5 meters long animal from the air. Its back was visible above the water, and when it submerged, it displayed a large vertical tail, distinguishing it from whales which have horizontal tails.

Pop Culture: The Iliamna Lake Monster appears in the trading card game *MetaZoo: Cryptid Nation*. Additionally, *The History Channel's* show *Missing in Alaska* discusses the case of a missing kayaker, speculated by some to have encountered the legendary creature.

Beastly Theories!

A Landlocked Giant: The Lake Iliamna Monster has many identities. Some researchers think it might be a large land-locked white sturgeon, which can grow up to 20 feet long. There are historical reports of big sturgeon in other North American lakes, which support this idea. The deep, cold waters of Lakes Iliamna and Clark in Alaska are suitable for such fish. If these creatures exist, they are likely to be very large white sturgeon. In the past, giant sturgeon have been identified as the source of some lake monsters in North America, making this a reasonable explanation for the creatures in Iliamna and Clark lakes.

A Prehistoric Survivor: Another idea is that the creature could be an undiscovered species or a survivor from prehistoric times. The large size of the lake, its diverse environment, and limited access make it intriguing to consider what might be living in its waters. One exciting possibility is that it could be a plesiosaur, a marine reptile that is known to have gone extinct about 70 million years ago. Plesiosaurs needed to come to the surface for air, so a creature of that size would be more visible.

SUPER SHARKS

Def.

Super sharks consist of undiscovered cryptid species, outsized known species, and sharks that inhabit unusual environments such as lakes, rivers, and ponds.

MALPELO MONSTER

What's in a Name? The Malpelo Monster, also referred to as Bongo or El Monstro, is named after Isla de Malpelo, situated 285 miles off the Colombian coast.

Monstrous Measurements: The Malpelo Monster can reach lengths of up to 6 meters, particularly in females. It is characterized by large eyes and a dorsal fin positioned above the pectoral fins. While it superficially resembles the ferocious shark (*Odontaspis ferox*), which typically grows to 4 meters, the Malpelo Monster exhibits distinct differences in size and morphology. These variations suggest it may represent either a new species or a distinct subspecies resulting from an isolated population.

Beastly Behaviours: The species typically prefers deep waters below 50 meters, making encounters rare due to its shyness and the challenging conditions of heavy storms and strong currents in its habitat. Its large size and larger eyes may be evolutionary adaptations to navigate the increased pressure and reduced light at these depths.

Deadly Diet: Despite its fearsome name, it has small teeth not suited for capturing large prey and is believed to be harmless to humans.

This leads to the assumption that, like its smaller relative the sand tiger, it poses no danger to divers or swimmers.

Watery Abode: Found in the eastern Pacific Ocean, particularly around the Malpelo archipelago, which lies 285 miles off the Colombian coast. This mysterious fish prefers colder waters beneath the thermocline, typically at depths below 160 feet.

Scary Sightings

Early 2000s: Initial sightings of an enigmatic giant shark occurred in the early 2000s, prompting Colombian biologist Sandra Bessudo to investigate its existence in 2001 after an encounter during a dive at National Malpelo Park.

Beastly Evidence

Beset by Pirates! This creature, occasionally observed and photographed, captivated diver, Sandra Bessudo, leading her to seek its identity. Bessudo's quest led her to organize a daring expedition in early 2002 aimed at uncovering more about the Malpelo Monster. However, her journey was fraught with challenges including a destructive storm that hindered access to the shark's habitat, and a violent pirate attack that resulted in the seizing of her vessel and gear.

Beastly Theories!

A Super Sand Tiger! The identity of the Malpelo Monster remains a subject of debate. While some experts propose it may be an unidentified species of sand tiger shark, characterized by larger eyes and significant size, research indicates it is a variant of the smalltooth sand tiger shark. This conclusion is supported by both morphological observations and DNA analysis, suggesting it does not constitute a distinct species.

LORD OF THE DEEP

What's in a Name? "Lord of the Deep" refers to a large shark-like creature believed to inhabit the South Pacific Ocean, with its English appellation potentially originating from a Melanesian word for a demon shark in their folklore.

Monstrous Measurements: The megalodon, a colossal marine predator, is characterized by a greyish dorsal surface and pale white underside. Estimates indicate it may exceed lengths of 30 feet, with some reports suggesting sizes of up to 100 feet. Its formidable triangular teeth range from 4 to 6 inches in length, enabling it to potentially consume large prey, such as entire cows.

Beastly Behaviours: Fishermen report that their heavy equipment has been mysteriously towed away by this powerful predator. Additionally, injured whales have been found with marks indicative of an attack by a massive shark.

Deadly Diet: Believed to feed on various marine life, including giant squids, whales, other sharks, and large fish. Observations indicate it also has a taste for shellfish and will occasionally commandeer crayfish from fishermen's traps.

Watery Abode: Its habitat is primarily in the South Pacific Ocean, especially along the eastern coast of Australia, where it inhabits deeper waters to hunt for prey.

Scary Sightings

1918: Some fishermen near Port Stephens, New South Wales, reported a significant encounter with an immense shark to ichthyologist David G. Stead. They claimed their crayfish pots, about 3.5 feet in diameter, were towed away by a ghostly shark. Estimates of its length ranged from 115 feet to an exaggerated 300 feet. In his 1964 book, *Sharks and Rays of Australian Seas*, Stead noted that these experienced fishermen, familiar with marine life, described violent water disturbance as the shark passed. Their fear prompted them to abandon fishing for several days, suggesting a genuine and unsettling encounter.

1927/28: In his 1931 work, *Tales of Tahitian Waters*, Zane Grey described a sighting of a massive shark while sailing near Rangiroa in 1927 or 1928, which exceeded the length of his 35-40-foot boat and had a square head, large pectoral fins, and a greenish-yellow body speckled with white. Following this, his son Loren claimed to have observed a similarly gigantic shark approximately 100 miles northwest of Rangiroa, estimated to be 40 to 50 feet long, featuring a massive head (10 to 12 feet across) and a large brown tail. Initially mistaking it for a whale, Loren quickly recognized it as a shark and later reiterated that it was distinctly different from whale sharks. In a 1994 interview with the Los Angeles Times, Loren recounted how birds were behaving erratically over a yellow patch of water during the sighting, reinforcing the unique characteristics of the creature he witnessed.

1930: A 37-foot great white shark was trapped in a herring weir at White Head Island near Grand Manan, New Brunswick, Canada.

1945: Six Cuban fishermen from Cojimar set out three miles offshore and encountered a large great white shark after hours of fishing without success. Recognizing the value of the catch, they improvised a fishing line using braided ropes and a wire leader with a half-eaten tuna as bait. After a lengthy struggle, they successfully harpooned the shark, which retaliated by damaging their boat. They brought the shark ashore, measuring over 21 feet and weighing around 7,100 pounds. This encounter, known as "El Monstruo de Cojimar," continues to spark debate over the shark's true size.

1954: A ship off the southern coast of Adelaide, South Australia, was attacked by a large shark. The bite mark on the hull measured 2 meters in diameter, with teeth impressions that were 10 centimetres long and 8 centimetres wide at the base. These dimensions suggested the shark was approximately 24 meters long.

1960s: B. C. Cartmell reported that the captain and crew of an 85' ship sailing the outer edge of the Great Barrier Reef witnessed an enormous shark, comparable in size to their vessel. They described the creature as whitish and noted their astonishment at its length, asserting that it was not a whale despite their extensive maritime experience.

1961: In *Shark! Unpredictable Killer of the Sea* (1961), Thomas Helm recounted an encounter with a giant shark in the Caribbean. He estimated the shark's length at "not less than thirty feet" as it swam beneath his 60-foot trawler, with its pectoral fins visible on either side. Although Helm and his companions could not identify the species, it bore a close resemblance to a great white shark.

1970s: Dave and T. Brinks reported an encounter with an unusually large great white shark while sailing their 40-foot vessel approximately 100 miles west of Monterey Bay, California. The shark swam alongside their boat, matching its length. It then swam beneath the vessel, causing it to rise, before disappearing.

1980: A shark estimated at 27 meters in length was reported multiple times off the coasts of Queensland and New South Wales, Australia.

Beastly Evidence

Beasts of the Big Screen: The concept of a living megalodon gained attention leading to several media forays into the subject such as the 2013 mockumentary *Megalodon: The Monster Shark Lives*, *Monster Quest's* feature episode investigating sightings of a large, dark shark, El Demonio Negro, in the Sea of Cortez, a potential melanistic great white, and *The Meg* movie franchise starring Jason Statham based upon the hit novel series of the same name by the author Steve Alten.

Fangs for Nothing! Fossilized megalodon teeth found off Victoria, Australia, are about 5,000 years old, but some older teeth retrieved by *H.M.S. Challenger* in 1875 sparked debates about the species' survival. Russian scientist Wladimir Tschernezky dated them to 24,000 and 11,000 years, but later studies criticized his methods as unreliable. Coeval fossils suggest a Mio-Pliocene age for these teeth. Although reports of sightings exist, no solid evidence supports the megalodon's continued existence.

A Clickbait Cryptid! Numerous videos and photographs claiming to depict the megalodon have surfaced on platforms like YouTube and in news reports; however, the majority are found to be hoaxes or misidentifications of basking sharks.

Beastly Theories!

A Mysterious Meg: The megalodon, a giant shark that existed 25 million years ago and is believed extinct 10,000 years ago, could grow 12 to 16 meters long and weigh up to 200 tonnes, with jaws 1.80 meters wide. Though classified as *Charcharocles megalodon*, it is often compared to the great white shark. Legends among Polynesian fishermen reference a massive sea creature called the "Lord of the Deep," suggesting that megalodons may still roam the oceans.

When You 'Monster' a Monster? A giant 20-foot shark, dubbed "Submarine," was once thought to be a megalodon off False Bay, South Africa, but was later identified as a large great white shark (*Carcharodon carcharias*), the largest predatory shark today. Great whites typically range from 11 to 13 feet, with rare individuals reported up to 37 feet. Some cryptozoologists speculate that larger shark sightings may indicate the existence of megalodon, while others remain sceptical. Notable incidents include a 37-foot great white reported in New Brunswick, Canada, in 1930 and a claimed 41.2-foot specimen caught west of the Azores. Reports persist of larger individuals, such as a great white attacking a smaller shark near Stradbroke Island in 2009 and another incident involving a human in January 2010 off South Africa. While large great whites are rare along the Gulf Coast of Texas, typical specimens occasionally appear, suggesting the possibility of larger sharks visiting the region.

Tall Tales From the Turn of the Century: During the early 20th century, tales of sea monsters captivated the public imagination, fuelled by sightings like those of crayfish fishermen and reports from the Great Barrier Reef. Critics suggest these accounts might be hoaxes, especially given inconsistencies in descriptions. The appearance of the megalodon remains uncertain due to limited fossil evidence, indicating it may have had a different morphology than the great white shark.

GIANT COOKIE CUTTER SHARK

What's in a Name? The cookie-cutter shark also referred as the cigar shark, is named for its unique feeding behaviour, which involves removing circular sections of flesh from larger prey, resembling the action of a cookie cutter on dough.

Monstrous Measurements: This shark typically measures between 16.5 and 22 inches in length. However, there is speculation regarding the existence of larger, unidentified species capable of delivering significantly larger bites than those associated with known specimens. This raises the possibility that these unnamed sharks exceed typical size ranges, as inferred from their alleged bite marks. It is also suggested that such bites might be misidentified feeding signs from larger species, such as sleeper or Greenland sharks, further indicating the presence of sizeable animals.

Beastly Behaviours: Found in deep-sea habitats, takes circular bites from various prey, including tunas and dolphins. While encounters with humans are rare, some documented attacks have occurred. This small shark features adaptations such as a buoyant liver and bioluminescent organs that help it ambush prey. Reports of bites on humans, including those of drowned individuals, indicate potential risks in open water.

Deadly Diet: The cookie-cutter shark has a diverse diet, preying on both large animals, from which it extracts circular chunks, and smaller species like squid. Its sharp lower teeth facilitate this unique feeding strategy.

Watery Abode: The cookie-cutter shark inhabits warm, oceanic waters globally, particularly around islands, and can be found at depths of up to 12,000 feet. It exhibits a vertical migration pattern, approaching the surface at dusk and retreating during daylight hours, including areas like Arctic waters off Alaska.

Scary Sightings/Beastly Evidence

Take a Bite! The distinctive bite marks left by cookie-cutter sharks on larger marine animals serve as undeniable evidence of their feeding practices. These marks, which resemble clean, circular holes, indicate the shark's unique method of preying on much larger animals and illustrate its ecological role in the ocean. While working in Alaska, a colleague of Eugenie Clark reported that a dead narwhal (*Monodon monoceros*) was pulled up alongside their research boat for examination one night. In the morning, as the scientists began to examine it, they found round bites on the animal that strongly resembled those left by the cookie-cutter sharks. However, they were much bigger than bites made by known cookie cutters.

Beastly Theories!

An Outsize Species? The role of gigantism in a stealthy species like the cookie-cutter shark raises intriguing questions. While such an anomaly could theoretically exist, it would be more useful for scavenging large carcasses rather than for ambushing prey. Moreover, larger marine animals are often found in cold environments, where their size and sedentary behaviour provide a buffer against harsh conditions and high pressure in deep waters. Both species of cookie-cutter sharks typically reach lengths of only 18 to 20 inches. This prompts speculation about the possibility of an undiscovered subspecies or hybrid that could explain a significantly larger cookie-cutter shark.

A Secretive Six Gill? The Pacific sleeper shark often scavenges on whale carcasses, while the Greenland shark leaves distinct circular bites on narwhals and seals. The exact mechanism behind these bite patterns is unclear, but it may relate to their unique jaw structure and feeding behaviour. Understanding their feeding biomechanics could reveal insights into their ecological role and interactions with prey. More research is needed to clarify this phenomenon and its impact on predator-prey dynamics.

GROUND SHARK

What's in a Name? The ground shark, belonging to the *Carcharhiniformes* order, is named for its distinctive ambush technique, where it lies motionless on the ocean floor to capture unsuspecting prey.

Monstrous Measurements: The ground shark surpasses the great white shark, which typically measures around 14 feet in length. However, unlike the great white, it lacks a prominent dorsal fin.

Beastly Behaviours: The species employs a patient hunting strategy, remaining concealed among the ocean floor's natural features to ambush passing fish. There are reports of these sharks exhibiting predatory behaviour towards humans, particularly in shallow waters.

Deadly Diet: Their diet comprises different fish species, which they capture through ambush from hidden locations. This opportunistic approach enhances their efficacy as hunters.

Watery Abode: The ground shark is found in the Timor Sea, a shallow body of water bordered by Timor, the Arafura Sea, and Australia. It typically resides at an average depth of 406 meters (1,332 feet) and can reach a maximum depth of 3,200 meters (10,500 feet).

Scary Sightings

Monster or Misidentification? While sightings of ground sharks have been reported, particularly in popular beach areas, these may often stem from misidentification. For instance, a typical shark like the wobbegong can appear disproportionately large in confined spaces such as tidal pools, leading to exaggerated accounts of giant or oversized specimens.

Beastly Theories!

Woe-Be-Tide the Wobbegong! The spotted wobbegong, a large species of shark native to Australasian waters, can grow up to 10 feet 6 inches. Primarily a bottom feeder, it occasionally poses risks to waders and anglers in tidal pools. A hypothesis suggests that a larger variant of the wobbegong shark, potentially exceeding 10 feet, may exhibit aggressive behaviour when provoked, raising concerns for beachgoers.

THE BLACK DEMON

What's in a Name? In Spanish, this creature is known as "El Demonio Negro," meaning "The Black Demon," based on eyewitness descriptions of its coal-black colouration and monstrous size.

Monstrous Measurements: Measuring between 20 to 60 feet long and weighing between 50,000 and 100,000 pounds. It is distinguished by its dark colouration and a notably large tail fluke resembling a great white shark.

Beastly Behaviours: This shark is a formidable predator, known for capsizing boats, attacking whales, and allegedly consuming large groups of sea lions in one bite. Its unpredictable behaviour has fuelled local legends. Notably, its enormous tail fin rises 5 feet above the water.

Deadly Diet: Its diet consists of whales, other cetaceans, and sea lions. Incidents of half-eaten whale carcasses washing ashore lend credence to its predatory behaviour. Additionally, there are accounts of the creature targeting and overturning boats, subsequently consuming the crews.

Watery Abode: Infrequently sighted in the Sea of Cortez, or the Gulf of California, between the Baja California peninsula and the Mexican mainland.

Scary Sightings

2008: A sports fisherman reported an encounter with the Black Demon while fishing off the coast of Baja, California. He claimed the creature rocked his boat, with its tail fin extending approximately five feet above the water's surface.

2012: In April, fishermen discovered a 20-foot-long great white shark weighing two thousand pounds in the Sea of Cortez, further fuelling the local legends of a giant shark referred to as "El Demonio Negro."

2013: Researchers, led by Hoyos Padilla, were tracking great white sharks off Guadalupe Island when they encountered a large female shark, later known as Deep Blue. This event highlighted the shark's significant size and was recorded, forming part of a *Shark Week* documentary.

2019: Deep Blue was documented consuming a whale carcass near Hawaii for a *National Geographic* film. Diver Ocean Ramsey also captured footage of her interaction with Deep Blue, igniting debate within the shark research community. These incidents may contribute to the legend of the Black Demon and its association with verified sightings of large, great white sharks.

Beastly Evidence

Questing for Cryptids! Expeditions, such as the 2009 *Monster Quest* episode, have investigated the Black Demon, a massive shark in the Sea of Cortez. However, they have found no evidence to support the creature's existence. Despite numerous eyewitness accounts, no definitive proof or confirmed reports of attacks associated with this alleged shark exists. Nevertheless, rumours of an aggressive shark linked to marine mammal deaths in the area continue to grow year after year.

Beastly Theories!

A Mexican Meg: The megalodon, a colossal shark that existed 2.6 to 23 million years ago, measured up to 60 feet and weighed over 50 tons. Although fossils, like the teeth found in California, inspire legends of its survival today linked to the sightings of the Black Demon, it is unlikely that such a large predator could survive unnoticed in our modern age.

A Super White: Deep Blue is a female great white shark, approximately 20 feet long and over 5,500 pounds. First encountered in 2013 near Guadalupe Island, she is believed to be over 50 years old. Not tagged for tracking, she was spotted feeding off in Hawaii in 2019 and returned to Guadalupe during the elephant seal migration. While she is the largest recorded great white, she is still smaller than the extinct megalodon, though may continue growing for another 25 to 30 years.

Demon Lore: The legend of the Black Demon has been a part of the local folklore for generations. However, there is currently no conclusive evidence or photographic documentation to support its existence. Supporters of the legend often reference the occasional discovery of half-eaten whale carcasses along the coastline as indications of the creature. Still, these could be nothing more than deceased cetaceans that great whites and other large sharks have scavenged. It is worthwhile to remember that many so-called mythical beasts, such as the giant squid, Komodo dragon, platypus, and gorilla, were once considered figments of folklore and fiction, only to be later confirmed as bonafide fauna, often even exhibiting attributes that exceed their original folkloric portrayals.

DEER ISLAND SHARK

What's in a Name? It is named after Deer Island in New Brunswick, Canada, where it has been sighted.

Monstrous Measurements: Eyewitnesses report a shark approximately 30 feet long, featuring a tail similar to that of a thresher shark.

Beastly Behaviours: This creature generates substantial disturbances in the water through powerful side-to-side thrashing motions, unlike the up-and-down movement of a whale's tail. Witness accounts describe the intensity of the splashing as comparable to a whale breaching, highlighting its significant size and presence beneath the surface.

Deadly Diet: This shark is believed to prey on schools of fish, similar to other large predatory shark species.

Watery Abode: Primarily seen near Deer Island, New Brunswick, within the productive fishing areas of the Bay of Fundy.

Scary Sightings

1999: Witnesses Bill Curtsinger and Heather Perry observed a 30-foot shark with a thresher-like tail while diving near Deer Island, New Brunswick. Curtsinger, a retired navy seaman and experienced diver, noted that the tail's shape and movement resembled that of a thresher shark, describing a distinctive scythe-like tail thrashing side to side. This sighting occurred after hearing significant splashes in the water, leading them to estimate the shark's length at 10 meters and its tail height at 2-3 meters. Curtsinger remarked that he had never encountered anything similar in his three decades of ocean experience.

2018: In June 2018, a New Brunswick couple encountered a great white shark while canoeing in Passamaquoddy Bay. Initially mistaken for a porpoise, the shark's dark grey colouration and size of about 4.5 meters prompted the realization of its true identity. The shark circled their canoe and followed them back to shore, causing significant distress. After consulting a local expert, they received confirmation of their identification. Chris Fischer of Ocearch noted that the East Coast is increasingly frequented by great whites during mating season, with several tracked in Atlantic Canadian waters.

2020: A great white estimated at 19 to 20 feet long was sighted in Passamaquoddy Bay, where an observer initially mistook it for a basking shark until it approached their boat, demonstrating a size that surpassed that of the skiff. This sighting is part of a growing trend, with an increase in great white shark encounters noted over the past decade, linked to rising water temperatures. While concerns about shark attacks persist, such incidents remain rare, prompting experts to emphasize caution among humans entering shark habitats, as they can resemble seal prey. The shark observed was untagged and could be up to 80 years old, highlighting the necessity for further research to understand better the life history and migration patterns of great white sharks in the Atlantic.

2021: Passengers on the Fundy Tide Runners Whale Watching tour recorded a large porbeagle shark swimming off Deer Island during a Sunday morning excursion.

Beastly Evidence

Mistaken for a Monster! Experts have validated the probability of great white shark encounters in Atlantic Canadian waters, particularly during mating season. However, the potential for misidentification exists, as various shark species inhabit the region, with their appearances varying significantly. This murkiness necessitates careful examination of eyewitness descriptions to accurately identify the species involved.

Beastly Theories!

Outsized Thresher Shark: Thresher sharks inhabit the Bay of Fundy, and the characteristics of the Curstinger Shark closely resemble those of a common thresher, albeit on a larger scale. The long, thin upper tail lobe is a notable feature in this sighting. While the recorded tail length falls within the known species range, the possibility of an undiscovered shark species with similar adaptations for preying on larger fish remains.

Basking Shark: The Bay of Fundy is home to various shark species, notably the basking shark, recognized for its large dorsal fin and substantial lunate tail, which can be observed when swimming near the surface. Basking sharks are prevalent from late spring to fall and are known to breach. Additionally, a sighting of a whale shark occurred in the bay in 1997, although it was not in close proximity to the shore and features distinct markings.

PHOTOS & ILLUSTRATIONS

As you dive into this book about bizarre and mysterious water monsters, you'll notice that clear photographs or illustrations of these creatures are tough to come by. This scarcity of visual evidence makes it tricky to paint a vivid picture of what these enigmatic beings might look like.

Even so, I've included the best examples I could find, connecting these creatures to their cryptid cases whenever possible, with the goal of helping the reader better understand these fascinating subjects, even if the images are limited.

Figure 1: A Toy Nessie on Rocks - taken on the shore of Dores Beach, Loch Ness Scotland. Photo copyright - Andy McGrath, August 2023

Figure 2: The author in traditional highland costume at Loch Ness. Photo by Andy McGrath (2023)

Figure 3: Dr. Clemente Onelli, director of the Buenos Aires Zoo, and hunter of the monster of Lago Nahuel Huapi -: By Unknown - here, Public Domain, https://commons.wikimedia.org/w/index.php?curid=141974331

Figure 4: Lago Nahuel Huapi, Argentina - Home of Nahuelito! By David - originally posted to Flickr as View from the Golf Course at Llao Llao, CC BY 2.0, https://commons.wikimedia.org/w/index.php?curid=6950396

Figure 5: Photograph of Igopogo, taken by an observer in 1976 (Source Unknown)

Figure 6: Rattlesnake Island in Lake Okanagan, a reputed haunt of Ogopogo! By Extemporalist - Own work, CC BY-SA 4.0, https://commons.wikimedia.org/w/index.php?curid=38417555

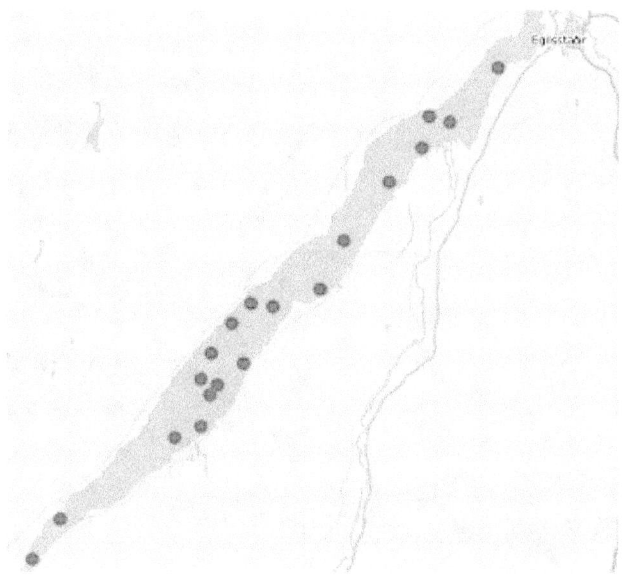

Figure 7: Map of Skrimsl sightings in Iceland - By OpenStreetMap - http://www.openstreetmap.org/?lat=65.33459&lon=-14.62119&zoom=16#, CC BY-SA 3.0, https://commons.wikimedia.org/w/index.php?curid=21349663

Figure 8: Lake Monster researcher, Scott Mardis, pictured with a life-sized recreation of 'Altie', the monster of the Altamaha River, Georgia.

Figure 9: Could this be a carving of the Canavar on the walls of Akdamar Church, Akdamar Island, Lake Van, Turkey? By Feldstein - Own work, CC BY-SA 4.0, https://commons.wikimedia.org/w/index.php?curid=35348038.

Figure 10: Is Kusshi, just a small part of a pantheon of Japanese lake monsters? Photo - Lake Kussharo in Teshikaga, Hokkaido prefecture, Japan, By 663highland - Own work, CC BY 2.5, https://commons.wikimedia.org/w/index.php?curid=23474609

Figure 11: Guai Wu, commonly known as the Lake Tianchi Monster, is believed to inhabit Heaven Lake, which encompasses Jilin Province of China and Ryanggang Province of North Korea. (Source Unknown)

Figure 12: Whimsical costume of Chessie the Chesapeake Bay Monster at the 4th annual Maryland Faerie Festival, 2008. By Frank D. Vassallo - Not previously published, CC BY-SA 3.0, https://en.wikipedia.org/w/index.php?curid=18273492

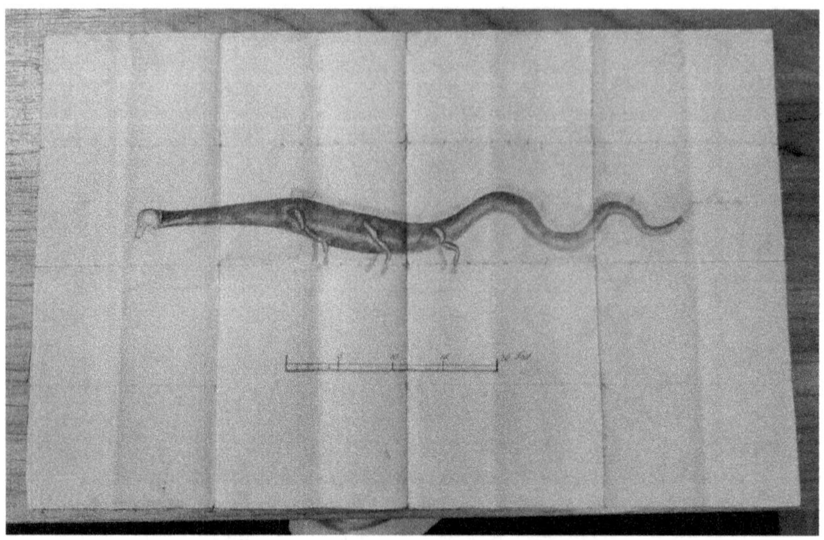

Figure 13: An original sketch of the Stronsay Beast from the archives of Orkney Museum. Eyewitness George Sherar described the Beast to Mr. W.S. Petrie, who created sketches from Sherar's detailed account. Photo by Andy McGrath (2025)

Figure 14: Could Old Ned have simply been an errant basking Shark that became lost in the lake? Basking_shark_Harper's_Weekly_October_24, _1868. Wikicommons. http://upload.wikimedia.org/wikipedia/commons/f/fe/ Basking_shark_Harper%27s_Weekly_October_24%2C_1868.jpg

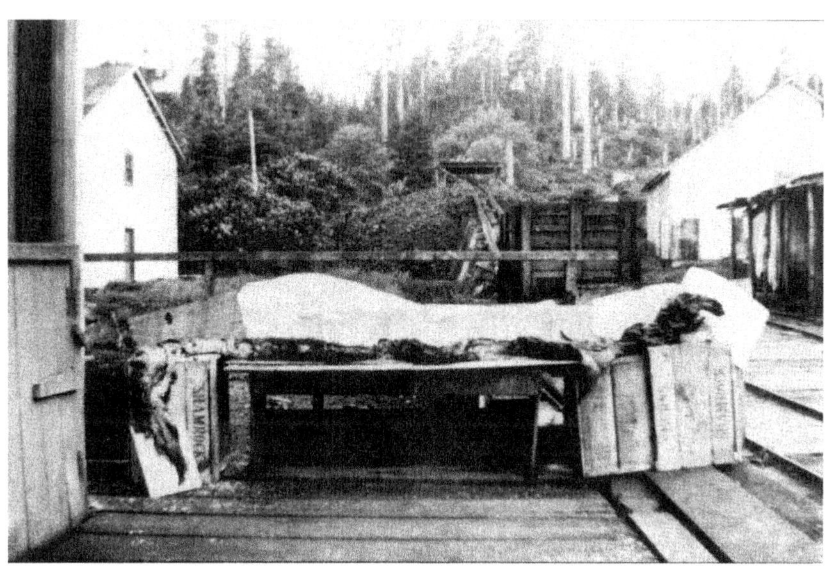

Figure 14: The Naden Harbour "Cadborosaurus" carcass, or 'Baby Caddy'. retrieved from the stomach of a sperm whale in Naden Harbour, British Columbia, Canada. By Boorman - http://lordgeekington. wordpress.com/cadborosaurus/, Public Domain, https://commons. wikimedia.org/w/index.php?curid=19654068

264 THE ILLUSTRATED LONDON NEWS. [Oct. 28, 1848.

THE GREAT SEA-SERPENT.

Figure 15: Gibson, J. (1887). Monsters of the Sea: Legendary and Authentic. Thomas Nelson and Sons, London. 138 pp. By Edwin Weedon / After Frederick James Smyth - Gibson, J. (1887). Public Domain, https://commons.wikimedia.org/w/index.php?curid=66567247

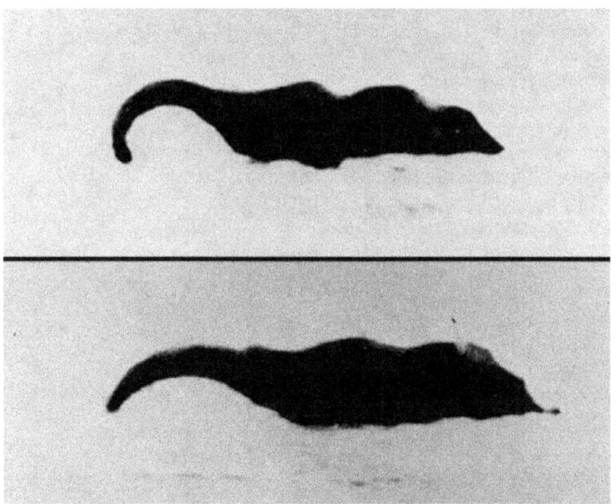

Figure 16: 'Mary F' photos of Morgawr, taken from Rosemullion Head near Falmouth in the February of 1976 and anonymously sent to local newspaper the Falmouth Packet. Mary wrote of her encounter: "It looked like an elephant waving its trunk, but the trunk was a long neck with a small head on the end, like a snake's head..." (Source: Anonymous)

Figure 17: A sketch of the creature witnessed by Marvin McCamis in October 1969 while diving in the DSV Alvin submarine at approximately 5,300 feet off the coast of the Bahamas. McCamis' sighting was documented in Charles Berlitz's 1977 book, Without a Trace.

Figure 18: "Kraken of the Imagination". By Edgar Etherington - Gibson, J. (1887). Monsters of the Sea: Legendary and Authentic. Thomas Nelson and Sons, London. p. 83, Public Domain, https://commons.wikimedia.org/w/index.php?curid=1404801

Figure 19:: The Carta Marina (Latin "map of the sea" or "sea map"), drawn by Olaus Magnus in 1527-39, is the earliest map of the Nordic countries that gives details and place names. By Olaus Magnus - http://cipher.uiah.fi/forum/materials/carta_marina?lang=en, Public Domain, https://commons.wikimedia.org/w/index.php?curid=159434453

Figure 20: A "colossal octopus" attacking ship, pen and wash[1] by Pierre Denys-Montfort, engraved by Étienne Claude Voysard, 1801. By Pierre Denys de Montfort (1766–1820) /Public Domain, https://commons.wikimedia.org/w/index.php?curid=66224971

Figure 21: The gigantic remains of a preserved Hoan Kiem Turtle, once believed to be a cryptid species and now sadly extinct, are on display in the Temple of the Jade Mountain in Hanoi, Vietnam. Photo by Casablanca1911 on Vietnamese Wikipedia. Transferred from vi.wikipedia to Commons by Phó Nháy using CommonsHelper. Public Domain. https://commons.wikimedia.org/w/index.php?curid=14538

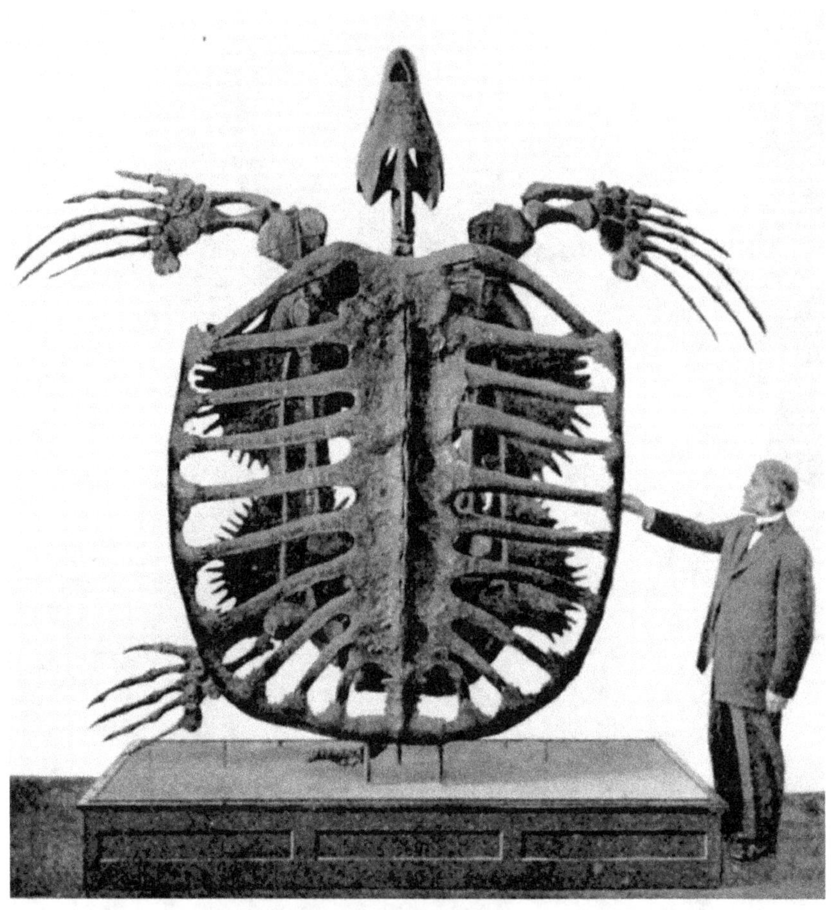

Figure 22: Could the 'Father of All Turtles ' be a living Archelon? An extant chelonian believed to have lived during the cretaceous era. Fossil skeleton of Archelon by Frederic A. Lucas - "Animals of the past" http://www.copyrightexpired.com/earlyimage/bones/display_animalspast_archelon.htm, Public Domain, https://commons.wikimedia.org/w/index.php?curid=2895807

Figure 23: Illustration of a Bunyip by J. Macfarlane (1890). ABORIGINAL MYTHS. - THE BUNYIP (caption) - photomechanical reproduction: halftone. State Library of Victoria Accession Number: IAN01/10/90/12 Image Number: mp006089 Notes: Print published in the Illustrated Australian news. Title printed below image l.c. Publication: Melbourne: David Syme & Co.

Figure 24: The skeleton of the extinct Steller's Sea Cow in the Bone Hall at the Smithsonian National Museum of Natural History, Washington, D.C., USA. - By Ryan Schwark - Own work, CC0, https://commons.wikimedia.org/w/index.php?curid=145925348

Figure 25: Artist Impression by Eye Witness, Sean Corcoran. This creature was encountered on Omey Island, Connemara, Co. Galway, Ireland. By Bango Art at en.wikipedia, CC BY-SA 3.0, https://commons.wikimedia.org/w/index.php?curid=16848874

Figure 26: The Aztec ruler Ahuitzotl (here written "Ahuiçuçin" = Ahuitzotzin, an honorific form), in the Codex Mendoza. Public Domain https://commons.wikimedia.org/w/index.php?curid=1350422

Figure 27: The River Wye is 155 miles long, flowing between its source at Penlimon to the Severn Estuary. Could an infrequent ocean visitor account for the mystery of the Beast of Bodalog? By River Wye from the toll bridge at Whitney-on-Wye by Nick Mutton, CC BY-SA 2.0, https://commons.wikimedia.org/w/index.php?curid=104353040

Figure 28: The High-finned Sperm Whale, also known as the High-finned Cachalot, is a variant of the sperm whale distinguished by its notably tall dorsal fin. CC BY-SA 3.0, https://en.wikipedia.org/w/index.php?curid=8987940

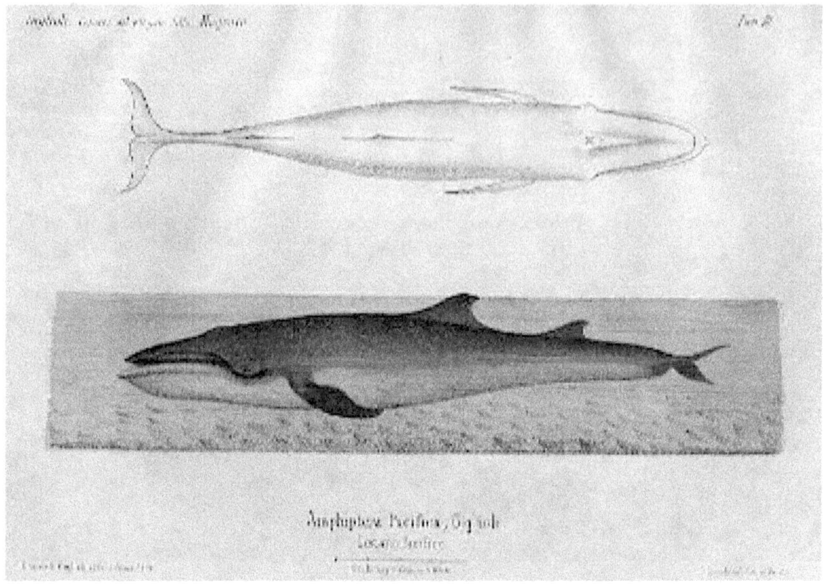

Figure 29: Giglioli's whale, scientifically named Amphiptera Pacifica, is also named after the ship Magenta, where the first reported sighting occurred. It honours Italian zoologist Enrico Hillyer Giglioli, who documented the species in the 19th century. By Enrico Hillyer Giglioli - http://perso.orange.fr/cryptozoo/dossiers/deuxdor2.htm, Public Domain, https://commons.wikimedia.org/w/index.php?curid=15474947

Figure 30: The rhinoceros dolphin, scientifically called 'Delphinus Rhinoceros' and later proposed as Cetodipterus Rhinoceros, recognized for its horn-like second dorsal fin near its head. Two separate dolphins appearing as if they are one dolphin by perspective - By Bob Jones, CC BY-SA 2.0, https://commons.wikimedia.org/w/index.php?curid=13486884

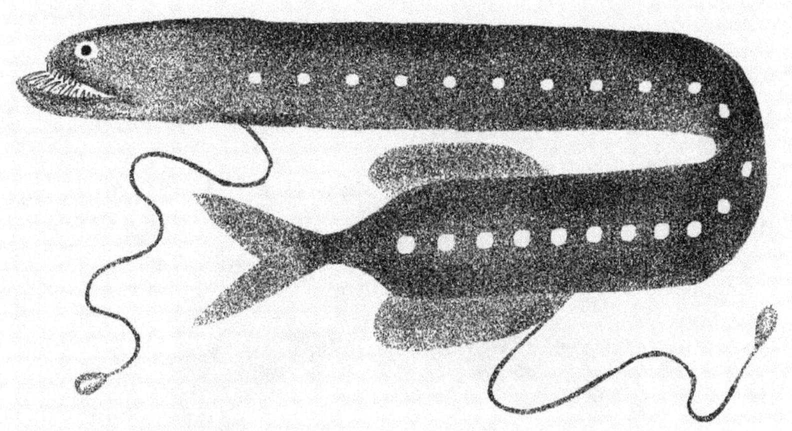

Figure 31: A fish described by William Beebe as he descended into the depths using his self-made submersible. This fish, like all others described on that dive, has never been seen by anyone else. Collectively these are known as the "untouchable fish" - By The Great Mule of Eupatoria - Own work, CC BY-SA 4.0, https://commons.wikimedia.org/w/index.php?curid=115956903

Figure 32: Beebe's bathysphere, Bathysphere rigged for a contour drive - Nat. geogr. Magazine, Beebe 1934. By Leo Wehrli - This image is from the collection of the ETH-Bibliothek and has been published on Wikimedia Commons as part of a cooperation with Wikimedia CH. Corrections and additional information are welcome., CC BY-SA 4.0, https://commons.wikimedia.org/w/index.php?curid=68590475

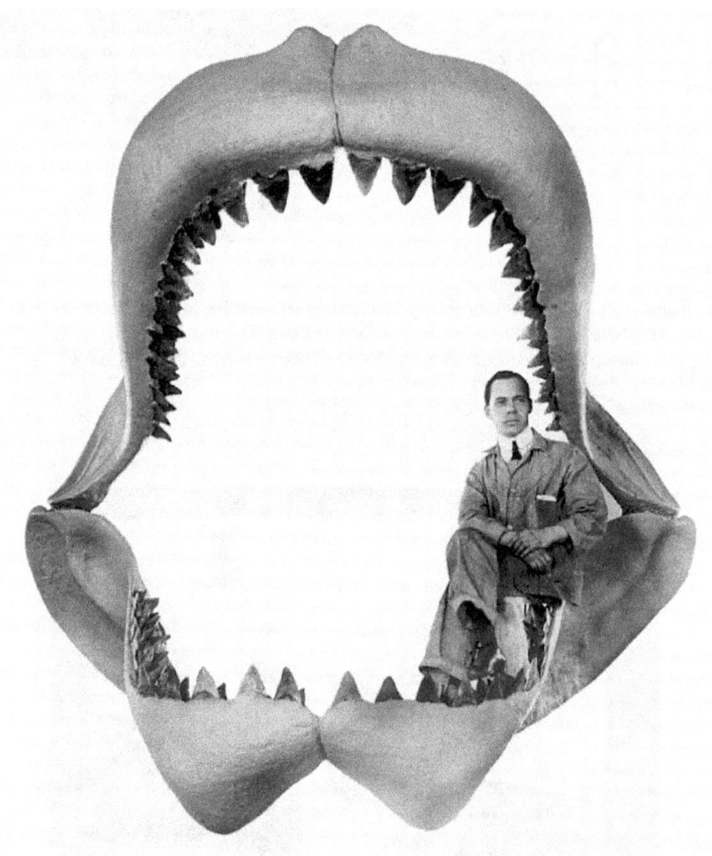

Figure 33: Is the Lord of the Deep a living megalodon? Reconstruction by Bashford Dean in 1909. Basal Miocene South Carolina. 60 ft. in length., enhanced photo - https://archive.org/stream/americanmuseumjo09amer/#page/n279/mode/1up, Public Domain, https://commons.wikimedia.org/w/index.php?curid=4387521

Figure 34: Could Giant Thresher Sharks Exist, and the Deer Island Shark be One? - World's Record Thresher Shark, Weight 922 lbs, caught 21.3.37 at Bay of Islands, New Zealand by Mr. W. W. Dowding of London from Launch "Alma G", Boatman, Francis Arlidge. Fought 2 3/4 hours. Archives New Zealand Reference: AEFZ 22625 W5727 2598 / 3103/0203. By Archives New Zealand –https://ndhadeliver.natlib.govt.nz/delivery/DeliveryManagerServlet?dps_pid=IE17097825, CC BY 2.0,

Figure 35: Is the ground shark a sub species of wobbegong that has grown to gigantic proportions in the rich seas surrounding Timor? By Richard Ling - Flickr, CC BY-SA 2.0, https://commons.wikimedia.org/w/index.php?curid=1886168

Under the Influence

No book such as this—woven with folklore, fables, cold cases, and real-time sightings—could ever exist without the enduring influence and dedication of those who ventured before me. They laboured tirelessly, sifting through tales from both the living and departed, straining their eyes in dim libraries, poring over ancient tablets, and relying on that indispensable yet algorithmically flawed wonder of the information age: the search engine! With deep gratitude, I recognise the following personages whose obsession and resolve have enabled me to glean the essence of this intricate sub-genre, this oft-forgotten child of zoology, which enchants both the learned and the curious alike. And... if amidst the flurry of acknowledgement, I neglect to grasp the hand of one to whom I owe my academic growth; I earnestly hope that the teacher, in question, forgives the shortcomings of a pupil nurtured by the wisdom of many deserving mentors.

That said, the following names shine brightest as worthy of tribute—

Adrian Shine. Alan McKenna. Ann Richardson Davis. Arlene B. Gaal. Austin Whittal. Matt Everett. Bernard Heuvelmans. David C. Xu. Denver Michaels. Edward L. Bousfield. Erik Pontoppidan. Gary Mangiacopra. Gary Opit. George M. Eberhart. Japetus Steenstrup.

John Kirk. Karl Shuker. Mark A. Hall. Matt Bille. Michel Ballot. Michel Raynal. Olaus Magnus. Paul H. LeBlond. Peter McQuahe. Phillipe Coudray. Pops McGrath. Richard Ellis. Roland Watson. Roy P. Mackal. Rupert T. Gould. Sabine Baring-Gould. Scott Mardis. Steve Alten. Tim Dinsdale. William Beebe. William Gibbons. Pops McGrath and Mumsy and Les.

To my wife and beautiful daughters, I do everything for you!

Love, Aba
Xxx

BIBLIOGRAPHY

Alexander, H. B. (1920). *Latin-American [mythology]*. Marshall Jones Co.

Alvarez, G. (1968). *El tronco de oro; Folklore del Neuquén*. Editorial Pehuén.

Ameghino, F. (1899, Juni 15). A Current Survivor of the Ground Sloths of the Ancient Pampas. *La Pirámide*.

An Octopus in the Hand... (1972). *The INFO Journal*, 2(4).

Andean „Plesiosaurus" May Be an Armadillo Or Modern Megatherium, Onelli Thinks. (1922, März 16). *The New York Times*. https://www.nytimes.com/1922/03/16/archives/andean-plesiosaurus-may-be-an-armadillo-or-modern-megatherium.html

Anderson, A. O., & Anderson, M. O. (Hrsg.). (1961). *Adomnan's Life of Columba*. Thomas Nelson and sons.

Arment, C., & LaGrange, B. (2000). A Freshwater Octopus? *North American BioFortean Review*, 2(3).

Ballard, R. D. (2000). *The Eternal Darkness: A Personal History of Deep - Sea Exploration*. Princeton University Press.

Bandelier, A. F. A. (1910). *The Islands of Titicaca and Koati*. Hispanic Society of America.

Beebe, W. (1924). *Galápagos, World's End*. G.P. Putnam's Sons.

Beebe, W. (1934). *Half Mile Down*. Harcourt, Brace.

Behrman, D. (1969). *The New World of the Oceans: Men and Oceanography*. Little Brown.

Benedict, A. (2018, August 18). Folklore Profile: The Amikuk. *THE PINE BARRENS INSTITUTE*. https://pinebarrensinstitute.com/cryptids/2018/8/18/cryptid-profile-the-amikuk

BERNARD, H. (1958). *Dans le sillage des monstres marins - I: Le Kraken et le poulpe colossal*. PLON.

Bernardino, de S. (1950). *General history of the things of New Spain: Florentine codex*. University of Utah.

Berzin, A. A., Tikhomirov, E. A., & Troinin, V. I. (1963). Ischezla li stellerova korova? *Priroda*, 52(8), 73–75.

Bille, M. A. (1995). *Rumors of Existence: Newly Discovered, Supposedly Extinct, and Unconfirmed Inhabitants of the Animal Kingdom*. Hancock House.

Borges, J. L. (1969). *The Book of Imaginary Beings*. E. P. Dutton.

Bowles, D., & Vela, N. (2012). *Mexican Bestiary: Bestiario Mexicano*. VAO Publishing.

Boyd, I. L., & Stanfield, M. P. (1998). Circumstantial evidence for the presence of monk seals in the West Indies. *Oryx*, 32(4), 310–316. https://doi.org/10.1046/j.1365-3008.1998.d01-61.x

Bright, M. (1989). *There are Giants in the Sea*. Robson Books.

Bringsvaerd, T. Å. (1970). *Phantoms And Fairies From Norwegian Folklore*. Johan Grundt Tanum Forlag.

Bruyns, W. F. J. M. (1971). *Field Guide of Whales and Dolphins*. Tor.

Bugge, K. (1934). *Folkeminneoptegnelser: Et utvalg*. Norsk folkeminnelag.

Bullen, F. T. (1899). *The Cruise of the Cachalot „round the World After Sperm Whales"*. Tauchnitz.

Bulpin, T. V. (1965). *Your Undiscovered Country*. Total Oil Products.

Burn Murdoch, W. G. (2012). *From Edinburgh to the Antarctic: An Artist's Notes and Sketches during the Dundee Antarctic Expedition of 1892–93*. Cambridge University Press.

Burton, M. (1960a). Muck and Monsters. *Illustrated London News, 237*, 570.

Burton, M. (1960b). The Soay Beast. *Illustrated London News 236*.

Burton, M. (1961a). *The elusive monster: An analysis of the evidence from Loch Ness*. Rupert Hart-Davis.

Burton, M. (1961b). Was the Soay Beast a Tourist. *Illustrated London News 239*.

Carwardine, M. (1995). *Whales, Dolphins, and Porpoises*. Dorling Kindersley.

Cavada, F. J. (1914). *Chiloé y los chilotes*. Imprenta universitaria.

Cavinder, F. D. (2003). *More Amazing Tales from Indiana*. Indiana University Press.

Cayton, A. R. L., Sisson, R., & Zacher, C. (Hrsg.). (2007). *The American Midwest: An Interpretive Encyclopedia*. Indiana University Press.

Churubusco Farmer Pumping Water From Lake To Catch His Giant Turtle. (1949, September 14). *Warsaw Daily Times*. https://news.google.com/newspapers?id=aDVHAAAAIBAJ&sjid=wnsMAAAAIBAJ&pg=5649,1186442&dq=churubusco&hl=en

Clarke, R., Aguayo L., A., & Campo, S. B. del. (1978). Whale Observation and Whale Marking off the Coast of Chile in 1964. *Scientific Report of the Whales Research Institute, 30*, 117–177.

Colon, H. (1969). The Life of the Admiral by His Son, Hernando Colon. In J.M Cohen, *The four voyages of Christopher Columbus* (S. 127–128). Penguin.

Coluccio, F. (1983). *Diccionario de creencias y supersticiones (argentinas y americanas)*. Corregidor.

Confirm Finding of Prehistoric Monster in Ice. (1930, November 28). *New York Sun*.

Cook, J. (1777). *A Voyage Towards the South Pole and Round the World—Volume I*. Strahan and Cadell.

Cornes, R., & Cunningham, G. (2018). *The Seal Serpent*. CFZ Press.

Costello, P. (1974). *In search of lake monsters*. Coward, McCann & Geoghegan.

Couch, J. (1856). *Remarks on the Species of Whales which have been Observed on the Coasts of Cornwall* (No. 24; S. 27–46). Transactions of the Royal Polytechnic Society of Cornwall.

Dinsdale, T. (1973). The Rines/Egerton picture of Loch Ness. *The Photographic Journal*, 162–165.

Dinsdale, T. (1975). *Project Water Horse: The True Story of the Monster Quest at Loch Ness*. Routledge & K. Paul.

Displaced Critters. (1955). *Doubt, 48*, 341.

Dorson, R. M. (Hrsg.). (1986). *Handbook of American Folklore*. Indiana University Press.

Dunkel, U. (1961). *Abenteuer mit Seeschlangen*. Kreuz-Verlag,.

Ellis, R. (1996). *Deep Atlantic: Life, Death, and Exploration in the Abyss*. Alfred A. Knopf.

Ellis, R. (1998). *The Search for the Giant Squid*. Lyons Press.

Esler, L. (2017, November 30). Whale species discovery at Mason Bay, 1933. *The Southland Times*.

Ferdinand Anders. (1978). Der altmexikanische Federmosaikschild in Wien. *Archiv für Völkerkunde*, *32*.

Fienup-Riordan, A. (1995). *Boundaries and Passages: Rule and Ritual in Yup'ik Eskimo Oral Tradition*. University of Oklahoma Press.

Fraser, F. C. (1935). Zoological notes from the voyage of Peter Mundy, 1655-56, (b), sea elephant on St. Helena. *Proceedings of the Linnean Society*, *147*(2), 32–37.

Gable, A. D. (1997). Two Possible Cryptids from Precolumbian Mesoamerica. *Cryptozoology Review*, 2(1), 17–25.

Gatschet, A. S. (1899). Water-Monsters of American Aborigines. *The Journal of American Folklore*, *12*(47), 255–260. https://doi.org/10.2307/533052

Geddes, T. (1960). *Hebridean Sharker*. H. Jenkins.

Gessner, C. (1604). *Historiae Animalium*. In Bibliopolio Andreae Cambieri.

Gordon, C. H. (1940, Juni). The Chequered History of Dusky Bay. *New Zealand Railways Magazine*, *15*(3).

Goss, M. (1987). Do giant prehistoric sharks survive? *Fate*, *40*(11), 32–41.

Gould, R. T. (1934). *THE LOCH NESS MONSTER AND OTHERS*. Geoffrey Bles.

Haley, D. (1978). Saga of Steller's Sea Cow. *Natural History*, *87*, 9–17.

Hall, M. A. (1991). *Natural Mysteries* (2nd Aufl.).

Hall, M. A. (2001). Mysteries of West Virginia. *Wonders*, *6*(4), 113–126.

Heinselman, C. (2000). Hoan Kiem Turtle: A Tale of the Sword. *Crypto*, *3*(3), 15–18.

Heseltine, N. (1960). *From Libyan Sands to Chad*. Museum Press.

Heuglin, T. von. (1868). *Reise nach Abessinien, den Gala-Ländern, Ost-Sudán und Chartúm in den Jahren 1861 und 1862*. H. Costenoble.

Heuvelmans, B. (1968). *In the Wake of the Sea-Serpents*. Hill and Wang.

Heuvelmans, B. (1978). *Les derniers dragons d'Afrique*. Plon.

Heuvelmans, B. (1986). Annotated Checklist of Apparently Unknown Animals With Which Cryptozoology Is Concerned. In *Cryptozoology 5*.

Heuvelmans, B. (1995). *On The Track Of Unknown Animals*. Routledge.

Hill, E. (2012). The Nonempirical Past: Enculturated Landscapes and Other-than-Human Persons in Southwest Alaska. *Arctic Anthropology*, *49*(2), 41–57. https://doi.org/10.1353/arc.2012.0021

Holiday, F. W. (1968). *The Great Orm of Loch Ness*. Faber.

Hyde, S. (2003, August 6). *„Inn" the news*. Brigadoon Bed and Breakfast. https://web.archive.org/web/20100925042635/http://mackinawbrigadoon.com/newsletter.phtml?id=12

ICE BARES STRANGE ANIMAL; Alaskans Suggeat Prehistoric Origin—Museum Here Investigating. (1930, November 26). *The New York Times*. https://www.nytimes.com/1930/11/26/archives/ice-bares-strange-animal-alaskans-suggeat-prehistoric-origin-museum.html

Indian Ocean. (1988). *The Marine Observer*, *58*.

Ives, M. (2016, Januar 22). Vietnam's Sacred Turtle Dies at an Awkward, Some Say

Ominous, Time. *The New York Times*. https://www.nytimes.com/2016/01/23/world/asia/vietnam-turtle-hoan-kiem-lake.html

Jacobson, S. A. (2012). *Yup'ik Eskimo Dictionary Second Edition: Volumes 1 and 2*. University of Chicago Press.

Kirk, J. (1998). *In the Domain of the Lake Monsters*. Key Porter Books.

Kitching, G. C. (1936). The Manatee of St. Helena. *Nature, 138*(3479), 33–34.

Klumov, S. K. (1962). Do large unknown animals still exist on the earth? *Priroda, 8*, 65–75.

La Leyenda del Ahuizótl; Era un ser terrible y mitológico de los aztecas. (2017, Oktober 6). *Metro Mty*, 44.

Latcham, R. E. (1924). *La organización social y las creencias religiosas de los antiguos araucanos*. Imprenta Cervantes. https://www.nypl.org/research/research-catalog

Ley, W. (1941). *The Lungfish and the Unicorn: An Excursion into Romantic Zoology*. Modern Age.

Lydekker, R. (1899). On the supposed former Existence of a Sirenian. *Proceedings of the Zoological Society of London, 67*(3), 796–798. https://doi.org/10.1111/j.1469-7998.1899.tb06895.x

Mackal, R. P. (1980). *Searching for hidden animals*. Doubleday.

MacKal, R. P. (1987). *A Living Dinosaur?: In Search of Mokele-Mbembe*. Brill Academic Pub.

Magin, U. (1987). In the Wake of Columbus' Sea Serpent: The Giant Turtle of the Gulf Stream. *Pursuit, No. 78*, 55–56.

Maigret, J. (1986). Les cétacés sur les cotes ouest-africaines: Encore quelques énigmes! *Notes Africaines, 189*, 20–24.

Mangiacopra, G. (1976). A Monstrous Jellyfish? *Of Sea and Shore, 7*(3).

Mangiacopra, G. S. (1976). The Great Ones: A Fragmented History of the Giant and the Colossal Octopus. *Of Sea and Shore, 7*(2), 93–96.

Mangiacopra, G. S., Raynal, M. P. R., Smith, D. G., & Avery, D. F. (1995). Octopus giganteus: Still Alive and Hiding Where? Part III- Lusca and Scuttles of the Caribbean. *Of Sea and Shore*.

Mareš, J. (1997). *Svět tajemných zvířat: Kryptozoologická encyklopedie*. Littera Bohemica.

Matters, L. (1922, Juli). An Antediluvian Monster: Is the Argentine Plesiosaurus a Fake or a Scientific Marvel? *Scientific American, 127*(1).

McLintock, A. H., & Bagnall, A. G. (1966). Animals, Mythical. In A. H. McLintock (Hrsg.), *An Encyclopaedia of New Zealand*.

Meurger, M. (1999). Francesco Negri: The Kraken and the Sea Serpent. *Fortean Studies, 6*, 238–244.

Michaels, D. (2016). *Water Monsters South of the Border*. CreateSpace Independent Publishing Platform.

Michel Raynal. (1994). Do Two-Finned Cetaceans Exist? *INFO Journal, 70*.

Molina, J. I. (1986). *Ensayo sobre la historia natural de Chlie*. Ediciones Maule.

Monster in Ice Has Long Snout. (1930, November 28). *New York Sun*.

Montfort, P. D. de. (1802). *Histoire naturelle, générale et particulière, des mollusques, animaux sans vertèbres et à sang blanc: Ouvrage faisant suite aux Oeuvres de Leclerc de Buffon, et partie du Cours complet d'histoire naturelle rédigé par C.S. Sonnini*. F. Dufart.

Moon, M. (1977). *Ogopogo: The Okanagan mystery from Indian lore to contemporary evidence, the facts about the legendary monster of British Columbia's Okanagan Lake*. J. J. Douglas.

More Details Needed. (1946). *Doubt, 16*, 242.

Mortensen, T. (1933). On the "Manatee" of St. Helena. *Videnskabelige Meddelelser fra Dansk Naturhistorisk Forening, 97*, 1–9.

Nelson, E. W. (o. J.). *The Eskimo about Bering Strait* (Eighteenth Annual Report of the Bureau of American Ethnology to the Secretary of the Smithsonian Institution, 1896-97, S. 3–518).

Nordenskiöld, A. E. (1881). *The Voyage of the Vega Round Asia and Europe* (A. Leslie, Übers.; Bd. 1). Macmillan and Co.

Nuttall, Z. (1895). A Note on Ancient Mexican Folklore. *The Journal of American Folklore, 7*(38).

Octopus Caught by Two Boatmen on Kanawha River. (1933, Dezember 25). *Charleston Gazette*.

Octopus Story Just a Hoax. (1933, Dezember 29). *Charleston Gazette*.

Orrick, C. (1999). Commentary on Stejneger's Sea-Ape Review. *North American BioFortean Review, 1*(2).

Osborne, H. (1968). *South American Mythology*. Paul Hamlyn.

Owen, T. R. H. (1960). *Hunting Big Game with Gun and Camera in Africa*. Herbert Jenkins.

Palmer, R. (1987, Januar). In the lair of the lusca. *Natural History*, 42–46.

Peterson, V. (2009, Mai 26). *The 1949 Story of the Hunt for Oscar, the Beast of Busco, According to the Indianapolis Star*. Busco Voice. https://web.archive.org/web/20110612134840/http://www.buscovoice.com/2009/05/26/the-1949-story-of-the-hunt-for-oscar-the-beast-of-busco-according-to-the-indianapolis-star/

Philippe Coudray. (2009). *A Guidebook to Hidden Animals: A Treatise on Cryptozoology* (Margaret Webb, Übers.).

Picasso, F. (1998, Dezember). South American Monsters and Mystery Animals. *Strange Magazine, 20*.

Pitman, R. L., Aguayo L., A., & Urbán R., J. (1987). Observations of an Unidentified Beaked Whale (mesoplodon Sp.) in the Eastern Tropical Pacific. *Marine Mammal Science, 3*(4), 345–352. https://doi.org/10.1111/j.1748-7692.1987.tb00321.x

Pitman, R. L., & Lynn, M. S. (2001). Biological Observations of an Unidentified Mesoplodont Whale in the Eastern Tropical Pacific and Probable Identity Mesoplodon Peruvianus. *Marine Mammal Science, 17*(3), 648–657. https://doi.org/10.1111/j.1748-7692.2001.tb01010.x

Poli, F. (1959). *Sharks are Caught at Night*. Henry Regnery Co.

Pollock, G. A. (1970). The South Island Otter—A Reassessment. *Proceedings of the New Zealand Ecological Society, 17*, 129–135.

Pontoppidan, E., Berthelson, A., & Blackburne, J. (1755). *The natural history of Norway*. A. Linde.

Quoy, J.-R. C., & Gaimard, J. P. (1824). *Voyage autour du monde*. Pillet Aîné.

Raynal, M. (1987). Does the Steller's Sea Cow Still Survive? *INFO Journal*, *51*, 15–19.

Raynal, M. (1994). The Case for the Giant Octopus. *Fortean Studies*, *1*, 210–234.

Raynal, M., & Sylvestre, J.-P. (1991). Cetaceans with two dorsal fins. *Aqualic Mammals*, *17*(1), 31–36.

Roesch, B. S. (1997). *Do Giant Cookiecutter Shark Exist?* ncf.carleton.ca. https://web.archive.org/web/20060709113403/http://www.ncf.carleton.ca/~bz050/HomePage.giantcookiecutter.html

Russell, E. F. (1967). *Great World Mysteries*. Mayflower Dell.

Rutkowski, C. (1993). *Unnatural History: True Manitoba Mysteries*. Chameleon Publishers.

Sarano, F. (2001, August 23). The Malpelo monster, a new species of shark? *PHOTOCEANS*. https://web.archive.org/web/20020320050126/http://www.photoceans.com/anglais/mag/index.cfm?id_act=243&id_rub=71

Scared by a Sea Serpent. (1898, Oktober 10). *Daily Mail (London)*.

Schafer, L. S. (1986). The Deepstar 4000. *The Compass: A Magazine of the Sea*, *56*(1).

SCOTS SEE SEA MONSTER; Furry Beast 20 Feet Long Is Washed Ashore Lifeless. (1944, Oktober 3). *The New York Times*. https://www.nytimes.com/1944/10/03/archives/scots-see-sea-monster-furry-beast-20-feet-long-is-washed-ashore.html

Sehm, G. G. (1996). On a Possible Unknown Species of Giant Devil Ray, Manta sp. *Cryptozoology*, *12*, 19–29.

Seler, E. (1909). Die Tierbilder der mexikanischen und der Maya-Handschriften. *Zeitschrift für Ethnologie (ZfE)*, *41*(6), 784–846.

Shenton, E. H. (1970). Where Have All the Submersibles Gone? *Oceans*, *3*(6).

Ship Reports Giant Sea Turtle. (1956, Juni 8). *New York Herald Tribune*.

Shuker, K. (1993). Hoofed Mystery Animals and Other Crypto-Ungulates, Part III. *Strange Magazine*, *11*, 25–27.

Shuker, K. (1995). In the Spotlight: The Dobhar-chu. *Strange Magazine*, *16*, 32–33.

Shuker, K. P. N. (1994). Giant Jellyfish. *Fate*, *47*.

Shuker, K. P. N. (1998). A Supplement to Dr Bernard Heuvelmans' Checklist of Cryptozoological Animals. *Fortean Studies*, *5*.

Smeeton, M. (1969). *The Misty Islands*. George Harrap.

Soule, G. (1968). *Undersea Frontiers: Exploring By Deep - Diving Submarines*. Rand McNally & Company.

Soule, G. (1970). *The Greatest Depths; Probing the Seas to 20,000 Feet and Below*. Macrae Smith Co.

Soule, G. (1981). *Mystery Monsters of the Deep*. F. Watts.

Stead, D. G. (1963). *Sharks and Rays of Australian Seas*. Angus and Robertson.

Steenstrup, J. J. (1857). Oplysninger om Atlanterhavets colossale Blaeksprutter. *Forhandlinger ved de Skandinaviske Naturforskeres*, *7*(1856), 182–185.

Steenstrup, J. J. (1962). *The Cephalopod Papers of Japetus Steenstrup*. Danish Science Press.

Stejneger, L. (1887). How the Great Northern Sea-Cow (Rytina) Became Exterminated. *The American Naturalist*, *21*(12), 1047–1054. https://doi.org/10.1086/274607

Stejneger, L. (1936). *Georg Wilhelm Steller, The Pioneer of Alaskan Natural History*. Harvard University Press.

Steller, G. W. (1751). *"De Bestiis Marinis", in Novi Commentarii Academiae Scientarium Imperialis Petropolitanae, volume II.* Press of the Academy of Sciences.

Steller, G. W., & Frost, O. W. (1988). *Journal of a Voyage with Bering, 1741-1742* (M. A. Engel, Übers.). Stanford University Press.

Steller Idea. (1985). *ISC Newsletter 4(3)*, 9–10.

Sterling, E. J., Hurley, M. M., & Minh, L. D. (2007). *Vietnam: A Natural History*. Yale University Press.

Swartz, T. (1997, Summer). Mystery of the Oil Pit Squids. *Strange Magazine*, *18*, 28–30.

Taming Monsters: Ahuizotl. (o. J.). Field Museum of Natural History.

Taylor, R. (1848). *A Leaf from the Natural History of New Zealand.* Robert Stokes.

The Gigantic Turtle of 1883. (1994, Januar). *INFO Journal, No. 70*, 14–15.

Thomas, P. (2007). *Indiana Off the Beaten Path: A guide to Unique Places.* Globe Pequot.

Tohall, P. (1948). The Dobhar-chu Tombstones of Glenade, Co. Leitrim. *Journal of the Royal Society of Antiquaries of Ireland*, *78*, 127–129.

Tregear, E. (1891). *The Māori-Polynesian comparative dictionary*. Lyon and Blair.

Trouessart, É. L. (1911). Existe-t-il dans les Marais du Lac Tchad un Grand Mammifere Encore Inconnu des Naturalistes? *La Natura*, *76*.

Urban, M. (2018). Maritime loanwords in languages of Pacific Meso- and South America? An exploratory study. In Katerina Harvati, Gerhard Jäger, & Hugo Reyes-Centeno, *New perspectives on the peopling of the Americas* (S. 27–60). Kerns Verlag.

Vilenov, V. (2010). *Tainy chetyrekh okeanov (Тайны четырех океанов)*. Veche.

Vladykov, V. D., & McKenzie, R. A. (1935). The Marine Fishes of Nova Scotia. *Proceedings and Transactions of the Nova Scotia Institute of Science 1934-35*, *19*, 17–113.

Wagner, R. (1982). The Ri-Unidentified Aquatic Animals of New Ireland, Papua New Guinea. *Cryptozoology*, *1*(1), 33–39.

Wagner, R., Greenwell, J. R., Raymond, G. J., & Nieda, K. von. (1983). Further Investigations into the Biological and Cultural Affinities of the Ri. *Cryptozoology*, *2*.

Welfare, S., & Fairley, J. (1980). *Arthur C. Clarke's Mysterious World.* Collins.

White, T. H. (1960). *The Bestiary: A Book of Beasts*. G. P. Putnam's Sons.

Whittall, A. (2009, Oktober 16). The water tiger. *Patagonian monsters.* https://patagoniamonsters.blogspot.com/2009/10/water-tiger.html

Whittall, A. (2013). *Monsters of Patagonia*. Zagier & Urruty Pubns.

Whittall, A. (2019, November 7). Freshwater stingray sighted in Lake Nahuel Huapi—Or was it a catfish? *Patagonian Monsters*. https://patagoniamonsters.blogspot.com/2019/11/freshwater-stingray-sighted-in-lake.html

Whyte, C. (1957). *More Than a Legend: The Story of the Loch Ness Monster*. Hamish Hamilton.

Williams, T. R. (1985). Identification of the Ri: Through Further Fieldwork in New Ireland, Papua New Guinea. *Cryptozoology*, *4*, 61–68.

Winer, R. (1974). *The Devil's Triangle.* Bantam Books.

Wood, F. G., & Gennaro, J. G. (1971). An Octopus Trilogy. *Natural History*, *80*.

Wood, G. L. (1982). *The Guinness book of animal facts and feats.* Guinness Superlatives.

Wright, B. S. (1967). The Lusca of Andros. *Atlantic Advocate*, 32–39.

ABOUT THE AUTHOR

Andy McGrath is a seasoned paranormal researcher and folklorist, bringing over 25 years of expertise to the intriguing realms of the unknown. As a speaker, investigator, podcaster, and author of works like *Beasts of Britain*, *Hairy Humanoids*, and *A Monster Kids Guide*, he is dedicated to uncovering the mysteries that lurk in the shadows. He also hosts the television series *Weird Britain* (History/Blaze), which celebrates the rich histories, captivating mysteries, and enchanting folklore of the British Isles.

Often dubbed the Sherlock Holmes of the paranormal, Andy masterfully weaves together contemporary encounters with ancient legends, crafting a vivid tapestry of elusive creatures and strange phenomena that may reside just beyond the boundaries of scientific understanding and human imagination.

In addition, he is the host of the *Beastly Theories Podcast*, a heartfelt endeavour to explore the triumphs and tribulations of paranormal research and obsession. Andy engages with some of the most respected researchers in the field, aiming to unlock the treasure trove of knowledge that resides within their formidable minds.

Regularly appearing on film, TV, radio, and various podcasts, Andy is also a dynamic keynote speaker specialising in folklore, cryptids, the paranormal, ufology, macabre history, and other intriguing fringe theories. Through his conferences, seminars, and workshops, he invites audiences to delve into the unknown and uncover the tales that shape our world.

Media, Marketing, and Licensing Inquiries:
For all inquiries, please contact:
Andy McGrath
Email: andyronmcgrath@gmail.com

BOOKS BY ANDY MCGRATH

Beasts of the World (Vol. 1): Hairy Humanoids

Beasts of Britain

Nessie: A Monster Kids Guide

Yeti: A Monster Kids Guide

AFTERWORD

Go to hangar1publishing.com to learn more about the Authors and stay up to date with their newest releases.

www.ingramcontent.com/pod-product-compliance
Lightning Source LLC
Chambersburg PA
CBHW061550120626
46550CB00004B/1441
* 9 7 9 8 8 9 3 2 5 0 8 5 5 *